GAME ON, PUPPY!

GAME ON, PUPPY!

The fun, transformative
approach to training your puppy

From the founders and creators
of Absolute Dogs, Tom Mitchell
and Lauren Langman

QUERCUS

First published in Great Britain in 2023 by

QUERCUS

Quercus Editions Ltd
Carmelite House
50 Victoria Embankment
London EC4Y 0DZ

An Hachette UK company

A CIP catalogue record for this book is available
from the British Library

TPB ISBN 978 1 52942 192 7
Ebook ISBN 978 1 52942 193 4

Illustrations by Absolute Dogs.

10 9 8 7 6 5 4 3 2 1

Typeset by CC Book Production
Printed and bound in Great Britain by Clays Ltd, Elcograf S.p.A.

Papers used by Quercus are from well-managed forests and other responsible sources.

To you, no doubt a dog owner
(if not now, you will be soon), this is for you.

Someone open to learn, eager to get the foundations right,
to inspire a relationship that will change your life.
There is nothing like the love of a dog, nothing like
the adventures on the horizon, with them at your side.
It is our absolute honour and privilege to be part
of this journey with you.

Contents

SECTION ONE:
Rising Star
(8-12 weeks)

SECTION TWO:
Super Star
(13-24 weeks and beyond)

INTRODUCTION
Hello, Gamechanger!

Congratulations on your new puppy! You've invited adventure, fun and the best friend a person could ask for into your life.

So, before we get into the training and talk about the potential struggles and challenges that you might encounter along the way, let's celebrate the amazing and wonderful fact that you have chosen to welcome this unique bundle of love into your home.

We'd also like to thank you for being the best owner for your dog. Over the next 24 chapters, we're going to cover everything you need to know in those first six months of living with your new puppy.

We're going to arm you with the knowledge, the skills and the information you'll need so that you and your dog can enjoy the best life possible together. At times, especially during the first few days, you might be asking yourself 'what on earth have I done?', but it's important to remember that all behaviour is changeable. Your puppy isn't always going to be excitable or nervous or pee on your favourite rug. It may feel like a rollercoaster from time to time, but we're here to support you. As we are going to show you, there's always a game you can play or something you can do to turn your puppy's struggles into strengths.

Above all, we want to make sure your training journey is fun for you and your puppy, so that you develop a truly beautiful relationship that will last a lifetime.

The Absolute Dogs Approach

Every puppy is born with a unique personality. Some puppies might be born naturally optimistic and take everything in their stride. Others may start out a little more pessimistic, wary of the world and need a bit more support to navigate life with confidence. Some puppies might be full of energy, always on the go and find life amazingly exciting. Others may be more chilled in nature.

There are three key concepts you want your puppy to have that we believe will equip them to make appropriate choices and enable them to be a calm, confident companion. They are calmness, optimism and proximity. If your puppy has the ability to be calm, sees new experiences and situations as nothing to be worried about and wants to stay close to you, it will give them a solid foundation to build upon.

But how do you teach these concepts to your puppy? We do this by playing games!

Train concepts, not behaviours

Absolute Dogs is all about a games-based approach to training, where we play games to build and strengthen those concepts that are going to set your puppy up for success. We call this concept training.

In the typical world of puppy training, you turn up for a puppy class and the first thing on the agenda is often teaching your dog a sit, a down and a stay. You might spend some time learning to walk on a lead around a church hall with minimal other distractions. The problem with this is that training your puppy a series of behaviours in a class environment doesn't prepare them for real life.

Your puppy might sit beautifully in class and even at home, but then you ask them to sit on a walk, or when a visitor comes to your door, and it's like they have never even heard the word 'sit' before! That behaviour doesn't translate to a real-life situation full of distractions and other options. It doesn't prepare them for the dog that's going to run up to them unexpectedly on a walk. It's not going to prepare them to listen to you when there's a really exciting squirrel close by. It just doesn't prepare them for life!

So what does?

There's a game for that!

What we've found is that to prepare our dogs for real life, we have to teach them the key concepts so they are ready for all those real-life situations.

Perhaps your puppy is very easily distracted at the moment and everything seems to grab their attention? You know what, Gamechanger? There's a game for that! You can play games that are designed to improve your puppy's focus so they become more focused on you and more able to deal with the distractions of day-to-day life.

Or maybe your puppy is a little pessimistic right now. Guess what? There's a game for that! Optimism games help make your puppy's outlook more positive so that in day-to-day life they're totally cool about everything, from loud noises that suddenly happen, to the dog that freezes in the distance and gives them ambiguous signals, to the bearded stranger they're not sure about at the shops.

The Absolute Dogs approach is all about having fun with your new puppy. We'll show you how to play games that will teach them the skills they need to navigate life with confidence and to make great choices, both at home and when out and about. And the best thing is, they're learning those skills through fun games in their own day-to-day environment in your own time. Your puppy is constantly learning, whether that's at home, in the garden or out on walks. As an amazing owner, you need to be sure your puppy is learning the right things that will set them up for success as they grow. That may feel a little daunting, and yet with our games-based approach it is both accessible and achievable. All the games in this book can be played with your puppy in the time it takes to boil a kettle. We want you to play games with your puppy without pressure. We focus on a fun time, not a long time. Puppies have short attention spans, so keep your sessions short. We believe no game should be any longer than 3 minutes and even if you only have time for one game a day, that's enough to help set your puppy up for success. You'll get results *and* have fun with your dog. So come on, Gamechanger, what are you waiting for?

The power of concept training

Concept training goes way beyond training a puppy to sit, down or stay. These things don't transfer to success in day-to-day life. Instead, if you focus on games that train concepts and enhance and shape your puppy's personality, you will achieve real-life results.

Your puppy will possess the skills to make awesome life choices without you having to provide constant input.

Rather than you needing to be one step ahead and to take all the responsibility for your puppy making the right decisions, they will have the skills and foundations to make those great choices without you constantly having to guide or nag them.

Imagine how much more you'll enjoy life with your dog if you're not constantly looking out for inappropriate things they might pick up and having to tell them to 'leave it!', or scanning the horizon on walks for things they might get distracted by or need to be called away from. The freedom to know that your dog will make those great choices comes from shaping their brain to value proximity and calmness, to be able to think in more sophisticated levels of excitement and to see value in disengaging from distractions.

That's the power of concept training.

Play games, train concepts, shape their personality and you're on to a winner!

Train FOR the situation, not IN the situation

This is another vital aspect of the way we train. Conventional training says you have to take your dog into real-life situations, and then teach them how to act. However, what commonly happens is the situation becomes too much for them and without the skills to cope, negative behaviours result. They're certainly not in a space where they can learn new skills. So instead of training them *in* the situation, we believe in training them *for* the situation.

Would you teach your child maths by forcing them to do a maths test? No, you'd teach them the maths that they needed beforehand, in order to take the test. Real-life situations are like the test for the puppy, and trying to teach our puppies skills while they're physically in that situation is rarely going to be successful. More often it leads to a frustrated owner who's working against their dog.

Not only that, rehearsal is powerful. The more your puppy practises not having the skills for a particular situation, the more they are going to rehearse inappropriate choices. It will make it more likely that they will do the same the next time they get put into that situation. The result is that you and your puppy end up trapped in a vicious cycle. First you go to the real-life situation, then it goes wrong and the puppy, without the skills to cope, rehearses a behaviour you don't want. Conventional training would encourage you to go back to the situation and try again, but all that happens is that the behaviour repeats, and may even get worse. Now you're stuck.

Perhaps you resort to puppy training classes, but as we're going to show you in this book, you don't need to go to these – and we're saying that as people who run them! Dog training classes are noisy and can often be overwhelming for a young puppy. When you take your puppy to a traditional puppy class, you're exposing them to a completely alien environment, forcing them to mix with other dogs and expecting all the puppies in that class – with their unique personalities – to get along and learn something. Why risk giving your puppy a bad experience when you can teach them yourself at home? We can guarantee that you'll see better results when you train your puppy away from situations that they might find challenging or overwhelming, so that when they do head out into the world, they already have the skills to succeed. We will give you everything you need to raise a calm, confident, optimistic puppy who has all the skills required to go out into the world making awesome choices.

With the Absolute Dogs approach, you get to teach your puppy the essential skills that will set them up for life, in your living room, your kitchen and your garden. This way, your puppy learns these skills before they ever even need them.

With each of the games in this book, you will play them at home first. Then when you take your puppy out, you're going to be revisiting games your puppy already knows. Because they have played the games and already developed the skills at home, they will be able to tackle any situation with ease, make the best choices and feel like a winner.

So, Gamechanger, let's get started!

The lingo

We use a lot of crazy lingo here at Absolute Dogs. Here are some of the terms and catchphrases we're going to use throughout this book.

A fun time, not a long time – This is our mantra when it comes to playing games with your puppy. Puppies have short attention spans so it's better to keep games short and fun. As a rule of thumb, no game should be longer than 3 minutes.

Arousal – We describe this as being like a volume dial on your puppy's brain. It adds intensity to emotions, whether they are positive or negative. For example, it could turn calmness into excitement or worry into fear.

Disco pants – Your puppy is constantly deciding what is an appropriate energy level for a situation. Sometimes your puppy might turn up expecting a disco (something high energy and fun to be happening) but actually it's not disco time and you want them to be calm. So in these sorts of situations, we talk about your puppy taking off their disco pants and swapping them for their pyjamas!

Duration – Once your puppy has mastered a game, we might ask you to add duration. This simply means asking your dog to carry out a task for longer before rewarding them. In the beginning, you reward your puppy pretty quickly. But as they progress, you can start to add duration. It can even be just a couple of seconds more. Your puppy will get so consistent you will find they do things for longer anyway because they are happy and want to.

Enrichment – This is how we refer to calming food activities such as bones, long-lasting chews and lick mats. They help to calm and relax your puppy by using their natural instincts to lick and chew.

Gamechanger – That's you! We refer to anyone who reads this book, plays games and follows the Absolute Dogs approach as a Gamechanger.

Gated community – This is creating a small, safe area for your puppy using baby gates, puppy pens and crates. You can use your gated community to manage where your puppy has access to as well as giving them a quiet, contained area to rest and sleep. We'll even discuss having multiple barriers or safe spaces around your home to give even more learning opportunities.

Management – Our approach is always about setting your puppy up for success by arranging their environment in a way that limits their opportunities to make inappropriate choices – we call this management.

Rehearsal is power – Dogs will become more of what they practise. So that's about making sure your puppy practises really great skills like confidence but also preventing them rehearsing negative behaviours such as barking or biting.

Rehearse the room – If your puppy practises a certain energy level in a particular room of the house then they will always have that energy level in that room. So if you are consistently playing high-energy, exciting games with your puppy in your living room, that room is never going to be a calm space until you rehearse calmness instead, and implement the strategies we'll show you.

There's a game for that – Whatever struggle your puppy is facing, there will be a game that can help you transform it into a strength.

Zoomies – Random bursts of energy that your puppy might have in which they run frenetically around, usually in circles.

CHAPTER 1

Before You Get Your Puppy

You might be reading this before you choose your puppy or perhaps in a few weeks you're due to collect your dog from the breeder or rescue centre. Either way, you're probably bursting with excitement and can't wait to welcome this little bundle of love into your life. In fact, this is an ideal time to start preparing for your new arrival.

This waiting period is a great opportunity for you to skill yourself up, make some key decisions and really try and get an understanding of puppies and how they react and behave before your new family member arrives and turns your life upside down.

How to choose your puppy

If you haven't chosen your puppy yet, then it's worth doing your research to make sure you select a breed that most suits you and your lifestyle. There are no right or wrong choices but each breed has certain traits and characteristics that might make them a better match for you.

- **Think about your lifestyle**

How much exercise and training input do certain breeds that you like require and can you realistically make time for that?

- **Where do you live?**

Do you live in a flat or a house with a garden? Are you in the city or in the countryside? Do you have lots of space or is your home on the smaller side? These things should all affect your decisions when you're considering what breed to choose, as some dogs will need a larger area.

TIP: The bigger the dog, the bigger the cost

One thing that a lot of people don't consider when they get a large breed is that the costs are going to be significantly higher – both with food and vet's bills. Everything is done on body weight, so caring for and keeping a larger dog is naturally more expensive.

Getting your puppy from a rescue centre

Most rescue centres will want to know about your lifestyle – if you are out at work all day, the time you have available to walk a dog. They will also consider the size of your home and any outside space when they are working on matching you with the right dog. Some rescue centres might even want to do a home visit.

- **Be honest**

The best thing you can do when getting in touch with a rescue centre is to have an honest conversation about your life and situation so you can be appropriately matched. They can only go by what you tell them. Sometimes, potential owners feel like they have to sell themselves, and end up painting a picture that's very different from the reality. Be brutally honest about how much time and space you have and how many times a day you'd be able to walk a dog. It's OK to say you want a breed that may have fewer requirements, but equally, you need to be aware that every puppy has needs and the centre will be sure to tell you all about them. The more honest you can be, the better. There will be a dog out there for you. You need to make sure it's the best dog matched to your situation, not the first dog you see. Don't be tempted to pick a puppy just because they look cute. Be honest with yourself too. Training is a lifelong commitment and no matter how old your dog is, they're always going to need your love, help and input. Always be curious, and ask many questions.

- **Be open**

Meet lots of dogs. Talk to the staff about the character traits that you like rather than being fixed on one particular breed.

Getting your puppy from a breeder

A good breeder, like a rescue centre, will want to know about your lifestyle and what you can offer a dog. Some might have a 20-page application form, others will just chat to you over the phone. Neither is right or wrong; different breeders have different approaches.

- **Talk to the breeder**

Good breeders will be honest with you. Tell them what kind of personality you're after and by 5 weeks old, they should be able to tell you more about each of their puppies. Often, it's the breeder who is best placed to match a puppy to the right home and family set-up. After all, having spent the last 5 weeks with your puppy, they know them best. When you go and visit a breeder to see a litter of puppies, remember that you are only seeing a snapshot. A puppy who seems really calm and chilled might only be that way because it has spent most of the day playing and it's exhausted. It's really hard to judge on that small snapshot in time so try and visit a couple of times if you can, and ask the breeder for regular updates.

- **Observe the mum**

Know the facts. Ideally, puppies should be with their mum for approximately the first 8 weeks, and you want the mum to be confident and happy. A good breeder should also be able to tell you about the puppy's dad and why he was selected as a sire, and show you any relevant health history, DNA and certificates for the lineage of both parents. Again, do ask the questions.

- **Get the paperwork**

Ensure you get what you need. It's a legal requirement for a breeder to give you microchip documentation for your puppy. If your puppy is a pedigree, you may be able to view or get a certificate from the breeder that details their ancestry. These days, sometimes these are digital. A breeder will treat their puppies for worms before they leave for their new home so they should be able to give you information about this too. (There are some great ongoing anti-parasite

13

treatments, such as BUG-K9 from A-OK9, which can safely go in with your puppy's food long-term). Most breeders will also have a puppy contract that explains both your and their responsibility for the puppy. Again, this is a good thing and the sign of a good breeder ensuring that all eventualities are covered.

• **Ask questions**
A good breeder should always be open to answering your questions. Useful things to ask might be 'What do you work on before the puppies go to their new homes?' or 'What's a typical day in the life of the puppies at this age?' They should also be able to tell you what type of food your puppy is eating. Raw food is increasingly used by many breeders, so don't be at all put off if this is the case; it has many benefits and is very much worth doing your research on.

Our top ten puppy essentials

While you're waiting for your puppy to arrive, there's a temptation to go on a mad spending spree, but you don't need to go over the top. There are only a few things that we would say truly are essentials.

1. A soft collar with ID
It's a legal requirement that a dog has an ID tag with their owner's phone number on it, which must be worn on their collar. We prefer either tags that fit flush on your puppy's collar, usually with a flexible band, or a collar with the phone number embroidered into it (there are many companies offering this online). A hanging tag that jingles when your puppy moves can leave your puppy more

vulnerable to other dogs you come across if they have learned to associate the jingling of an ID tag with another dog approaching, so we don't use these.

2. A crate

We'd always recommend having a crate and it's going to be useful throughout your dog's life. It is your puppy's safe space and a place for them to have downtime. The best and safest way to get your puppy home from a breeder or rescue centre is to pop them in a crate that you can secure on the back seat of a car, and have someone sit next to them on the journey home to check that they're comfortable. As you'll see in future chapters, you'll use your crate to teach your puppy all sorts of things, from how to be calm and how to be happy spending time home alone to how to sleep through the night.

Puppies are young and excitable and, like children, they don't always know when they need a nap or when they need some calm time. A crate makes that choice for them. In their crate, they have no option other than to chill out. You can think of this a little bit like when you go to a spa and you're not allowed to have your mobile phone with you. When distractions are removed, you can truly relax. For more information about different types of crates and how to choose one, see chapter 9.

3. A dog bed

This doesn't have to be anything fancy or costly. A soft bed can be a great option for sleep time and can be used in the corner of a puppy pen or gated area. Some puppies will chew soft bedding though, especially during that painful teething stage (see page 210 for more on this), so a more indestructible plastic bed with a soft pad inside it might be a better option. Raised cots or beds with legs are also great for teaching boundary games (more on this in chapter 9) because they provide a very clear, defined area.

You might choose to have more than one bed in different areas of the house, or move the bed around depending on where you want your puppy to settle.

Safety first

Never leave any age of dog with anything inside their crate (whether that's bedding, food or toys) that they could accidentally ingest or get tangled up in. Always remove your puppy's collar or harness before putting them inside the crate. There should be nothing in there that your pup can accidentally get caught in. You can put some washable bedding inside to make it cosy for your puppy (see information below).

---

4. Easily washable bedding

Your puppy will need some bedding to make their crate or puppy pen comfortable. Accidents will happen while your puppy is toilet training so choose something that is easily washable. Vet bedding is a popular option as it's washable and isn't easy for your puppy to chew or shred, but old towels or blankets are a great alternative.

5. Baby gates/puppy pens aka your 'gated community'

These can be used to manage where your puppy has access to in your house and to create their own defined area, particularly in the first few weeks. As you will see as you progress through this book, they are extremely useful when you're training your puppy and we will refer to them as your 'gated community'. Preventing free access to stairs is really important in those early months to avoid accidents and protect those growing puppy joints. A puppy's joints aren't fully developed until they're mature. It depends on the breed, but it can take up to 2 years for some dogs. Until then, you want to try and avoid repetitive movements like running up and down stairs.

Limiting your puppy to certain parts of your home also means they won't get overwhelmed by too many options or have opportunities to make less appropriate choices when you're not able to keep your eyes on them all the time. The majority of owners tend to choose the kitchen at first, as the floor is easily cleanable. This will also keep your puppy safe if there are areas of your house that have things they could get into mischief exploring or hurt themselves with if they chew.

It's also important for your puppy to learn to spend time away from you, which we'll explore in chapter 13. Gates and puppy pens are also brilliant for helping to teach your puppy that it's OK to be able to spend parts of the day separated from you and that this isn't scary.

6. Water bowl

Your puppy should always have access to fresh, clean water. Choose a ceramic bowl that is heavy enough to stop your puppy tipping it over. These are also easier to keep clean and hygienic than plastic or metal. A silicone collapsible bowl can be useful when you are travelling.

7. Calming food activities

Puppies love to mouth and chew so things like chews, bones and long-lasting treat dispensers such as lick mats and Kongs are essential. Kongs are snowman-shaped rubber food toys with a hollow centre that you fill with food for your puppy to chew and lick out. Lick mats are textured mats that challenge your dog to lick up every last bit of food (see the A-OK9 website for some options). They help to keep your puppy calm and they can also help soothe painful teething. We'll be talking more about them in chapter 4. We like to refer to these calming food activities as enrichment.

8. A puppy long line

This is a lightweight, thin nylon line that you attach to your puppy's collar when they're inside the house and leave trailing on the floor the majority of the time. As you're about to find out, puppies are into everything, so a long line is very useful for those first few weeks. Grabbing their collar can be scary for them so if they're heading for trouble or about to eat something they shouldn't, then you can pick up the line to gently lead them away instead. Long lines can also be useful as extra security when you're taking your puppy off lead for the first time. Use them as and when you feel is useful throughout your dog's life. We sell long lines on our website, www.absolute-dogs.com.

9. A harness

When you do head out for walks, it's better for a puppy to wear a harness rather than a collar. Puppies have their thyroid gland and a lot of important nerves in their neck that could be damaged by pulling or straining on a collar. A well-fitted Y-shaped harness allows their shoulders to move so it doesn't impinge on their neck. You'll need more harnesses as your dog grows so ask fellow dog owners if they've got any hand-me-downs or buy second-hand.

10. A double-ended lead

A double-ended lead with clips at both ends gives you two points of connection. One end normally attaches to the back of your puppy's harness, while the other end attaches to a clip on the chest of the harness or to your puppy's collar. This allows you to walk in a more balanced way and helps to gently steer your puppy. We're also going to introduce you to some games where a double-ended lead comes in handy. We sell double-ended leads on our website, www.absolute-dogs.com.

Other useful items

• Coats and jumpers

Depending on where you live and what time of the year it is, some puppies will need an extra layer when they go outside. For tiny breeds such as Chihuahuas, this is particularly important.

• Toys

As you're going to find out, one of your main aims is to build calmness in your puppy. If you fill their space full of toys, then switching off and relaxing is going to be more challenging for them.

In chapter 5, we look at how you can use toys in your training to build engagement and your puppy's relationship with you, and allowing free access to them will undermine this.

On a more practical note, toys are expensive and you really don't want your puppy to be destroying them. Leaving a dog unattended with toys could also mean a trip to the vet when parts of them suddenly end up stuck in your pup's tummy.

• **Interactive puzzle feeders**
These are plastic disks or trays that your dog has to flip, push or roll around to unlock food. They are a great option for engaging your puppy's brain, building their problem-solving skills, letting them use that powerful nose and varying the way you deliver your puppy's meals (more on this in chapter 4).

Form your team

Your choice of puppy will shape the team you need. You'll need to find a vet and possibly a groomer before your puppy arrives. You're paying these people for their knowledge and advice, so you want your team to consist of those you trust, respect and get along with. Get recommendations from other dog owners. It's a good idea to meet a few vets, chat to them, ask questions and look at their facilities rather than waiting until your puppy has a tummy upset or is due their first inoculations, and then suddenly having to find someone at the last minute. Not all breeds will need a groomer – for example, a smooth-coated dog may only need you to become skilled at doing their nails. If you do need a groomer, bear in mind that being groomed can be a stressful experience for dogs, and as a result good groomers get booked up.

Preparing your home

This isn't about rearranging your whole house but about having realistic expectations, particularly in the first few weeks after you bring your puppy home. Puppies navigate the world with their bodies and their teeth. They don't know that certain things are off limits or understand that they shouldn't chew things in your home, so you do need to move things out of their way. If you're going to leave your puppy in a particular room, check first what you're leaving in there with them.

It's important to set yourself and your puppy up for success and help them to make great decisions. If you don't want your puppy to have access to certain rooms or areas of the house, put a baby gate up. If you don't want them to chew socks or shoes, then make sure there are none on the floor in your puppy's pathway. Always be vigilant. If you can't supervise your dog, create physical boundaries so that they can't roam the house freely.

It is also important to think about setting aside some areas of your home that are just used as calm spaces for your puppy where they can chill out and rest. As you're going to be teaching your puppy how to be calm, it makes sense to have some areas in your home that are just calm spaces. Think about having some rooms where you train your puppy and play games, and others where you just chill out – we call this rehearsing the room. We'll delve into this in more detail in chapter 8.

21

Basic puppy-proofing

Here are some things you might want to put out of reach in those first few weeks when you're starting to train your puppy:

- Shoes
- Charger cords
- Children's toys
- Chemical/cleaning products
- Medications.

KEY QUESTIONS

Before you get your puppy, there are some key questions you and your family should ask yourselves:

- Do you want your puppy to sleep in your bed?
- Is your puppy going to be allowed to go upstairs?
- Do you want your puppy to go on your furniture?

There are no rights or wrongs. Work out what suits you as an individual or household and check everyone's on the same page. It can be really confusing for your puppy if different members of your household have different rules. Nothing is set in stone, but making sure everyone is clear on what the rules are is going to avoid any conflict or uncertainty further down the road.

We don't allow our dogs on the furniture without being invited and that's something we taught our puppies from day one.

Pupternity leave

Realistically, you can't expect to bring home a puppy on a Sunday and then go back into the office for a full day on the Monday. You're not going to know until you get your puppy how easy it's going to be to transition them to being left home alone. Even though we'd encourage you to get back to whatever the norm is as soon as you can, there is inevitably going to be a lifestyle shift when you get a dog.

To begin with, your puppy is going to need very regular toilet breaks (see chapter 7). As you progress with toilet training and your puppy begins to have a little more control over where and how often they go to the toilet, 3–4 hours is still the longest a puppy can wait, so you're going to need to factor that into your plans while your puppy is young. Even as an adult, it's not healthy for your dog not to be able to go to the toilet for hours on end if you're out of the house all day.

Every puppy is different and it's a case of getting to know them and working out what they can and can't handle, but you can probably anticipate there's going to be at least 2 weeks of adjustment.

Many of us have flexible working lives these days and working from home if you can is an ideal solution with a new puppy. You're going to need to be around a lot those first few days as your puppy adjusts and you'll probably want to be around too, to get to know them.

A winning mindset

Finally, we'd like to cover some ways to adjust your mindset when you welcome your puppy.

Reframe your thinking

Sometimes we'll talk to owners about their new puppy and they'll list all the things that they don't want: they don't want their puppy to wee on the floor, chew the furniture or sleep on the beds. We always try and get them to reframe their thinking and consider what they DO want instead. Don't say 'I don't want my puppy to wee on the floor,' do say 'I want my puppy to wee on the grass outside'. Or don't say 'I don't want them to sleep on my bed,' instead do say 'I want my puppy to sleep downstairs and enjoy doing so.'

Decide what you do want and frame it that way, then set up a scenario in which your puppy learns the required skills. Then you can focus on how to achieve those skills, and reward your puppy when they do.

This switches the mentality from one of problems to one of solutions. If you only focus on what you don't want, then your only approach is to try and stop these things from happening. Instead, if you know what you do want, this allows you to have a positive mindset and see all the opportunities to reward your puppy.

New owners often become very frustrated and overwhelmed when they get trapped in a world of what they don't want rather than focusing on what they do want. Rather than getting stuck on a problem – he's barking, he's weeing, he's chewing my sofa – think about what you do want and come up with a solution for that.

24

The relationship bank account

Your relationship with your puppy is a bit like a bank account with deposits and withdrawals coming in and out of it as you interact with your puppy throughout the day. Deposits are any positive interactions that you have with your puppy, such as playing a game or stroking them. Withdrawals are anything they might see as negative or might not enjoy, such as a visit to the vet or giving them a bath or clipping their nails.

When you reward your puppy for something they've done correctly, you're depositing good things into your relationship bank account. Your puppy is starting to understand that you're incredibly valuable to them and that being with you and interacting with you is fun. If you get frustrated with your puppy and scold them, you're withdrawing from the bank account. Puppies don't realise they've made a mistake. They don't understand the difference between right and wrong so it's important to try and avoid those interactions so the positives always outweigh the negatives.

Praising your puppy

When you first get your puppy, observe your dog and get a feel for what lights them up. Use what they like as a reward – that might be food, or it could be praise or stroking. These are all positive interactions that pay into the relationship bank account.

We love to praise our puppies and we believe you should verbally praise your dog from day one. Some dogs love to be stroked and cuddled while others are less keen. Be aware that different kinds of stroking have different effects on your puppy. Long, slow strokes are more calming, whereas more rapid pats would get your puppy more excited.

Certain withdrawals from your relationship bank account are inevitable, such as vet visits, for example. Withdrawals can happen without you meaning for them to happen too. We are all human, and even the best-intentioned human can fall short on occasion. Don't feel bad. Things will go wrong with your puppy at times but how you deal with it and how you move on from it is what matters. Always be aware of your relationship bank account and the importance of depositing wonderful interactions and value into your relationship with your puppy. That way, when you do make a withdrawal (trimming their nails or giving them a bath, for example), the balance is still tipped in the right direction because there's such an amazing history of support and of you being the bringer of awesomeness and joy.

CHAPTER 2
Your Puppy's Bucket

In this chapter, we're going to look at what is possibly *the* most important concept that you can understand about your puppy. It's the one thing we think every dog owner should know and this ground-breaking, exciting idea will completely transform the relationship you have with your dog for the rest of their life.

Every puppy has an imaginary bucket. Throughout the day, lots of different things will fill up that bucket and once it reaches capacity and overflows, it will lead to less desirable behaviour from your puppy. Your aim as an owner is to help keep your puppy's bucket at a manageable level.

What fills the bucket?

- **Excitement** – events or interactions that get your puppy excited will contribute to how full their bucket gets. This might be playing with a toy, going for a walk, or experiencing something new for the first time.

- **Fear** – depending on your puppy's personality, what they find scary could be anything from another dog barking at them or a visitor at your house to a trip to the vet. What one puppy finds exciting, another may find worrying, and this adds to their bucket.

- **Physical or medical issues** – if your puppy is itching because they've got fleas or allergies then their bucket is going to be more full than usual. If they're sore or in pain, this will fill their bucket too. Often a puppy's tummy will get a little upset by all the changes that happen when they first move from the familiarity of the breeder to their new home with you, so it's worth knowing that this can fill their bucket too.

Imagine this: You take your puppy for a walk. Your puppy gets excited when they see you picking up the lead because this predicts the exciting walk that is coming, so their bucket is already a little bit full, even before you leave the house. Then you walk to the park and spend 10 minutes throwing a tennis ball. Your puppy finds this really exciting and their bucket fills a bit more. On the walk back, another dog barks at your puppy. Because your dog finds this a bit worrying, their bucket fills even more. At this point, you see a postal worker coming round the corner, which surprises your puppy. All of these experiences have been pouring into your puppy's bucket and at this point, it's close to overflowing. Then you walk a little further and just before you get to your house, you approach someone pushing a crying baby in a pram. This adds the final measure to that bucket, the bucket overflows and your puppy barks or lunges at this person. As owners, we sometimes find ourselves saying 'I'm sorry, they've never done that before!' Then we might start thinking 'I need to keep my puppy away from crying babies as they're obviously a trigger for them'. But your puppy isn't

29

reacting to that specific event or situation, but to everything that's led up to that moment. Too many experiences have filled your puppy's bucket and it has overflowed.

We can all relate to this. You know when you've had 'one of those days'? Perhaps you overslept, then you had a long and busy day at work where things went wrong and a lot was thrown at you, then you got stuck in traffic on the way home. Then you finally get home and your partner says something to you and you just lose it. That's your bucket overflowing. It's not really about what your partner said, it's just an accumulation of things that have happened throughout the day and your partner's comment was the final straw. We describe that as a bucket overflow moment. It's not because of anything happening in that specific moment, it's the lead-up to it – either that day or even the day before.

Bucket basics

- Every puppy has a bucket, which fills from a variety of different causes.
- Positive stress and excitement pay into it.
- Negative stress and fear pay into it.
- Pain, itching and tummy troubles pay into it.
- Depending on your puppy, different events will pay different amounts into the bucket.
- How a puppy reacts might not necessarily be about the situation that they're in. Instead, it could be the result of what has happened that day or even that week.
- Any out-of-the-ordinary change in your puppy's behaviour could be a sign that they have a full bucket.

Full-bucket behaviour is NOT a training issue

If your puppy usually knows how to behave, the problem isn't that they haven't been taught a certain skill. The problem is that their bucket is full. Any attempt to resolve the problem through training is going to be doomed to failure because the underlying issue (a full bucket) persists.

What does a full bucket look like?

- Barking/more vocal.
- Lunging towards things that are scary or exciting.
- Struggling to settle in the house.
- Pulling on the lead.
- Jumping up.
- Distracted or struggling to focus on you.
- Humping.
- Irritability with you, your children, other pets.
- Hiding away and avoidance.

Emptying and filling

Every dog has a different sized bucket. The physical size of a dog doesn't determine the size of their bucket. A Chihuahua can have a huge bucket whereas a Great Dane can have a tiny one. Your puppy's bucket is in part due to their genetic make-up and their personality and in part a result of the events and experiences they are exposed to on a daily basis. Some puppies have very small

31

buckets, but we can grow them over time. Other puppies have huge buckets and that means they can endure difficult encounters and yet rarely experience those bucket-overflow moments (of course, this is uncommon!).

The other thing to bear in mind is that every puppy's bucket takes a different length of time to empty and they can only do that when their brain isn't being stimulated or exposed to things and everything is nice and calm.

Some puppies can get overstimulated, their bucket overflows, at which point perhaps they bark or react to another dog, but half an hour later their bucket has emptied again and they have recovered from that event. For other dogs, it can take much longer for the bucket to empty back to a level where they are more able to respond appropriately to events and less likely to be 'reactive'.

Observe your puppy

As you get to know your puppy, you'll begin to get a sense of when their bucket is starting to fill. Notice how their behaviour changes at certain times. As their bucket fills, you'll often find their choices deteriorate. Let's say you've been struggling with your puppy nipping. It's likely that as their bucket fills, that nipping will get worse. If you've got a puppy who barks, they'll potentially bark more as their bucket fills, or they might find it harder to settle. If you think their bucket has overflowed, consider what has happened in the lead-up to that moment so you can do everything possible to avoid that happening again in the future.

There are three important factors to consider when it comes to your puppy's bucket:

- Lifestyle choices
- Emptying the bucket
- Growing and inspiring calmness.

1. Lifestyle choices

Life and the general busyness of your household can naturally be bucket filling, so think about what else you are exposing your puppy to on a daily basis. It's really important not to overwhelm your puppy, so if you think their bucket is nearing full, be mindful of what you're doing. Perhaps it's not a good idea to take them to the school gates this afternoon or on an exciting walk this evening.

Be aware of your puppy's bucket and work with it rather than against it. Be smart about what situations you put your puppy in. It's important to match the situation to the size of their bucket. If there's a mismatch between their bucket size and the environments you put them in, then it will lead to an overflow. You might be desperate to take your new puppy to the pub, but it's important to ask yourself whether this is in their best interests. Do they have a bucket that will accommodate all the stimuli of that environment? Make sure you're not putting your puppy in a situation that is beyond their capacity.

It's OK to say 'no'

Your aim as an owner is to adapt your puppy's lifestyle to suit the capacity of their bucket. Much of the time a puppy's owner is a major contributor to the bucket, often without even realising. We want to do so much with our puppies – play with them, take them out and meet lots of people – and sometimes this can mean we're not giving them enough of a break. Think about the situations

33

you're putting your puppy in and adapt plans if you think they've had enough.

Try and think ahead about what's coming up in your puppy's life.

If you know you've got to take them to the groomer or friends are coming to visit, limit other activities that are likely to pay into their bucket in the lead-up to that event so that they're more likely to have the capacity to deal with it.

Puppies are a magnet for people. They're small and super cute and everyone is going to want to hold them or stroke them. When you get a new puppy, all your dog-owning friends are going to be ringing you asking you to meet them for a walk.

But now you know about their bucket, take a step back and consider whether a particular situation is right for your puppy. Are they (and their bucket) going to be able to cope with it? Going for a walk with a friend and their dog might not be appropriate, because you've identified that your puppy needs to be a little calmer or a little more confident before they are put in that situation.

You know your dog best. Being your puppy's advocate is about knowing when to say no and being brave about it. It's about feeling confident in saying to people: 'my puppy won't enjoy that experience'.

2. Emptying the bucket

Left alone, we have found that a typical puppy's bucket can take 72 hours or longer to empty – and that's without other things happening in the meantime. So the big question is, how do we speed up that process?

If you need to relax, do you head to the disco or the spa? You go to the spa, of course, and that's what we need for our dogs. To help that bucket to empty, you need your puppy to chill out. There are lots of things that you can do to help:

- Take a bucket holiday. Aim for 3 days of calm, where you try and minimise your puppy's exposure to anything that's going to fill the bucket or prevent it from emptying. Remember that both exciting and scary things will pay into your puppy's bucket. If there are unavoidable commitments for your puppy in those 3 days that you can't cancel or change, think about how you can limit their exposure to sounds, sights and interactions that are going to pay more into their bucket. That might be as simple as finding somewhere for your puppy to settle quietly in a covered crate and a long-lasting chew to help them tune out what's going on around them.

- The key is to become your dog's expert observer. Know what works for your puppy and what their positive and negative stressors are. Notice what has an impact on them and recognise and identify any changes in the norm, then give them a few days of rest and relaxation.

- Engage them in activities that are naturally calming, such as enjoying a Kong or a long-lasting chew. See the 'Ditch the Bowl' section in chapter 4 and chapter 8 on calmness for more ideas.

- Replace any exciting games and activities with calmness games, which we'll talk about more in chapter 8.

3. Growing and inspiring calmness

The third factor to consider when it comes to your puppy's bucket is the importance of calmness. In fact, calmness is so important to your puppy's emotional well-being and to their ability to make great choices that we've dedicated a whole chapter to it. You'll find this on page 106.

The human bucket

We humans have our own buckets and as a new dog owner, we want you to be mindful to empty your bucket as well as your puppy's.

Typically when people get a dog, it becomes all-consuming. Their entire day is filled with doing things for or with the dog or worrying about them and that can be stressful. Make sure you have moments each day where you do something that isn't dog-related. Even something as simple as running yourself a bath or going for a walk without your puppy can help you to empty your own bucket.

You will overcome this

Things won't always go right with your puppy but try to stay calm and keep a positive mindset. Remind yourself that one negative event is not a predictor of everything in the future. Just because you have one walk with your puppy where they barked at another dog doesn't mean that from now on they are going to bark at every dog they see.

If you're feeling a little stretched by the demands of your puppy, make a conscious decision to have a solution-focused mindset. Think 5 per cent problem, 95 per cent solution. If your puppy barked at another dog, think about what skills your puppy would need that would stop them from reacting that way next time. That way, you immediately focus on the solution – which is that they need to be calmer and more optimistic. There are lots of games you can play with your puppy to teach them those skills. Remember, everything is changeable and there is always a game for that!

Don't be too hard on yourself

New owners often feel a great sense of guilt around their dog. We encourage you to get rid of those emotions and focus on the fact that it doesn't have to be perfect. Your puppy is really lucky to have you as an owner. The fact that you are reading this book means you are a brilliant owner who wants the best for your puppy.

Knowledge is power

As an owner, you can adapt your puppy's lifestyle to suit their bucket.

You can also play games with your puppy that will help increase the capacity of their bucket and enable them to cope with a variety of situations without an overflow. Throughout the book, we're going to show you so many games to play with your puppy to build calmness, grow their optimism and help them think better when they're excited – all of which will help prevent their bucket getting too full.

Having an awareness of your puppy's bucket and keeping it as empty as possible means you're going to have a fun, enjoyable and more harmonious life with your dog. Your puppy will be happier, more relaxed and better able to enjoy daily life. That in turn keeps their bucket empty and allows them to go about their business happily. You can't get better than that!

CHAPTER 3
Puppies, Babies and Children

Welcoming a new puppy into your family is exciting, and this can be especially true if you have young children. At Absolute Dogs, we believe that children and dogs should have fun together and that little ones can be willing participants in helping to train their new furry friend. Introducing a dog to your family can be an incredible opportunity for children to learn about responsibility, communication and respect for boundaries. However, that relationship will take time to grow and develop, and if it is going to flourish it needs to be built on the right foundations.

When people decide to add a puppy to their household, they often have an idyllic picture of a dog completing their family and being a best friend to their children, and yet in many cases the reality is very different to begin with. We see so many families who have brought home a puppy and found their behaviour challenging. If you take a step back, you can easily see why. What you tend to get when you introduce a new puppy to a family is over-excited children, running around and making noise. That creates an excited puppy who does the same. The puppy starts to become overstimulated and tired and might jump up at the children, nip them or grab their clothes. Understandably, the children scream and run away and the puppy, thinking this is an awesome game, gives chase. This continues and everyone gets stuck in a vicious, chaotic cycle. Alternatively, your puppy might find the advances of the children in a household quite worrying, resulting in a very full bucket and a pessimistic little puppy who hasn't learned the skills they need.

It's worth remembering that the puppy teething phase can be one of the most challenging times, especially for young children who don't understand why puppies bite, and who can quickly flip from excitement about their new friend to fear of those sharp puppy teeth. See chapter 14 for more on mouthing, nipping and biting.

Preparing children for the awesomeness of a new puppy

When a puppy is joining your family and children are already part of the household, preparation is key to success for all involved. Consider your new puppy's age and size, as well as the age and maturity level of your children, and factor this into the first introduction and all subsequent interactions between them. Whether your puppy is coming from a breeder or a rescue centre, it's vital that you don't pressure them to be part of your family life at first. Everything will be new and strange and possibly a little scary. They are very likely to have a full bucket and must have an opportunity to decompress.

You could have the friendliest of puppies, and they may still not be happy with children getting in their space right from the moment they come home. So it's really important to set up that first introduction in a way that ensures everyone is comfortable and to manage the expectations of very excited (or possibly wary) children.

Before a certain age, children cannot understand why they should act in a certain way around a dog. No matter how much you try to explain to your toddler why they shouldn't crowd your puppy, get into its space when it is eating, or ride it like a horse, these things are all too tempting to a child. They just don't get that your puppy will not appreciate this type of play. You should always carefully manage any interactions between them and your children.

Set expectations

Before your puppy comes home, explain to your children that your dog has just left their mummy and brothers and sisters and they might be feeling anxious and worried. Depending on the age of your children, relate it to something they might have been through, such as their first day at nursery or school, so they understand how nervous their puppy might be coming somewhere new with people they don't know.

Involve them in the conversations

In chapter 1, we talked about all the things you might need to consider before bringing a puppy into your home. If your children are old enough to understand, it's great to involve them in these discussions. Talk about things such as:

- Where your puppy will sleep.
- Which rooms they're going to be allowed to go in.

- Which areas of the house you're going to play games and train in and which are for rest and quiet time.

Set ground rules and explain why you're putting them in place. Write a list together of things your children need to remember and stick it on the fridge. Using your puppy's name makes it personal and can help everyone start to feel a bond with their new family member before they even come home. Let's call him 'Fido'.

The list might include:

- I can sit calmly on the sofa and watch Fido play.
- I will walk calmly and quietly past Fido so that he doesn't get scared.
- I can stroke Fido if Mum/Dad/a grown-up says it's OK.
- I should wait for Fido to come to me and remember that he might feel worried if I get too close.
- I can help with Fido's training when a grown-up is there to supervise.
- I can play calm games with Fido that don't make him too excited or make him want to jump up at me.
- I will remember to give Fido lots of space when he's eating or sleeping.
- I can learn what Fido's body language is telling me about how he's feeling. (See the box later on in this chapter for more information.)
- I can have lots of fun doing things that don't involve Fido so that he gets time to relax.

Explain the bucket

Right from the start, it's a good idea to get your children involved in the bucket analogy. In simple terms, explain that your puppy will be very tired and overwhelmed and that each day he or she will need lots of rest time and calmness. Again, it will help to relate it back to something your children understand. That might be reminding them that babies and toddlers need nap times, or that older children need time to chill out and watch TV or read a book.

Have strategies in place

Before your puppy arrives, it's worth explaining to your children things that your new puppy might do and how you're going to respond to them. Talk about how your puppy might mouth or jump up and explain how that is normal behaviour for an excited or teething pup. Come up with solutions beforehand. If your puppy mouths or nips, suggest how it would be a good idea to direct them to something else, like a toy or a chew. If your puppy jumps up, explain that you're not going to scream or run away. Instead, you're going to pop some food on their bed and lead them over to it calmly, or scatter a few pieces of their food on the floor.

Think about your puppy as an adult dog

Before your puppy comes into your family, it can be helpful to think about how you want your puppy to behave as an adult dog and all the things that you DO want. Perhaps you want your dog to walk calmly on a lead when you take them out and not jump up at people when they're fully grown because they will be too big. This gives you something to reference later if your children are encouraging the puppy to jump up: 'Remember we talked about when puppy's a big dog we don't want them to jump up.' Explain how confusing it will be if you encourage them to do that now, and the rules change when they're bigger.

Make sure you include fun things too. You might want your dog to be able to retrieve a ball or play tug.

Gentle introductions

When you first bring your puppy home, keep your first introduction to young children short and calm. Remember, your puppy might never have seen children before. It's really important to allow your puppy time and space to choose to engage with you. Some puppies might not want to interact with children, just as some children might want to keep their distance from dogs, so don't force it.

There are lots of things you can do to make this introduction go well.

Supervise every greeting stage and be ready to intervene at any point if either your puppy or children look uncomfortable.

We love boundary games for dogs (see page 130), but they can also be super helpful for children! Ask your children to stay within appropriate boundaries (the sofa, a chair, a rug on the floor) when introducing your puppy to them for the first time. This will keep everyone calm and prevent sudden movements that might startle your puppy. It can be helpful to have them sitting on the floor so they're at the same level as the puppy. We discuss boundary games in more detail in chapter 9.

Remind your children to let your puppy come and say hello in its own time and not to grab the puppy or try and pick it up. If the puppy does come over to them, then gentle stroking is OK.

If you have more than one child, it can help to do introductions one at a time so it's not too overwhelming for your puppy.

Strategies for success

Use your gated community

If dogs and children are together all the time, that can very quickly lead to overflowing buckets all round. This is when you are most at risk of things going wrong. Dogs and children should have their own spaces to coexist safely. Make sure there are periods every day where your puppy has time away from the children and the constant happenings of the household to relax, sleep and empty that bucket. As we'll talk about in chapter 9, that might be a puppy pen, a crate, a bed or a quiet room.

Think about where you place your puppy's bed or crate and try to make sure it's away from the noise and activity in the house so your puppy can genuinely rest. Tom's niece, Lily, would not leave her two dogs alone when they were in their crates because of where they were positioned. They could easily see each other so both the puppies and Lily were tempted to interact instead of sleeping. Simply moving the location of their crates solved that. Covering the crate can also help to deter young children from disturbing a sleeping puppy.

Let your children have a puppy-free area too. You might make their bedroom or a playroom off limits for the puppy so they can play safely and more energetically without worrying about how the noise is going to affect the dog. Lauren's daughter Eliza often wanted to grab hold of their dogs Blink and Eazy, or ride them like ponies. Rather than allow this to become a constant source of worry, Lauren employed gates, puppy pens and boundaries, and bought Eliza a hobby horse. This allowed for distraction and space to manoeuvre. Everyone needs a strategy!

Always supervise any interactions

Whatever their age, children should never be left to interact with a puppy without some form of supervision. This is especially important with a younger child who won't understand or even notice a change in a dog's body language. A crawling baby or a toddler has no understanding of how to read a dog and invading their space, crawling on them, grabbing at their fur, ears, skin and tail can easily create a disastrous situation where the dog feels it must defend itself. It is crucial that when a child isn't old enough and doesn't know how to respect a dog's space, they have no free access to it.

Giving your dog a safe place away from interruptions when eating and sleeping will help them feel secure. Never allow a child to take any item (food or toy) off a dog.

Signs that your puppy might be uncomfortable

- Eyeballing
- Ears back
- Staring
- Prickling fur
- Stillness

- Growling, snapping, barking
- Trying to get away
- Wiggling and squirming
- Lowering to the floor
- Peeing while interacting.

Teach your children how to handle your puppy

Teaching children about respecting a dog's space and helping them learn what their new furry friend might enjoy – and more importantly, what they might not enjoy – is really important.

Every dog is different, and you will get to know your own puppy's preferences over time. Talking to your children about the different areas of your puppy's body – and explaining which ones are more appropriate for petting – can help grow a healthy respect for your dog's boundaries and keep everyone safe.

It might be helpful to compare this to things your children enjoy or dislike. Perhaps your child dislikes having their underarms tickled or loves being hugged by you but dislikes being embraced by people outside your immediate family. The same is true of dogs. Some dogs feel very uncomfortable being petted by strangers but really enjoy pets from members of their family. Other dogs love to be fussed and stroked by everyone!

The safest places to pet a dog are usually on their chest, their shoulders, and gently under their chin – but again, every dog is different and it will take time to get to know what your puppy likes and dislikes. See chapter 16 for more information on how to get your puppy used to being handled.

Just like Tom's niece Lily, children will often want to try and pick a puppy up. This can be unsafe, especially for younger children, so it's good to have a rule that all four paws need to stay on the floor at all times. Always keep handling calm and gentle and wait for the puppy to initiate any interactions.

Get your children involved in games

Children love to play, so get them involved in some games that they can play with your puppy (see this chapter for some awesome suggestions). Games create a common language for children and puppies to communicate with each other. Explaining to your children in simple terms why you don't feed your puppy from a bowl and how you can use your puppy's food to help them learn all the skills they need as they grow up can be another great way to get your children involved. If your children want your puppy to go somewhere or to move away from something, encourage them to lure with a little bit of food. Explain that whenever you spot your puppy being nice and calm, you're going to reward them with some of their dinner. You could even teach your children to notice any time your puppy chooses to hang out calmly on their bed, and gently drop a few pieces of food beside them to show your puppy what a great choice they made.

You can make toilet training a game too. Have a chart on the fridge like you might use when you are potty training a toddler, and give your children the very special job of putting a sticker or a star on the chart every time the puppy goes to the toilet outside.

Reward your children for being a great owner

If you spot your children doing something right – whether you notice them having a nice, gentle interaction with your puppy or ignoring your puppy because they know it needs to rest – be sure to acknowledge that. Let your children know they are doing a great job and that they are being a super owner.

When you're training a puppy, it's so easy to see the things that people do wrong and miss those little opportunities to reward them for doing something right. Spotting all the great choices your kids make around your puppy will make those things much more likely to happen again in the future.

Games are an awesome way to grow the relationship between your children and your puppy. Here are some great games they can enjoy together.

MAGIC WAND

A 'magic wand' here is a ball chucker or, as we like to call it, a wanger (see page 165 for the grown-up version of the wanger game). If you don't have a ball chucker, then get creative – soup ladles or large serving spoons also work well and can be washed after the game. Explain to your child that this is the perfect game to help your puppy to learn to walk nicely by your side while you're all out and about together.

Step 1: To turn on their magic wand, get your child to put a piece of your puppy's food into the 'cup' end. Hold out their wand away from their body with the cup end nearest the puppy. Get them to try and keep it level with their mouth. When your puppy looks towards where the piece of secret food is hidden, get them to lower their magic wand so the puppy can eat the tasty food. Get them to try and keep your puppy standing up if they can, rather than sitting or lying down.

Step 2: Once they have their magic wand working nicely, they are going to try and add some extra sparkle by moving the wand up just a little bit higher to see if your puppy can still smell the food. When puppy's head is under the wand, get them to turn their magic wand and tip the food into puppy's mouth. Will they catch it? It's OK if they don't – they get to chase after it on the floor, which is also fun. Remember to turn on their wand again with another piece of food and then lower the wand when puppy looks up so that they can eat the tasty food – yum!

Superstar level: Has your puppy been really clever at Step 1 and Step 2? Have your child and the puppy been practising hard together? Explain they are now ready to unleash the wand's magical powers and start moving around. In the beginning, get them to move slowly and watch for your puppy to follow them. Once your puppy is standing under the cup of their wand, get them to tip it and see how clever their puppy is at catching!

MAGIC CATCH

Magic Catch is a super game to keep your puppy near you and teach them that playing games is way more fun than running off after other dogs, birds or even squirrels.

Step 1: Before you get your puppy out to play this game, **encourage** your child to practise throwing their food first. Get them to imagine where your puppy's mouth might be if they are standing in front of them, and practise throwing pieces of food towards them so they can catch it.

Step 2: Once they've practised their throwing, get them to take a couple of pieces of food and call puppy over to them. Now they need to try to throw it so that your puppy can catch it! Explain to your child that it's great for your puppy to win every time, so even if they don't catch it, they can tell them 'good try' and let them eat it from the floor.

STIR THE CAULDRON

A 'cauldron' is something your puppy can walk around. You can use a cone, a bucket, a watering can or a bin. A 'cauldron' shorter than your puppy is helpful if your dog is just learning this game. When you start the game, get your child to hold your puppy gently by their collar/harness. If your child or your puppy are not OK with this, step in to hold your puppy still.

Step 1: Once you have your puppy gently held at one side of your cauldron, have your hand with some food ready on the opposite side. Make sure you are standing really close to the cauldron so that your puppy can't 'cheat' and squeeze between you and your cauldron or jump over the top to get to your hand. Let go of your puppy's harness or collar and encourage them to go around the outside of the cauldron to get that yummy food.

Step 2: Once your puppy understands the idea of going round the cauldron to get the food, you can gradually start moving the reward so they have to chase it around the cauldron. If your puppy catches on quickly, you can also stand a little further away from the cauldron and see if your puppy can still go round it.

Step 3: When your puppy has learned to go around the cauldron in one direction, try the other direction too!

Introducing your puppy to a new baby

Sometimes, introductions need to happen the other way round. If your family is expanding with more than just a furry addition, you may be thinking about preparing your puppy for the arrival of a new baby.

Bringing a baby home is a huge adjustment for everyone and dogs are no exception. The complete disruption of routine can be overwhelming. We refer to babies as 'novelty machines' – they make strange sounds and smells and unexpected movements, especially when they become mobile and start crawling, walking and grabbing. This can be really testing for dogs, so it's important to start preparing your puppy for your new arrival as soon as you can.

Strategies for success

Ditch the routine

Make sure you don't have a set routine with your puppy before the baby arrives because there's going to be very little routine when they do. Your life is going to change massively and be driven by the needs of your tiny human! You may not be able to take your puppy out at precisely the same time each day. There may be days when you can't manage it at all. In chapter 23, we'll talk about the benefits of ditching the routine.

Play Novelty Party – the baby edition!

One thing you can guarantee is that the arrival of a baby will mean the arrival of many new and novel items, from cots and cribs to play pens, musical mobiles and noisy baby toys. Imagine how overwhelming all this can be for a puppy. Have you ever noticed your puppy startle at a perfectly normal household object simply because it's been left somewhere different? Perhaps a room has taken on a completely new look as you've turned it into a nursery. Has your puppy taken that in their stride, or are they showing signs of being a little stressed by the arrival of all this unfamiliar equipment? Grow calmness and confidence around all the new items that have started to appear – a car seat, a bouncy chair, a pram, a Moses basket or crib – by scattering some of your puppy's daily food allowance around them (not in them). You want to get your puppy used to seeing these things and being around them and to pair those items with a positive outcome so your puppy learns they are not something to worry about.

Get your puppy used to baby noises

Play baby noises on YouTube or Spotify at a really low volume. At the same time, give your puppy a Kong, a bone or a long-lasting chew. Over time, slightly increase the volume so they learn to see these unusual sounds as no big deal. Make sure you incorporate a range of unfamiliar sounds into these sessions. Every baby will make unique noises, so you are not aiming to condition your puppy to a specific sound. Variety is key!

Teach your puppy to disengage

Play Disengagement Pattern (see page 346 for more details) with your puppy away from the pram or the crib (or wherever you think your baby might be spending most of their time) so that your puppy learns the value of disengaging from spaces and places you need them to stay away from, before the baby is even there.

Keep things calm and optimistic

If you already have a puppy who is calm and optimistic, then a baby is just a test of that. If you have any doubts, put work into those skills and read chapters 6 and 8 before the baby arrives.

Take it slowly

Great relationships are formed at a distance to start with. Your tiny baby has the ability to scare your puppy. It's such a fragile relationship and one you really need to grow carefully. Don't be in a rush to introduce them.

Those early days can quickly feel overwhelming – for you, your children and for your puppy. It can be difficult knowing how best to set your puppy up for success as they learn to adjust and settle into their new home, and how to manage your own expectations and, more importantly, those of your children.

Yet, with the right preparation and a foundation of calmness, children and dogs can have a truly magical relationship. What could be more awesome for your little ones than growing up with a furry friend by their side.

CHAPTER 4
Feeding Your Puppy

When it comes to feeding your new puppy, the first thing we want you to do, and something we do with all our own puppies and dogs, is DITCH THE BOWL.

What does 'Ditch the Bowl' mean?

Dogs love to learn. Did you know that they also *prefer* to work for their food rather than just being handed it on a plate? Ditch the Bowl is a life-changing concept where you get to toss out the routine of feeding your puppy by putting their food into a bowl twice a day. Instead, you use it for training, for building calmness and as a way of reinforcing all the brilliant choices your puppy is going to make throughout the day.

Start as you mean to go on. Right from the very first day that you get your puppy, we want you to ditch the bowl and use your puppy's daily allowance of food to reward them for making super choices. This will help to form good habits and create rewarding experiences by playing games and growing the skills they need to set them up for a lifetime of success. Dogs love experiences, and this is a way of enriching their lives further and creating a robust and well-behaved companion!

If you feed your puppy from a bowl, you're just wasting that value. Imagine you've got a bowl containing 20 pieces of kibble (dry dog food). That's 20 opportunities to reinforce and reward your puppy for making an amazing decision!

In chapter 1, we talked about the relationship bank account. By playing games with food as a reward, you pour all that value into the relationship bank account instead of into a bowl. It's food your puppy would have eaten anyway, but delivered in a way that's much more fun for both you and your puppy.

As well as boosting your relationship, Ditch the Bowl increases the value of that food by creating fun experiences and allowing your puppy to use their natural instincts. What's not to love about that?

It doesn't matter what sort of food you feed your puppy (kibble, raw, semi-moist). You choose the food you want to feed them and then you work out how to use it. So go on – ditch that bowl!

Without a bowl, food is split three ways:

- Playing games – to build skills that your puppy is going to need as they grow and to put value into those all-important concepts like calmness, optimism and proximity.
- Rewarding choices – food is a great way of communicating to your puppy that they made a great choice.
- Enrichment – providing your puppy with opportunities to be physically, emotionally and mentally satisfied through calming food activities such as Kongs and chews.

Ditch the bowl and boost your relationship

When you don't use a bowl, feeding your dog becomes a positive interaction and helps to boost your relationship. In fact, it's the foundation for all the reward-based training you're going to do with them. Your puppy gets used to food being delivered from you. They want to be close to you so you become the centre of their world and they associate you with everything fun. Win-win!

How to ditch the bowl

Each day, measure out your puppy's daily allowance of food and then look for opportunities to play games and reward their awesome choices. Your puppy doesn't need to have set mealtimes and no two days need to look the same. Spreading their food out over the course of the day, and delivering it in lots of different ways, will give you many opportunities to provide input where your puppy needs it most.

There are so many ways you can use your puppy's food. It's not all going to be about games and high-energy activities. That would be pretty exhausting for you and your puppy! As you learn more about the importance of growing calmness (see chapter 8), building optimism (see chapter 10) and putting value into proximity (chapter 11), you'll quickly discover that there are hundreds of ways you could use this daily pot of value.

How do I know how much to feed my puppy?

It's worth remembering that the feeding guidelines on any packet of dog food are simply that – guidelines. Judge what you're feeding your puppy based on what you observe: their appetite, body condition and bowel movements are pretty good indicators of whether they're eating the right amount.

If you feed a little more one day because you played some extra games, or because your puppy needed a little more input to keep their bucket healthy, that's OK too. Just reduce what they get a little the following day to balance it out. Ultimately, you decide what your puppy eats. A bit like humans, sometimes your dog might have more calories one day than the next; each day doesn't have to be exactly the same. It tends to even out over the course of the week.

How do I know that my puppy is eating a healthy amount?

Rather than weighing your puppy, we believe that looking and feeling your dog gives a better assesment of their overall health. There are three areas that you can check:

1. Ribs
Place your hands either side of your puppy's ribcage. You should be able to easily feel each of their ribs but you shouldn't be able to see them through their fur (with the exception of the last one or two ribs, which you may sometimes be able to see).

2. Waist
Looking at your puppy from above, they should have a discernible waist. You are looking for an hourglass shape.

THE POO SCALE

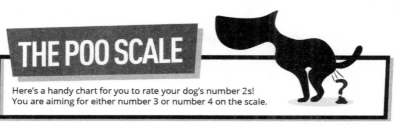

Here's a handy chart for you to rate your dog's number 2s!
You are aiming for either number 3 or number 4 on the scale.

TYPE	DESCRIPTION		WHAT DOES THIS MEAN?
1	Separate hard lumps, hard for your dog to pass		Severe constipation
2	Sausage-shaped, but lumpy		Mild constipation
3	Sausage-shaped, but with cracks on the surface		Normal
4	Sausage-shaped, smooth and soft		Normal
5	Soft blobs with clear cut edges, easy for your dog to pass		Lacking fibre
6	Fluffy pieces with ragged edges, a mushy stool		Mild diarrhoea
7	Watery, no solid pieces, entirely liquid		Severe diarrhoea

3. Tummy

Looking at your puppy from the side, they should have what vets describe as an obvious 'abdominal tuck'. This is where the transition from their chest to their abdomen clearly goes upwards. In simple terms, their chest should hang lower than their belly.

Don't be daunted

Ditch the Bowl is a lifestyle. It's both a training strategy and a feeding strategy and it's something that we do from the first moment with our puppies and continue throughout their lives.

It might feel like hard work not feeding your puppy from a bowl but honestly, once you give it a try, you'll see how easy it can be. If you've had a busy week at work and don't have time for a game, then use chews, Kongs and puzzle feeders to deliver your puppy's food and dip in and out of the games when you can. Even as little as playing one game a day with your puppy can bring about huge changes. Remember – it's about a fun time, not a long time! All it takes is a few minutes a day.

Will my puppy get hungry?

As humans, we can either eat lots of smaller meals throughout the day or have three big meals. If you snack throughout the day, you are probably going to be less hungry than if you have three bigger, more spaced out meals. Puppies have small stomachs and expend a lot of energy, so eating more frequently actually suits them better than having larger structured meals in a bowl.

Won't my puppy get frustrated?

We find that when dogs are fed from a bowl, some will only eat a little bit of it and the rest of the food will just sit there because it's no fun. By ditching the bowl, you are making their food an experience.

Discover what your puppy enjoys and what motivates them. Every puppy is different. Some dogs will find it most exciting to chase food that's been flicked along the floor. Some will enjoy sniffing it out. Others will find the very best experience is to try and catch food that's been tossed through the air. Roll it (meals on wheels, anyone?), cage it with your hand, throw it, drop it or hide it. Get creative and find out what lights your puppy up and gets them most engaged. You will come to discover that this gives you some really valuable clues to the type of experiences your puppy is going to find most enjoyable in other areas of life too.

Until you do something with it, every piece of your puppy's dinner is just a piece of food. You get to create experiences with it. If you have a puppy who is less interested in food and who you're struggling to encourage to eat, this is the very best way to grow their motivation for food.

If you find your puppy is a little lacklustre to begin with or seems overwhelmed, don't be disheartened. Even just chewing is quite exhausting for a young puppy. Keep your sessions short and inject them with fun, and before you know it your puppy will be joining the game.

Experiment with types of food too. There is nothing to say that your puppy needs to be restricted to one brand or flavour of food. You'd find it pretty boring if your meals were the same every day.

When you're playing games with your puppy and shaping that puppy brain to make awesome choices, it's often helpful to have different values of food reward available.

You might discover that your puppy's absolute favourite food in the world is chicken, or steak – but it could also be cucumber! Just like people, every puppy has their own unique preferences. This information will be really useful when you need that jackpot reward to tell your puppy they just did something completely amazing – or when you need a little extra value to compete with the environment.

Two simple feeding games

Play these simple games with your puppy from day one and they will quickly learn the fun that comes from not being fed from a bowl and it will become part of day-to-day life.

FUN WITH FOOD

This is the very first step to getting your puppy engaged with food and discovering what experiences they enjoy.

Step 1: To begin with, simply place a piece of food on the floor. Can your puppy find it? If necessary, point it out.

Step 2: Now hold a piece of food in your hand. Does your puppy check it out? Will your puppy track and follow your hand if you move it, and seek that food out?

Step 3: When they've mastered that, roll a piece of food a little distance. Does your puppy follow it? If you need to point it out, that's OK.

Step 4: Gradually add a little more movement. Place the food further away as your puppy's tracking ability gets better. Can your puppy find it?

Step 5: Now try bowling some food away from your puppy and encourage them to chase after it. Increase the distance of your throws, depending on how well your puppy is tracking and locating that food. If they miss a bit, don't worry. It probably means you asked too much.

Step 6: Take your food game to different areas of your home. Playing in different rooms increases your puppy's optimism and flexibility.

SCATTER FEEDING

Scatter feeding is a great way to occupy your puppy's brain as they search for food, and for many puppies this is also a naturally calming activity. Snuffle mats are small rugs where you hide pieces of food in the tufts of fabric that your puppy has to sniff out.

Step 1: When you first introduce this game, you want your puppy to have success, so make sure that you start out nice and easy. You might begin by scattering a handful of your puppy's food on the carpet, in a snuffle mat, or in short grass in your garden. Use food that is pale-coloured and smelly (think chicken or cheese) rather than small pieces of kibble, to make it easier for your puppy to snuffle it out.

Step 2: You can increase the challenge by scattering the food over a larger area, in longer grass or using food that's harder to locate.

TIP: Not only can you do this at home in your house and garden, scatter feeding is also awesome to do when you're out and about on walks if you need to bring your puppy's energy down a little, or give them a focus when there are distractions in the environment.

What if my puppy eats raw food?

Ditch the Bowl is accessible to everyone. There's always a solution and you can still ditch the bowl even if your puppy eats raw. Try:

- Treat dispensers – there are all sorts of treat dispenser toys that you can buy in different shapes and sizes.
- Squeeze tubes – these are a bit like toothpaste tubes that you put wet food into. You squeeze out a tiny amount and your puppy licks the end.
- Freeze-dried or dehydrated food.
- Chunks of raw meat cut into smaller pieces.
- Raw meat fed from a small spoon.
- Raw food rolled into little meatballs (or use a mould) and frozen and given to your puppy still frozen.

Foods that are harmful for puppies

- Chocolate
- Grapes
- Raisins
- Xylitol (artificial sweetener found in chewing gum, peanut butter etc.)
- Cooked bones
- Caffeine
- Macadamia nuts
- Alcohol
- Onion

Enrichment Activities

These are some of the calming food activities we talked about in chapter 1, such as stuffable food toys like Kongs or long-lasting healthy chews.

Ditching the bowl is about way more than simply hand-feeding your puppy or using their food for games. When you ditch the idea of having to feed your dog from a bowl at set times of the day, you get to be so much more creative. It gives you opportunities to encourage mental stimulation by providing your puppy with food toys that can be filled or stuffed as well as long-lasting healthy chews. When they are not playing games, these are another great way to give your puppy some of their daily food allowance without having to use a bowl.

What you choose to feed your puppy is a personal decision, but wherever possible we would encourage you to choose natural options over anything that has been highly processed. While some of the suggestions that follow might leave you feeling a little squeamish, your puppy will love them! You can buy them from most pet shops.

Remember that chews, stuffed Kongs and all the other options that follow are part of your puppy's daily food allowance, so if you're using these as part of your Ditch the Bowl, deduct from your puppy's quota of kibble or other food to ensure you're not overfeeding them.

Chews

Chews are a great long-lasting treat and help with calmness. Here are some ideas for natural chews you might want to feed your puppy:

- Natural pressed tripe bones
- Bull pizzles/bully sticks (dried bull penis)
- Antlers – choose your size and style carefully though, as they can chip teeth
- Ears (raw or dehydrated from a rabbit/lamb/cow/pig)
- Fish skin braids/knots
- Paddy whacks (ligaments from cows and sheep, dehydrated or raw)
- Appropriately sized raw bones (necks/wings/ribs)
- Puffed jerky (pieces of beef lung puffed up using hot air)
- Plain/stuffed hooves
- Appropriate raw meaty bones, for example marrowbones.

Stuffable food toys

Kongs and other stuffable food toys, as well as natural stuffables like hooves and hollow marrowbones, are a great way to promote calmness and keep your puppy occupied when they're having quiet time in a crate or puppy pen (see chapter 9 for more about this). There are many options available, so find something that works for you and your puppy. They can be filled with raw or tinned food, cooked chicken, kibble soaked in water to soften it or anything else that is suitable for your puppy to enjoy.

Depending on your puppy's personality, some will be much more tenacious than others when it comes to working out how to access that yummy food, so you might need to start off with something really easy to avoid creating frustration. By increasing the difficulty at your puppy's pace and balancing the mental challenge of accessing that food with the calming nature of licking and chewing, you're building up your puppy's tolerance to frustration and ensuring that they don't give up. Awesome!

Step 1: Start by allowing your puppy to eat some food stuffed into an open-ended hoof or Kong. Ensure your puppy gets an easy win.

Step 2: If your puppy embraces this challenge, you can make it more challenging by freezing the hoof or Kong once it's been filled, or packing it more tightly. The longer you freeze it and the more compact the contents, the more challenging it becomes. Increase the difficulty gradually.

Step 3: If your puppy is comfortable, increase the challenge by using different fillings, packing the Kong or hoof more tightly, freezing for longer so your puppy needs to work harder at licking, or using different shapes and sizes of stuffable food toy to vary the challenge.

Lick mats

Lickable mats, also known as 'Calm' mats, are another great option. Licking is a naturally calming, soothing activity, so spreading some of your puppy's food on a mat for them to lick off can be another great way to feed some of their daily food.

Slow feeders/puzzle bowls

Many people use slow feeder bowls to stop their dogs from gulping down their food. These can be a brilliant addition to your enrichment activities and get that puppy brain working for their dinner.

Interactive/puzzle toys

These are super cool! Your puppy has to problem-solve in order to get the food. These toys aid cognitive development, keep your puppy stimulated and are a great mental workout. You can find loads of different ones online but you really don't have to spend a lot of money on them. Be inventive and create your own – see below for some ideas.

DIY Toys

Here are some brilliant ideas that have been suggested on our Facebook pages.

- Fill a shoe box with empty toilet rolls and hide treats inside. Your puppy will love trying to find their dinner.
- Place a few pieces of food in a muffin tin and cover them with tennis balls. When your puppy successfully moves the balls, they'll find a tasty reward underneath.
- Pop a few pieces of food inside a toilet roll inner, fold down the ends and watch your puppy work out how to get to the hidden treasure.

We promise you that your puppy will love the fact you're not feeding them from a bowl and can assure you they won't get frustrated at having to work for their food.

We don't consider it to be 'earning'. Our dogs are not working for us, it's more a case of us playing and working together. For most species, feeding has a social aspect. Dogs love to interact and becoming part of their mealtimes is an amazing way to bond and bring joy to the relationship. Dogs are driven to work for their food and they actively seek opportunities to hunt, stalk or chase. As owners, we often prevent many of these behaviours, so it's hugely rewarding for our dogs when we give them an alternative way to work for their meals and incorporate opportunities to enjoy those experiences within the context of getting their dinner.

Ditching the bowl creates a dog who LOVES to work for food

and work with you. Your puppy is looking for an interaction with you, and they enjoy playing games and having fun. The food is just adding extra value to that interaction. By ditching the bowl, you are growing a reward experience and enriching your puppy's life.

> **TIP: Although it varies from breed to breed, it's important to remember that up until they're six months old, a puppy's sight, hearing and coordination are still developing, so when your puppy is very young you will need to make it easy for them.**
>
> Puppies also have a tendency to be overexcitable and can be quick to go off task unless you keep them engaged. Have fun and remember it doesn't have to be perfect. You and your puppy are working together for the first time.

CHAPTER 5
The Power of Play

When we think about play, toys often come to mind, and yet play is so much more than toys. Play is at the heart of games-based training. It's a brilliant way of boosting your puppy's confidence, as well as providing mental and physical enrichment to your puppy's life. Play is also an awesome way of building your relationship and boosting your bond with your puppy. At its heart, play is about the joy of interacting with you, so whenever you play with your puppy, you want it to be fun, pressure-free and rewarding.

It's worth knowing that not every dog naturally embraces play or starts out life finding interactive play with humans rewarding. Some puppies may play very naturally with their littermates or with the environment but find the idea of playing with their owners a little less exciting or too pressured. Some puppies are more reserved and need lots of no-rules, low-pressure fun before play is something they start to really enjoy. Yet if you can find your puppy's passion for play by identifying what experiences they value, play can be something you love to do together, as well as adding a whole new dimension to your training.

We come across lots of owners who tell us their puppy doesn't seem interested in playing with them. They do, however, play with the environment – so they're keen to chase a squirrel or play with the leaves on the floor or even a blade of grass. What we often find is that these owners have put too much pressure on play, added too many rules and lost the fun. They have made it more about how they want to play rather than working out what their dog enjoys. The good news is that as soon as you peel away the rules, lower the pressure and act a bit silly with your puppy, little by little you will see their passion for play return.

It's also important to remember that play isn't always about getting into your puppy's space, putting too much intensity into the play or even about making things loud and exciting. Even the quietest, most gentle play session can have immense power. This can be as simple as stroking your puppy while they hold a toy in your lap.

Ultimately, your puppy is looking for fun experiences – and it's your job as their super cool owner to make sure they find them with you! The more passion you build in your puppy for wanting to play with you, the more likely they are to pick you over distractions and see you as the very best source of fun.

You don't always need toys

Play doesn't have to involve toys. It can just involve you!

While we love to incorporate toys into our play sessions, the most important thing to remember is that you are looking to create playful experiences your puppy enjoys and wants to engage with. Some dogs are naturally motivated by toys, while others show a preference for food rewards. Identify what your puppy finds rewarding and work with that. Ultimately, it's about the experience you provide. If your puppy loves to chase you and hunt you down, that's play too.

Tips for choosing toys

Identifying the type of toy your puppy finds most rewarding can be a gamechanger when it comes to building engagement and being able to reward them in ways they find joyful and reinforcing.

Anything can be a toy, providing it is safe and appropriate for your puppy to interact with. From sheepskin tugs and squeaky tennis balls to old tea towels, there are infinite options for creating rewarding play opportunities.

Styles of play

There are so many different styles of play. You may have noticed your puppy naturally exhibiting some of these. They might enjoy stalking a toy or food before pouncing and initiating more direct play. Your puppy might enjoy chasing food, a toy or even you! Many dogs love to tug. Hunting, sniffing and finding food are all forms of play too.

Although you want your puppy to love their toys, it's important to make sure that it's not just the toy your puppy wants. Your ultimate goal is for your puppy to value most of all the relationship experience with you that comes through the toy.

• **Keep it simple**

Keep toy play simple at first. Don't put too much thought into your play at this stage. Having fun without any rules is the very best way to ignite your puppy's passion for play with you.

Soft tug toys made of fur or fleece can be a great way of tapping into your puppy's natural desire to play and pounce. Think about using toys with longer handles so your hands aren't too close to those sharp puppy teeth! Remember that your puppy's eyesight and coordination will still be developing to begin with, so gentle play in really short sessions will keep it fun and rewarding. Also bear in mind your puppy's tiny teeth, which means they are going to struggle to pick up a toy that's too big or heavy or that requires a lot of bite.

> **NOTE:** While your puppy is teething, softer toys may be more comfortable on painful gums. Be considerate in the way you play too. Avoid lots of tugging during this period and keep your play more gentle.

• **Not every dog likes every toy**

Work with the dog in front of you. Some puppies will naturally love balls, while others may prefer tugs or squeaky toys or frisbees. To some extent, this will be influenced by your dog's breed. Herding dogs will often show a preference for toys they can stalk, while gun dogs may prefer toys they can pick up and carry. Don't forget, though, that your puppy is first and foremost an individual. It's vital not to force or pressure your dog to play with a particular toy, however much fun you think it looks! Watch how your puppy interacts with different toys and you'll quickly be able to identify their preferences. Depending on the puppy you are working with, you might choose a long-handled toy to keep them motivated and to allow them to play without getting too close. You might have a puppy who loves to chase rolling toys, carry soft toys, play with toys that move and bounce or even parade around with a pair of socks.

- **Think about what your puppy likes to do**
Watch how they interact with the world by observing their free play time. Maybe your puppy likes to chase leaves or perhaps they like to carry objects or tug on grass or plants. Use their natural preferences in your play session. Let your puppy lead the learning and pick what they enjoy. If your puppy is motivated more by food than toys, choose a toy that you can put food in to help them play.

- **Think about how you play**
The way you play with a particular toy can make a huge difference too! If your puppy is a little wary of playing close to you, then a tug with a very short handle is going to add a whole lot of pressure. A tug toy with a longer handle will allow your puppy to play with you without feeling crowded. You may discover your puppy has a very natural tendency to retrieve and loves nothing more than to return a toy to you for the opportunity to go and retrieve it again, or you may find that your puppy's ultimate reward is a game of tug. Become your puppy's expert!

- **Keep your toys as high-value rewards**
You might quickly discover that, left to their own devices, your puppy's ultimate reward is to take a treasured toy to a safe distance

and dissect it. If your puppy currently has free access to toys, that can hugely undermine the value of working (and playing) with you.

Keeping toys as a high-value reward will really help power up your play time with your puppy and make sure they're not learning to make their own fun that doesn't include you – which will quickly translate to a dog who finds anything and everything more exciting than you when they venture out into the world.

How to introduce toy play to your puppy

- Don't put lots of toys down at once, otherwise you'll have a dog that plays on their own and not with you. Your aim with play is to create an interactive experience where the source of fun is you. As your puppy's toy play develops, adding more toys into the picture and playing games like Toy Switch (page 386) helps your puppy understand that you always have the very best game, even in the face of distractions – as well as boosting that powerful concept of disengagement. We look into this in much more detail in chapter 22.

- Sit down on the floor with your puppy so you're playing at their level. When you're first introducing toys, experimentation and observation are going to be key so you can work out what your puppy enjoys – and just as importantly, what they don't.

- Don't pressure your puppy, especially if you're introducing a new toy, or playing for the very first time. Observe your puppy's reactions. Some puppies love toys that move, bounce or make noise, while others might be unsure. Your puppy might want to give the toy a good sniff to be sure nothing scary is going to happen before getting involved. Offer lots of verbal praise and encouragement to let your puppy know they're doing a great job. If your puppy is lacking confidence around the novelty of new toys and experiences, remember to keep boosting their optimism through all the games in chapter 10.

TIP: Don't force it! You want your puppy to enjoy the experience. If they don't seem interested, it's OK to try again another time.

- Once you can see that your puppy is interested and comfortable with the toy, add some gentle movement. Animating the toy so that it moves like prey can be a great way of getting your puppy engaged in the game. Motion is one of the best ways to get a dog interested in play and makes things instantly more exciting. Move the toy along the floor and see if you can get your puppy to chase it, or try tossing it in the air and see if they can catch it. Zigzag it around to engage your puppy in a game of chase. You want to see your puppy's eyes light up and their joy ignite! The secret sauce to successful play with your puppy is going to come when you tap into their passion.

- Don't overlook the value of balancing play with calmness or the importance of short sessions for keeping engagement high and for making sure your puppy's bucket doesn't overflow with all that excitement. Don't get too energetic, too soon. Keep things calmer at first. A fun time, not a long time, is always a good thing to keep in mind.

Above all, don't put any pressure on your puppy. They might want to follow the toy, sniff it or even hold it. Allow your puppy to lead the play and look out for the experiences they enjoy.

- Keep it varied. Don't just do the same thing or get out the same toy every session, otherwise your puppy will quickly get bored and lose interest. Remember that the allure of that squirrel (or whatever your puppy finds exciting) is its unpredictability!

- Be engaged. When you're playing with your puppy, always make sure that you're engaged and involved. No playing while you scroll on your phone or have half an eye on the television. Your puppy will quickly learn if your attention is elsewhere and will find their own fun with the environment and not with you.

- Those who play together stay together. Try and incorporate some element of play into every day. Keep your play sessions short – play for 2 or 3 minutes a couple of times a day. Your aim is always to end the session before your puppy gets bored (or too overexcited) so you leave them hungry for more play.

- Put the toys away when you finish playing. Your dog wouldn't be into squirrels if there were squirrels lying everywhere. That's a sure-fire way to make something lose its value. Scarcity adds the excitement and interest!

- Follow up with calmness. After a play session, give your puppy a rest – whether that's a toilet break, offering them a drink or a Kong in their crate. You want your puppy to have the ability to be calm and switch off at the end of a high-energy, exciting play session.

• Vary the locations where you play. Play with your puppy in different rooms of the house to boost their confidence and flexibility (remembering the importance of rehearsing the room and safeguarding those quieter areas where your puppy knows it is time to switch off and relax).

In the early stages of building your puppy's love of play, an easy, low-distraction environment is really important. This is all about setting your puppy up for success. However, distractions are a part of life, so as your puppy's play develops, take it outside into the garden or other outdoor environments.

> **TIP: Get someone to observe you playing with your puppy or film your play session on your phone, then watch it back. This can be really useful when you're trying to work out what your puppy does or doesn't like.**

Say no to sticks

Somehow, it's entrenched in many people's beliefs that to play with your dog you should throw them a stick. But did you know that sticks can actually be harmful for dogs, especially delicate puppy mouths? Dogs can easily fracture their teeth by biting or chewing on sticks, and small bits can break off and migrate through their body. Tom once treated a dog who had chewed a stick and 6 weeks later suddenly became really unwell as a fragment was lodged behind his shoulder blade. Stick fragments can even puncture a dog's lungs, so wherever you can, stop your puppy from chewing them.

Retrieve

Retrieve is a super foundation for so many skills you're going to want your puppy to learn as they grow. A rock-solid retrieve is the key to a truly reliable recall and it's brilliant for building value in proximity. If you've got a good retrieve, chances are you've got a good relationship too! For more on proximity, see chapter 11.

Building a great retrieve with your puppy will grow confidence, focus, flexibility, independence, grit and so much more. It's simply a core exercise, and it can be so much fun too. So, here is the low-down.

It can help to think of retrieve as a number of individual components that all layer together to get that final picture.

- Go out to get the item.
- Pick up and hold the item.
- Bring the item back.
- Deliver the item to you.

Underpinning all those layers is desire for whatever toy or item you're asking your puppy to retrieve.

Getting started on the foundational layers of a retrieve can begin as soon as your puppy is engaging happily with toys, and will give you a super basis on which to build and refine this skill as your puppy grows. Remember to let your puppy find the joy in carrying their toy back to you for reward. Be careful to avoid taking it off them, otherwise they are very quickly going to learn that bringing it back is a really bad deal.

Toy Switch (page 386) is a super foundation for building the basics of a retrieve. Using two toys of equal value, you can teach your puppy that bringing a toy back towards you is the way to make the fun game continue.

> ## Top tips for getting your puppy to retrieve
>
> Use a hallway or position yourself so you're throwing your puppy's toy into a corner to limit their choices and set them up for success.
>
> A few repetitions at a time is plenty! End the game while your puppy is still engaged and having fun.
>
> Playing on lead is a super way to avoid unwanted behaviours, such as stealing the toy. This way, not only do you get to limit the opportunities your pup has to rehearse undesirable behaviours, you also grow value in playing around you.

Protecting your puppy's joints

When you think of a traditional game of 'fetch', you probably envision dogs joyfully racing across the park after balls fired from ball launchers, which we call 'wangers'. You'll discover in chapter 11 how we prefer to incorporate wangers into puppy training. By throwing a ball at high speed way into the distance, not only are you taking value away from proximity, you could well be encouraging your puppy to run, twist, turn and brake suddenly, which puts a lot of impact on their joints. This isn't great for dogs of any age but is especially important to avoid while your puppy is still growing.

Encouraging your puppy to retrieve a 'dead' toy limits this

damaging impact, as does hiding toys for them to seek out – while giving their nose a super workout too.

Here are some puppy-safe retrieve options:

- Use a floppy toy that can't roll.
- Wait for the toy to stop moving (go 'dead') before releasing your puppy to get it.
- Hide a 'dead' toy for them to search out.

Tug

Some dogs love to tug while others don't enjoy it at all.

Like all forms of play, it taps into those natural instincts every dog has for hunting and using their mouths.

Played correctly, tug is a brilliant interactive game you can enjoy with your puppy that can have a hugely positive impact on your relationship. When you're playing tug games, present the toy horizontally to make sure that your puppy grabs it correctly. Don't dangle it vertically as they might accidentally nick you with a milk tooth. Allowing your puppy to 'win' the toy can boost their confidence and optimism and help them feel like a superhero, which is going to carry over into other areas of life. Balance that up with whipping the toy away periodically to build their desire. Sloppy mouths lose dinner!

A dog who enjoys tug and interactive toy play as a reward is much more likely to have a desire to retrieve, because bringing the toy back allows the game to begin again. In turn, this will boost your dog's recall, because coming back to interact with you is way more fun than any distraction the environment might be offering. For more on recall, see chapter 21.

Top tips for tug success

Consider your choice of toy. Tugs made of fur with longer handles allow lots of movement and give your puppy a soft area to grab and bite.

Just like any other form of toy play, animating the toy will get your puppy engaged.

Teaching your puppy where to bite (the soft fleece or fur area) and where not to plant those sharp teeth (the handle or your hands) is going to help your play sessions be fun and rewarding for you and your puppy. Presenting the tug horizontally while the handle is tucked out of the way, and engaging your puppy in a brief session of play when they mouth the correct part of the toy, will help them learn what's expected. Lots of verbal praise and encouragement is important too, especially when you're building your puppy's understanding of play.

Keeping some tension on your tug toy helps your puppy keep tugging, which will mean they are less likely to lose their grip and re-grip somewhere less appropriate.

Make sure you're not tugging upwards and jarring your puppy's neck, or playing so vigorously that you're tugging your puppy as well as the toy. Match your puppy's tug and remember to let them win.

Be all in! If you want your puppy to learn to play enthusiastically, you need to be able to do the same.

As your puppy's toy play develops, you will find that you can incorporate toys and interactive play into so much of your training. It adds a whole new dynamic to your relationship, as well as supercharging your training success. Above all, your ultimate aim is to have a joyful and rewarding experience with your puppy so that your dog is going to value you over anything else the environment might try to tempt them with.

SECTION ONE

Rising Star

(8-12 weeks)

CHAPTER 6
The First 24 Hours

So your puppy is finally home – but what do you do in those first 24 hours with them? Some puppies will arrive at their new home excited, curious and ready to explore and have fun. Others will be more cautious and unsure. They might have left brothers and sisters behind at the breeder or perhaps you've re-homed a puppy who started life in a stressful environment.

Remember that regardless of their background, your puppy has just had a big disruption in their life, so it's normal for them to be unsure. It's also normal for them to be very tired. Puppies are supposed to sleep 17 to 20 hours a day so don't worry if your new bundle of joy spends most of their time napping at first.

Toilet training is also something you'll need to tackle. As it's such a huge subject, please see the following chapter for how to start that.

What to do on your puppy's first day

Keep it calm

Don't try and do too much. Your puppy has just had a huge upheaval, so be mindful how that's going to impact on their bucket. You don't need to rush to take your puppy out or visit the vet for their first check-up.

As we talked about in chapter 2, don't be scared to say no to things that you don't think will benefit your puppy. As much as friends and family are going to want to come round and see your new arrival and you're desperate to show them off, try and keep things calm and mundane those first few days so it's not too overwhelming. If you're filling your puppy's days with excitement right from the get-go, then you're ultimately going to end up with a more excitable dog.

Keep it small

In chapter 1, we talked about setting up your 'gated community', so you will already have created a small area for your puppy with either a puppy pen or a baby gate. It's best to start their world small and then grow it, and this is where your puppy's going to spend most of their time at first so they don't feel totally lost in a big house. Make sure they've got access to a water bowl and their open crate so they've got somewhere safe and comfortable to relax and have a nap. There are no hard and fast rules where this area has to be, and it depends on your personal preference. Quite often, people choose the kitchen as the floor tends to be easier to clean in case of accidents. Try not to choose an area that is a busy thoroughfare with constant coming and going, as that is going to make it hard for your puppy to tune out and get that all-important rest.

Let them explore

Let them explore slowly and have a sniff of their new environment. Give your puppy some time to wander in the garden – on a lead if the space isn't secure – and around the house, with you supervising at all times. Watch for signs that your puppy is becoming overwhelmed and be ready to take them inside or reassure them.

Keep them close, visit often

Your puppy has experienced a major change, so keep them close to you those first 24 hours. They may have been used to having constant company and not be used to being alone. They're in a completely new environment with new people and new smells. Some puppies will be fine with you going in and out of the room, whereas others might want to be with you all the time that first day. If you're not with them, check on them often.

Puppy blues are a thing!

The dream is that you'll pick your new puppy up and fall instantly in love – and you probably will – but just like baby blues, puppy blues do happen. Puppies are overwhelmingly cute and adorable, but the reality is, they're also really, really hard work. The first few days and weeks of owning a new pup can be very stressful and traumatic. It's not uncommon to wonder if getting a puppy was the right decision when they're weeing on the floor, waking at all hours of the night or nipping your toes with their sharp little milk teeth. It's normal to feel overwhelmed when they're causing havoc in your house. You're probably also sleep deprived, which doesn't help.

In chapter 2 we introduced you to the concept of your puppy's bucket and the fact that, as an owner, you have one too. If you're feeling challenged by your puppy, consider whether other things are filling your bucket that could be impacting your ability to cope with your puppy. Even just identifying what's filling your bucket can help you put your puppy struggles in perspective.

Your puppy doesn't automatically understand the rules and expectations of a human household. Remembering that can help adjust your outlook.

It can really help to think about your language, your focus and your state, and try hard to reframe things. If you're feeling stressed (or, as we prefer to think of it, stretched), try and change your state of mind. Put some music on, have a bath, do some exercise or seek advice from a fellow dog owner who has been there them-selves. If you can do something that will change your energy and put you in a better mindset, you'll have a much better perspective on the challenges your puppy is bringing to your day.

Remember, your dog isn't difficult or being deliberately chal-lenging. What you're experiencing is normal puppy behaviour. These behaviours are temporary and it *will* get better. We're here to guide you through it and this book will help you tackle those destructive behaviours, crack your puppy's toilet training and set you and your puppy on the path towards a beautiful adventure together, so hang on in there.

Let the games begin!

Introducing your puppy to some simple games can help start to build your bond and relationship in a fun, low-pressure way.

GO COMMANDO

Go Commando is a simple yet fun game that makes close proximity to you a highly valuable, confidence-building and fun experience for your puppy. Let your legs be an assault course! Not only will this teach your puppy that being close to you is a rewarding and fun experience, it's also great for building confidence.

Step 1: Get comfy on the floor and then encourage any interaction your puppy offers.

Step 2: Use some of their daily food allowance to lure them under and over your legs and around your body. Is your puppy confident enough to climb over and across you? Reward them with their food as they do.

FOLLOW ME

Feeding your puppy from your hand is a great way to start building your relationship and teaching them that you are the source of great things. This should be really low pressure. It needs to be your puppy's choice to interact with you and take the food. Some will be right in there, while others might take a little longer to warm up to the idea.

Step 1: Take a piece of your puppy's food between your fingers and hold it out. If your puppy is hesitant, give them chance to sniff and work out that you're offering them something yummy. Starting with a small amount of high-value food such as chicken can help your puppy to begin with.

Step 2: Once your puppy is taking food happily from your hand, move a couple of steps away. Your puppy should follow. Feed again to show them they made a great choice to come and interact with you some more. Remember to switch hands so they learn that food comes from both hands.

Step 3: A few short repetitions are enough to begin with. If you find your puppy is a little too snatchy with the food, keeping your movements slow and calm can help limit excitement, which often leads to nipping.

The first night

Helping your puppy settle at bedtime can really make those daytime struggles feel more manageable. Puppies are cranky when they've not had enough sleep, but so are their humans!

Where will my puppy sleep?

We recommend that your puppy sleeps in a crate for those first few days or couple of weeks, and possibly even longer if that suits you and your lifestyle. At Absolute Dogs, we feel it's best to have your puppy near you – remember, keep them close and visit often. They should be close enough that you can put your fingers in their crate, to reassure them you are here. The crate should be closed at night and have some comfy bedding in it to make it super cosy (this also helps prevent toileting in their crate, as no dog wants to soil their own sleep area).

Crying and whining on the first night is normal and if your puppy is next to you, you can easily reassure them if they're unsettled. Owners are often told to 'start as you mean to go on', so they put their puppy in their crate in the utility room or the kitchen, close the door and let them cry until they eventually give in and fall asleep. But this is distressing for both you and your puppy and isn't the best way to teach your puppy that you are a team and that you're there to meet their needs. It also doesn't work! If they cry and cry and eventually stop, it could be because they have learned a state of helplessness and are still feeling anxious. If they cry and cry and don't stop, they are also experiencing continued and repeatable anxiety. Either way, this is not the best approach, and is a great example of 'training in the situation' rather than arming your puppy with the skills to thrive in any situation and make great choices. As you will already know from the introduction to this book, if a situation is too much for your puppy and they don't have the skills to cope, they are not in the right headspace to learn. So rather than leaving your puppy when they're struggling to settle, instead you can train 'for the situation' with super cool games and strategies. When introduced in the right way, your puppy can learn to love their crate and settle happily, both at bedtime and during the day. We cover this in lots more detail in chapter 9. Most of all, what your puppy rehearses, they become, and what they learn first, they learn best. Hence why it's so important to get this right. However, don't despair if you haven't started off doing this and your puppy is still struggling to settle. That's the beauty of it, even if you are coming to this with an older puppy or dog, you can still follow the same process and achieve success.

For those first few bedtimes, we would recommend one of two options. The most comfortable way for most people is to place the puppy's crate next to your bed and then move the crate away as your puppy becomes more settled over a number of days or weeks. So if you eventually want your dog to sleep in the kitchen, gradually move the crate away from your bedroom and downstairs.

Or you might prefer to do it the other way round, starting off with your puppy's crate in the location where you eventually want it to be, and sleeping next to them in those early days. However, sleeping on a hard kitchen floor for several nights has never really appealed to us!

A crate next to your bed will give both you and the puppy more sleep. Then if your puppy is unsettled, you can reassure them by popping a hand inside or speaking in a calm, reassuring tone.

Follow your puppy's lead about how quickly to move their crate. Some puppies are very settled at night after a few days, others take weeks. In chapter 9, we'll show you some games to play with the crate during the day so your puppy should gradually start to enjoy spending time in there and learn that it's a great place to relax, which will mean they're more settled at night too.

Night waking

We'll explore toilet training in a lot more detail in chapter 7, but a young puppy will need to go outside to wee at least once in the night for the first couple of weeks. Set an alarm for 2–3 a.m. on your puppy's first night so you can wake up and take them outside. That way, they learn to toilet outside and you are minimising any opportunities for them to have an accident in their crate.

When you're taking your puppy outside in the night, you need to make sure this is a non-event. When you've got a brand-new puppy, it's tempting to be upbeat and lively because you're so excited by this new bundle of fluff that has joined your family, but you don't want your dog to think it's OK to have a disco at 3 a.m.!

The trick here is to make sure your puppy is not inadvertently rewarded with lots of social interaction, sniffy time in the garden, a long walk or cuddles. Disturbing you in the middle of the night because they need to go is a perfectly reasonable thing for your puppy to be doing. Waking you up to play or because they've got their disco pants on and fancy a party in the garden is not!

Put your puppy on a lead, carry them outside, stand in one spot until they've been to the toilet, bring them back inside, pop them straight back in their crate and go back to sleep. If your puppy doesn't go to the toilet within a few minutes of being outside, bring them back inside. If they don't settle back to sleep, then try them again.

Don't engage with your puppy or give them any praise or reward, with the exception of the verbal cue you use to encourage them to go to the loo – see page 103 for more information.

You want them to learn that toilet trips in the middle of the night are exactly that. If you give your puppy cuddles, lots of attention and a fun run about in the garden, guess what? They are much more likely to wake you up another night for more of the same!

Top tips for a happy bedtime

Do take your puppy out for frequent toilet breaks during the evening, remembering to use a lead if they are getting easily distracted or aroused by the environment. If you don't have a garden, try to choose a calmer area outside your home if possible.

Do offer them unlimited access to water throughout the day but discourage any long drinks that will fill their bladder before bedtime.

Do give options for chewing or gnawing, such as filled bones/ Kongs and long-lasting chews.

Do pop your puppy in the area you are leaving them overnight with their chew while you are doing your final preparations for bed (but remember, safety first – never leave a puppy unattended with something that could be unsafe or present a choke hazard).

Do use a covered crate to help them settle. We'll cover different types of crates in more detail in chapter 9.

Do carry on with your day once you get up in the morning. Rushing straight to let your puppy out can quickly lead to progressively early waking and noise.

How to soothe an unsettled puppy

Don't be tempted to take your puppy out of the crate for cuddles if they are unsettled. If you are serious about wanting them to be able to settle calmly in their crate as part of their bedtime routine, the middle of the night is not the time to cave on this intention just so you can get some sleep. Equally, you don't want your puppy to be unnecessarily distressed. As discussed above, letting your puppy 'cry it out' is not an approach we would advocate and actually just teaches your puppy to feel helpless.

Instead, can you move the crate closer to you, so your puppy has the comfort of your presence but is able to settle in the crate? If the crate was at the foot of your bed, can you move it beside your bed so you can pop your fingers through the bars to offer some reassurance? Can you safely put the crate on your bedside table so your puppy can see you? If you keep your puppy's crate close by you, we generally find unsettled behaviour doesn't persist for more than a couple of weeks – although it's important to remember that every dog is different.

Overtired puppy tantrums

If all your puppy's needs have been met and they are still unable to settle (think overtired toddler), this is the time to try soothing music and covering the crate. Will they settle if you give them a Kong or something to promote those feelings of calmness? As you will learn more about in chapter 8, chewing and licking are calming activities for dogs.

Your puppy needs to learn and be secure in the fact that you are always going to meet their needs, but they are not always going to have access to you all of the time. We will explore this idea in more detail in chapter 13.

CHAPTER 7
Toilet Training

Your ultimate aim is for your puppy to let you know when they need to go to the toilet and for them to go in an appropriate place. However, accidents are inevitable at first as your puppy doesn't know any better. The key to effective toilet training is vigilance. From our own experience of training hundreds of dogs, if you're really focused and intentional for 3 weeks, you'll have toilet training pretty much cracked at the end of that time. If you're not as 'on it', you could find accidents go on for months.

Some things to bear in mind when you bring your puppy home:

- Some dogs might come from the breeder or rescue centre with an element of understanding, but they are unlikely to be fully toilet trained.
- They don't know that they should signal to their human when they do want to go to the toilet outside.
- Usually, a puppy won't go to the toilet where they eat or sleep. However, if they can pee in their crate or puppy pen and still find a nice dry spot to curl up, they probably will. You can help avoid this by making sure your puppy's crate or designated sleeping area isn't big enough for them to toilet

and still have room to snooze – and, of course, by making sure you take them out regularly while they are learning where it is appropriate to go.

- Toilet training can be affected by changes in diet, medical conditions such as a UTI, the weather (who wants to go outside in the rain?!) and the size of your puppy.

Physical limitations

In order for puppies to be able to hold their bladders and bowels, they need to have developed the necessary neurological ability. Some dogs, especially smaller breeds, don't achieve this until they're 12 weeks old, and smaller breed dogs inevitably have smaller bladders! If your puppy is 8 or 9 weeks old, then you should still start toilet training them and be consistent. But if you have been vigilant for 3 weeks and your dog is still not fully trained, be aware that they might not have the neurological ability to go with it. Be kind and don't get upset with yourself or your puppy if accidents keep happening. It varies from dog to dog when they will have that neurological ability – some puppies are capable at 7 weeks old.

> **TIP: As a minimum, you should be taking an 8-week-old puppy out to the toilet every hour except during the night, when it's around 3–4 hours.**

How do I know if my puppy might need to go to the toilet?

They have:

- Eaten within the last 15 minutes (sometimes sooner!).
- Played actively for more than 15–20 minutes.
- Drunk water within the last 15 minutes.
- Had a very active day and drunk more water than usual.
- Just woken up from sleeping, no matter how long their nap was.
- Had a fun training session or played some games within the last half an hour.
- Sniffed the ground and appear to be overly distracted.
- Started turning in circles – probably on your favourite rug!
- Moved towards the door or in the direction of the most frequently used exit.
- Experienced something exciting within the last half an hour, including visitors, time spent around another dog or interacting with excited children.
- Had a deterioration in behaviour (a puppy who needs to poo might become a little more nippy or cranky, or show signs that their bucket is a bit more full).
- Had a diet change. This can also increase a puppy's need to go to the toilet.

In summary, a good way to think about all of the above is that whenever your puppy transitions from one activity to another, for example, from eating to not eating, playing to resting, sleeping to being awake, it's likely they'll soon need to toilet or would like to be offered the opportunity to do so, in an appropriate place.

Five simple steps to toilet train your puppy

1. Be aware when they need to go out

Observe your puppy and notice any changes in their behaviour, such as sniffing or spinning or your puppy appearing agitated. As a rule of thumb, the smaller the breed, the more frequent the toilet breaks.

2. Choose an area

To begin with, it can help to pick a specific spot outside where you want your puppy to go to the toilet. Carry them to the area where you'd like them to go and place them down or take them outside on a lead or puppy line. This will stop them going anywhere along the route that might not be appropriate, and will help them focus on the task at hand. We often see owners struggling because they designate the whole garden as the area their puppy should toilet. Often, the garden is also a place they play games with their puppy and there might be toys all over the grass. This means the puppy goes out into the garden, associates where they are with fun and switches to the mood for playing. If they can't put their brain in the right gear for going to the toilet, as soon as they go back into the house they may immediately go on the floor. Take them to that space any time you think they might need to go and they will quickly catch on to the idea that their job is to go to the toilet, not to look for opportunities to play. Stay with them so you know when they have done their business, but be really calm and boring.

Once your puppy has associated outdoors with toilet time, it's also really important for them to be flexible so that if the need arises, they can go anywhere you ask them to. When you are out walking with your puppy, be on the lookout for new surfaces for them to toilet on – grass, concrete, tarmac, gravel, soil, even bark. Where safe, give your puppy chance to go both on and off lead. This will set your puppy up for success as they grow. You don't want a dog who can only go to the toilet in your garden or on grass. This can be really limiting if you find yourself somewhere without that surface and your pup can't or won't go!

3. Use a verbal cue

Teaching your puppy to go to the toilet on cue is so useful because it allows you to ask them to go to the toilet anywhere, and, like any other behaviour they know on cue, they will go! When we take our own dogs to the toilet, we always say to them 'hurry up'. Your verbal cue can be anything, but as long as you are consistent, over time your dog will learn to go to the toilet whenever they hear it. Start to associate toileting with your verbal cue from day one and your puppy will soon catch on.

4. Reward them

Reward your puppy when they go to the toilet in the place that you want them to go. The only exception to this is any toilet breaks that happen in the night. Remember, when it comes to your puppy, nothing fun happens after 10 p.m. Any toilet trips that come after that and before they wake up in the morning should be boring, uneventful and efficient. Put your puppy back to bed without reward, ceremony or fuss.

Wait until they've finished before you praise so you don't interrupt them. Puppies' attention spans are short and they might get distracted and forget what they're there to do!

Praise your puppy verbally in a happy but calm way. Stroke them gently for a few seconds, making sure you don't pet them in a way that produces too much excitement (deep, slow petting).

Reward your puppy calmly with a little bit of their daily food allowance. This isn't the time for excitement or super high-value food such as cooked chicken or ham. Your aim is to communicate to your puppy that they did a great job so they are more likely to do the same again in the future. Make your reward too exciting and your puppy might struggle to focus next time because they're anticipating the fun to come.

5. Supervise them or limit the space they're in
During the early stages of toilet training, having a crate or a puppy pen or a small puppy-proofed space can really help to make sure that your puppy doesn't have accidents. If your puppy can't avoid the mess, they're less likely to make it in the first place. At the same time, don't forget to give them plenty of opportunities to go outside so they can go when they need to.

Whoops!

Accidents do, and will, sometimes happen and they're not your puppy's fault. People often ask us what they should do if their puppy goes to the toilet inside. The answer is simple: stay calm, clean it up and carry on!

Take a deep breath and be forgiving. Put your puppy away in a pen or crate to give you chance to clean up (so they don't try and play with the cleaning materials) and use an enzyme-based cleaner to clean away the residual odour that might encourage your puppy to use that area again. Say to yourself, 'I am not alone. Other puppy owners have survived this and so will I!' Remember, you've got this. Before you know it, your puppy will have mastered toilet training and you'll forget just how time-consuming it was.

The conventional approach might be to chastise them or tell them off. Your puppy won't understand why you're punishing them, but if they associate an unpleasant reaction from you with occasions when they have toileted inside, they might learn to avoid going to the toilet when you are present, which will create a bigger problem.

Toileting is very much a rehearsed skill. You want to give your puppy as many opportunities as possible to rehearse going in the right place and reward them when they do, because that's what they will do more of in the future.

Every dog is different

Some dogs need longer than others to toilet. Some dogs like to sniff around for a bit and find that perfect spot, while others just prefer to get on and do their business. Every puppy is different, and you'll start to get to know your own dog and their habits. As long as you are consistent and make sure to set your puppy up for success, they will quickly learn what is expected and will have mastered the art of toileting outside on cue before you know it.

CHAPTER 8
Key Concepts: Why Calmness is King

In the introduction, we talked about the three key concepts – calmness, optimism and proximity – that you need to start working on with your puppy from day one, which we'll cover over the next few chapters. If you base your puppy's training on these three concepts, we know everything else will fall into place. The first, and arguably the most important, is calmness.

Calmness is the foundation to all of your puppy's learning. It is something that will make your puppy happier and your life easier. When your dog is calm, all of their choices become good choices. It's what makes it possible for your puppy to choose a quiet, relaxing activity over biting your feet or barking at the postman. Calmness is indeed king!

If your puppy is excited, frustrated or fearful, they are likely to show certain behaviours. That could be anything from barking and jumping up to biting and lunging. However, if your puppy is calm, then the behaviours they choose are always going to be good ones, such as resting calmly on a bed, walking loosely on a lead, ignoring distractions on a walk. If your puppy is calm, they are only going to make great choices and behave appropriately.

Calmness doesn't always come naturally

Some dogs are born valuing calmness, but the majority of puppies don't know how to be calm so we have to teach them. It's simply not part of their natural decision-making process to choose calmness over craziness at first. Your puppy might struggle with calmness because they are wary of the world and find new and novel events pretty challenging. Some puppies like to live life in the fast lane and they think everything about life is exciting – even breathing!

While excitement and desire to play games and enjoy fun activities is good in small doses, it is not a state you want your puppy to exist in all the time. Think back to what you learned in chapter 2 about your puppy's bucket. A dog who struggles to switch off and calm down has things constantly paying into that bucket. Their brain is switched to alert all the time and that's pretty exhausting. A puppy who is constantly on the go and can't switch off will have a very full bucket and can be pretty demanding to live with.

As we talked about in the introduction to this book, rehearsal is powerful and your puppy will become more of what they practise. If every day is full of high-arousal activities and non-stop excitement, your puppy will wake up the next day already set to anticipate excitement – even before anything exciting has happened. This quickly leads to a dog whose default state is anything but calm, and whose choices and responsiveness to the events of the day become less and less appropriate and harder to work with.

Again, don't despair if you haven't followed this method from the minute you got your puppy. Your dog will become more of what they practise every day so if you want to move them in the right direction, your aim is for them to practise more calmness. They might struggle at first but over a number of days, it will get easier and they will learn how to be calm.

Calm puppies make better choices because their bucket isn't constantly full or overflowing. Teaching your puppy to be calm keeps their bucket empty as a matter of course. Then, when exciting or challenging events do happen, the bucket doesn't overflow. Unexpected challenges may still pay into that bucket but, because your puppy has some go-to calm behaviours, they recover much more quickly when the inevitable exciting or worrying things do happen in their life, and their bucket empties again much more easily.

Lauren's story: The gift of calm

Over 10 years, Lauren has competed multiple times and with multiple dogs at events at Crufts, the largest dog show in the world, as well as Discover Dogs, the European Open and the FCI World Championships. Her dogs have enjoyed huge success and have won multiple times at Crufts. At dog shows, novelty is in great abundance, from children and different breeds of dogs to travelling on trains, hotels, cameras, television, and walking sticks. You name it, Lauren's dogs have seen it all! But having trained for calmness, the dogs simply lap it up, and on the occasions that they don't, Lauren always knows how to handle it.

Exercise ISN'T the key to calmness

It's natural to assume that an overactive puppy needs more exercise or you need to play more high-energy games with them in a bid to wear them out. It might surprise you then to learn that the oppo-site is actually true. If your puppy is excitable, energetic or struggles to settle because they can't relax and their bucket is full, exercise is going to fill that bucket even more and make them even fitter and more energetic!

If you have an energetic lifestyle, then you can bet in a couple of weeks your puppy will too. If you have a calm lifestyle, you can bet they'll be calmer. Instead of thinking you need to tire your puppy out, make sure your day is based around the following calmness strategies instead.

How to teach your puppy to be calm

Our dogs' lives shouldn't be all go, go, go or consist solely of high-arousal games or activities. Just like humans, puppies need periods of downtime and rest.

There are three different ways that you can encourage your puppy to be calm throughout their day. We refer to this as the calmness wheel or triad. Sleep is an essential part of your puppy's day so you should always give them a chance to nap at regular intervals.

Your puppy can dip in and out of these three ways as needed. It's flexible and will vary from day to day, depending on your plans.

1. Passive calming activities
Sniffing and licking are naturally calming activities for dogs of any age, so harness those natural instincts and use them to help your puppy to be calm.

If you put some relaxing music on and have a soak in a warm bath, you're going to feel calm afterwards. You need to be able to find an equivalent for your puppy by offering activities that help them to feel calm and relaxed. Examples would include giving your puppy a long-lasting chew or a stuffed Kong or scattering some food on the floor for them to sniff out and find.

When thinking about what activities are appropriate for your puppy, it's important to observe what works for them. Not every puppy will find scatter feeding a calm activity. For some puppies, long-lasting chews can be exciting or challenging and create frustration rather than calm. Your puppy might even enjoy a calming massage – try long, slow strokes in the direction of their fur. The most important thing is to discover what helps your puppy chill out and relax.

2. Calmness protocol

This is all about spotting moments when your puppy is relaxing and being calm and rewarding them with some of their daily food allowance. Marking the moment with a positive outcome tells your puppy they made a great decision.

This can feel a little counter-intuitive at first. Your puppy has just settled down and might be about to go to sleep. If you then reward them, aren't they going to wake up again? Here's the thing. Your puppy will learn that being calm is the way to get the reward, so being calm will gradually become the behaviour that they are willing to offer more often. You are reinforcing that choice to be calm and making it much more likely to happen again.

How you reward your puppy is also really important. Deliver any food in a calm way. You might place a piece of food gently beside your puppy, or move it slowly towards their mouth (imagine aeroplane feeding a child – see the Aeroplane Game below). If food is super exciting for your puppy and you find that you are undermining their calmness, sometimes a slow stroke or a gentle word of praise is more appropriate. Every dog is different, so find out what works for your puppy.

TIP: Beware of fake calm

Your puppy will soon learn that they get a reward for lying on their bed, which might prompt a deliberate performance where they pretend to be calm and relaxed when actually they're not. You'll come to recognise the signs as you get to know your puppy and can see by their body language that they're still alert and not yet properly relaxed. Look out for a head pressed down into their bed but eyes wide open, watching your every move. Fake calm alert! Make sure you're not rewarding that. True calmness is what you're aiming for – when your puppy switches off and isn't prompting you for interaction or food.

AEROPLANE (SLOW FEEDING)

Slow feeding is a super strategy for creating calmness and stillness. This entire game should be slow and calm, without too much excitement from you. You want your puppy to learn to be calm when being rewarded, but this is also a great way to encourage self-control, tolerance of frustration and to lower their arousal. If your puppy gets too excited, it could be that you are moving the food towards them too quickly, so slow everything right down.

Step 1: With your puppy settled on the floor in front of you or on their bed, start to bring a piece of food down to them, gradually. If they start to shift their weight towards the food, try to jump towards it or reach for it, move your hand back out of their reach.

Step 2: As soon as they settle again, continue moving the food towards their mouth.

Step 3: You may have to repeat pulling back and bringing the food forward several times before your puppy settles in for the ride. When they do, it's time to feed!

3. Active rest

Imagine being a puppy having to cope with all these new experiences and situations and having a lot of overwhelming information being thrown at you, every minute of every day. Active rest is about putting your puppy in a quiet space where there is no other option for them but to chill out, be calm and sleep. That might be achieved by popping your puppy in a crate or a puppy pen or designating a room of your house where people don't go in and disturb them so they can rest. Your home is a busy, noisy place to a puppy and they need some enforced downtime to help them tune out and choose calmness.

Calmness strategies

Having strategies available that will help your puppy learn to value calmness and give them plenty of time to tune out and chill is really going to set you up for success.

Create calm zones

When we looked at preparing your home for your puppy, we talked about having some areas in your home that are just calm spaces. Think about having some rooms where you train your puppy and play games, and others where you just chill out. If you frequently play tug or throw and fetch in your living room but then you want to sit down and watch a relaxing movie in the evening, there's no distinction for your puppy, who might spend the majority of the film sitting and staring at you, waiting for you to play. We call this rehearsing the room. Practise the energy that you want your puppy to choose when they're in there.

Create a cue

Having a cue for when it's time to train and focus is a good idea. This helps your puppy know when it's 'game on' and time to work. At the end of a session, it's also useful to have a cue to let them know that it's time to switch off, relax and chill out. Your puppy may take a little time to learn these cues, but it's good to start that association right from the beginning. Whenever we're training, we always cue the start of a session with 'OK, ready' or similar, and finish with 'Settle down now, we're done'. Over time, your puppy will come to know the commands and recognise your tone of voice and what they mean.

Sleep is golden

Making sure your puppy gets enough sleep is so essential to their ability to be calm. If you ever find that your puppy's behaviour is deteriorating and their choices are becoming less appropriate, they are more than likely overstimulated, tired and desperately need a nap. Just like children, puppies will often resist sleep, so helping them learn how to regulate their emotions and embrace calmness, even when the witching hour is calling their name, will help overcome almost any struggle.

You'll notice that your puppy's ability to take these deep, essential naps will grow less and less as they get a little older. This isn't because they need them less, but because the world has become much more stimulating and they're having a harder time tuning out all those distractions. This is why having a crate, puppy pen or puppy-proofed area is essential to your puppy's success. Covering the crate can also help to drown out or block any distractions.

It's vital to build a positive association with your puppy's crate and make it a place they are happy to hang out. We cover crate training in more detail in chapter 9.

Don't be predictable

You've already ditched the bowl, but just as important is ditching the routine. Dogs are good at predicting. It's a survival skill. Learning to predict where the food will be and when there's danger are both essential for survival. But prediction isn't always a good thing when it comes to calmness. Think about how you might feel when you're looking forward to a big or nerve-racking event. The planning, preparation and anticipation can be more overwhelming than the actual event itself. By the time that event comes, you're stressed and burned out. It's the same for puppies.

Dogs will very quickly start to predict excitement or worry at certain times of the day or as a result of particular routines or things you do. In fact, they are experts at it.

Your puppy might learn that when you put on your waterproof coat and pick up the lead, you're going for a walk. Or when you get their crate and carry it into the hall, you're taking them to the vet. Our puppies will always be on alert for reminders or cues that something potentially scary or exciting is going to happen.

That creates anticipation – or an increase in arousal. With a bucket filled by all that anticipation, your puppy is less likely to go into that event or activity feeling calm, so there's more chance their choices aren't going to be the best ones.

How to ditch the routine

To avoid predictability, be deliberate and intentional about ditching the routine. And keep this in mind throughout your dog's life, not just when they are little. Every dog will benefit from having no set routine. If your dog already has a routine then it's still possible to change it and start to mix things up. However, be sympathetic to what your dog already knows. Gradually move away from their routine – perhaps swapping out one activity each day - rather than going complete cold turkey and changing everything straight away.

Here are some suggestions:

- Open a door and close it again.
- Put your shoes on, sit down and have a coffee.
- Pick up your puppy's lead or harness throughout the day and then put it down again, so that the action of picking up the lead (and the anticipation of a walk that it triggers) is not immediately filling your puppy's bucket.
- Pick up your keys then answer some emails.
- Switch up when and how your puppy gets fed, making use of enrichment options, passive calming activities, games and play (see chapter 4).
- Take lots of trips to nowhere so that a car ride doesn't always lead to an exciting day out or trip to the vet.
- Drive to a favourite walk location, get your puppy out of the car, play a game and go home again.
- Pop your puppy in the car, sit in the driveway and have a coffee or check your emails, then go inside again.
- Play different games every day – and try to play at different times.
- Leave the house and then come straight back inside.
- Arrive home from work a little earlier or later than usual.

By eliminating these predictable events, you remove the anticipation. It is possible to halve a dog's regular bucket just by ditching the routine alone. This is an incredibly powerful concept.

REWARD NOTHING

Some puppies see little or no value in stillness and find the concept of doing nothing really hard. If you have a puppy who is always active and 'doing', this is a really valuable game.

In essence, you are using some of your puppy's daily food allowance to reward them for doing absolutely nothing at all! The only two rules in this game are:

1. That your puppy is calm and still when you deliver the reward.
2. That you only deliver the reward if they maintain 'doing nothing' as you move the food towards them.

Your puppy can be in any position they choose, but the key is that for those ten pieces of food you pick out for the session, they are doing absolutely nothing when that food is delivered. The aim is to capture that moment where they bring the energy down, switch off or relax their muscles.

Step 1: Prepare ten pieces of food.
Step 2: Sit down in front of your puppy.
Step 3: Every time you see them pause for a second, relax or take a breath, REWARD!

MOUSE

This is a brilliant game for teaching your puppy to regulate their impulses and develop some self-control. It's also a great calmness game. We think this is a good way of building a dog's enjoyment of working for their food, so if you have a puppy who is a little less 'foodie', it's one to try. You can also adapt the game to play with toys.

We often combine this with boundary games (see chapter 9).

Step 1: Start out with a single piece of food or a small pile of your puppy's dinner, placed on the floor in front of your puppy. As long as your puppy is calm and controlled around the food, it stays uncovered.

Step 2: Deliver pieces of food to your puppy from the pile. You might take a piece from the pile and feed it straight to your puppy's mouth or flick a piece towards them. To make it a bit more exciting, flick a few pieces in quick succession. Keep them guessing!

TIP: If your puppy tries to help themselves at any point, the food is covered (caged with your hand like you're caging a mouse) until they back off a little and calmness resumes. If your puppy catches you out – just laugh and carry on!

HEAD LOW

As well as being an exceptionally cute trick to teach your puppy, this is a great calmness game because it promotes that relaxed, sleepy position that many dogs opt for when they are truly chilled. The aim is to teach your puppy to drop their chin to the floor (or bed) and leave it there until you release them from that position (by asking them to do something else).

Any time you spot your puppy doing this behaviour naturally of their own accord, reward them then too. To teach it:

Step 1: Start with an object flat and wide enough that your puppy can put their chin on it. Coasters or the lids from tubes of crisps are great for this. Initially, warm your puppy up to the experience by having the object in one hand and, with food in your other hand, position the food in such a way that your puppy has to touch their chin to the object to get the food. Hold your target object off the floor a little distance in front of your puppy and begin by rewarding any interaction that your puppy offers with their head or chin (try to avoid encouraging them to get their paws involved). Mark verbally to communicate they are getting the right idea (use 'Good', 'Yes') and follow up with a piece of food.

Step 2: Take the object away (pop it behind your back), and then re-present it and see if they interact with it again. Once they get the idea, you'll often find they engage with the object much more readily.

Step 3: Pop the object behind your back again, and when you bring it out this time, hold it just beneath your puppy's chin. Watch to see if they now rest their chin on it. If they do, mark and reward! Take the object away again, and repeat.

Step 4: Once your puppy gets the idea, you can gradually lower the target towards the floor so that your puppy transfers that behaviour and starts putting their chin flat on the ground. If you've worked in a sitting position up to now, you may need to repeat some of the earlier stages with your puppy lying on the floor or on their bed.

Step 5: Build duration by pausing before you mark and reward.

Step 6: When your puppy has cracked this game, you can add a verbal cue just before you pop the target down, so that your puppy learns to associate hearing that cue with doing the behaviour. Any word works as long as you're going to remember to use the same one every time. We quite like 'Sleepy'!

Step 7: Eventually, you can remove the target and your puppy will offer their chin to the floor without it.

Calmness is such an important concept for your new puppy to learn and you can also use the same strategies to teach calmness to an older dog.

Once they have a great baseline of calmness, they will find it easier to go back to being calm even when their arousal is increased or they get more excited. Working on calmness every day will build such a solid foundation of great decision-making that it will be easier and easier for your puppy to control their impulses when opportunities arise. Remember that rehearsal is powerful. What your puppy practises most is what they will do most of. If calmness is what they practise, they will find it much easier to find that calm state, even when exciting or worrying things happen.

Calmness isn't only going to be important for puppies, though. It should be the foundation on which everything else is built throughout your dog's life – and getting that foundation in place now will get you and your puppy off to the very best start. Quite simply, a calm dog lives a happier and healthier life.

CHAPTER 9
Crate and Boundary Games

Keep calm and get a crate! Crates are a vital part of helping your puppy to understand and embrace calmness. They're a safe space where your puppy can learn to really switch off and relax.

It's not unusual to feel uneasy about expecting your puppy to spend time in a crate, or to have doubts about whether crate training is in your puppy's best interests. You will come across many and varied views on the use of crates and, in the end, it's down to personal choice.

Like any piece of equipment, a crate can be used inappropriately or be misused. A crate should never be used as a form of punishment. Your puppy should not be expected to spend extended periods of the day, every day, inside a crate. Often, owners are told to put their puppies in the crate, close the door and let them cry, but we believe that's traumatic and heartbreaking for both you and your puppy. If you do choose to use a crate, it needs to be used kindly and positively through games.

Before you embark on crate training, or decide that crates are not for you and your puppy, it can be helpful to think about all the reasons you might find a crate to be a useful part of your training plan.

- **Safety and security**

A crate is a great way to give your puppy a safe space to chill out, relax and feel secure. It can also give them a safe space away from visitors.

- **Vet time**

It's extremely helpful to acclimatise your puppy to being happy in their crate well before they need any vet stays or extended care.

- **Multi-dog households**

If you have other dogs, crates allow you to give your dogs time apart, which is important for keeping buckets empty and vital for dogs who don't always get along.

- **Toilet training**

Dogs don't like to toilet where they sleep, so a crate can be helpful when you're toilet training a young puppy.

- **Supervision**

Crates are useful for keeping your puppy safe when you're not able to watch them.

- **Safe vehicle travel**

Crates make it easier to travel safely and securely with your puppy.

- **Time away from home**

Getting your puppy comfortable spending time in a crate will ensure they are well prepared for vet visits, groomers, boarding or other environments where being in a crate might be necessary, or if they ever need crate rest after an injury. Their crate becomes their portable safe place that remains consistent even when the environment or location is not!

• **Bedtime**
Knowing your puppy is safe and secure at night in a comfy crate can be the best option for a good night's sleep for all.

Choosing a crate

When it comes to choosing a crate, there are many types and sizes available. Here are some considerations to help you choose the right one for your puppy. Crates generally cost from around £25 for a basic model and you can often pick one up second-hand.

Plastic or airline crates

We like this type of crate because they're made of soft plastic, are easily portable, and are small enough that they make puppies feel safe and secure. They are also a lot more comfortable – the puppy can lie against the soft plastic on the sides rather than wire – and there's no risk of them getting their mouth caught on the bars, which they can sometimes do in larger wire crates. We usually put some soft, washable, absorbent bedding in the bottom.

Wire-framed crates

If you mainly use your crate in one location, you might consider a slightly heavier metal wire crate. Some models have partitions that allow you to adjust the internal space as your dog grows. They weigh a bit more, but fold very flat. Some dogs are wary of the sound the base of these crates makes, so do bear this in mind. It's possible to purchase custom-made covers for wire crates if you find your puppy is happier not to be seen when they're settling into their crate for a nap.

Soft crates

These are lightweight and fold almost entirely flat. They are made out of a metal frame and water-resistant canvas, but puppies can easily chew them so they may not be the best choice to begin with.

Custom-built crates

Many companies offer bespoke crates that can be matched to the style and decor of your furniture and blend more seamlessly into your home.

Car crates

For safe travel, you may also consider investing in a crash-tested car crate. There are various brands available to fit different makes and models of car.

As a general rule, your puppy should be able to lie flat, turn around and sit up straight in their crate.

> ## All good things happen in the crate
>
> You can really boost the value of your puppy's crate by making sure all good things happen in there! If your puppy is having a Kong or chew, giving them this inside the crate will help your puppy learn this is a great place to hang out.

Crate training: Step by step

Help your puppy learn to love their crate and see it as a great place to hang out calmly and have a snooze by following these simple steps.

Don't test it too soon. Remember you are training FOR the situation, not IN the situation. When you have visitors or something else really exciting is happening won't be the best time to do a crate-training session. You might see lots of progress in some sessions and less in others. Some days your puppy might seem to have forgotten everything they had previously learned. That's OK! It can help to start each session just a little easier than you ended the previous one.

Step 1: Reward any interaction with the crate

When you first introduce your puppy to their crate, you might find they are a little hesitant – or they might immediately climb all the way in! Reward any interaction – sniffing, moving towards the crate, putting a paw inside – by feeding them some of their daily food allowance.

It can help to place a few pieces of food in the crate to encourage their choice to go in, and then throw another piece of food away from the crate to encourage them out again. This means you're not putting too much pressure on your puppy to get inside and stay inside, especially if they are a little cautious to begin with. You don't want your puppy to feel conflicted if they're uncomfortable going inside the crate but really want the food you've put in it.

Step 2: Reward any choice to go in the crate

Reward any choice your puppy makes to go into the crate. Ideally, you want to see that they are choosing to go in, and then reward this choice (rather than luring them in with food). Once your puppy is in the crate, start posting some pieces of food through the bars in the side. You want to create the idea that this is a great place to be. Be generous!

Step 3: The release cue

Encourage your puppy to come back out with a cue (e.g. 'OK', 'break', 'free'). The word you use doesn't matter as long as you're consistent – you could even say 'bananas' if you really wanted to! A second or two after you give the verbal release cue, throw a piece of food for your puppy to follow, so they start to pair the word with coming out of the crate.

Step 4: Add a little duration

As your puppy starts to learn that the crate is a great place to be, you can work on a little duration and get them to stay in there longer. Keep it fun, low pressure and unpredictable and don't always make it harder.

If your puppy is ping-ponging in and out of the crate, the crate needs more value. If they are getting stuck in the crate and not coming out when you say your release word and throw a piece of food, focus a bit more on that. Be flexible, adaptable, and most of all, have fun.

Step 5: Be unpredictable

Now your puppy knows going into the crate is a good thing (which means moving away from you), move around and try feeding them from different angles. Stand to one side of the crate and feed through the gaps, then the other side, or straddle the top of the crate and see if they will happily go in with you feeding them from above.

Once your puppy is totally fine going into the crate from different directions, half close the door and see if they can still figure out how to get inside. If they persevere, reward them and show them they made a super choice.

Play around with the door. Close it briefly, then open it and see if your puppy continues to go into the crate and reward them when they do.

Step 6: Close the door

The crate door can quickly become something your puppy doesn't like, because when it closes they can't get to you and they can't get out. Now your puppy is seeking out the crate and wanting to be in it, close the door completely and continue to feed them through the door. You want them to see the door closing as a good thing. When the door closes, the food bar opens! Open the door briefly and stop feeding, then close the door and reward with food again inside the crate. You want your puppy to know that the door closing is a predictor of great things rather than seeing it as a bad or scary thing.

Step 7: Visual access

This is about your puppy being fine in the crate without being able to see you. You're aiming to teach your puppy to relax happily in their crate away from you, even if they can't see you and you're not close by. This is an important step between your puppy being happy in the crate and you leaving the room.

Put a towel or blanket over the crate and position yourself so that your puppy won't be able to see you when they enter the crate. Will your puppy happily leave you to get into the crate? When they choose to do so, lean over and drop some food through the door, so your puppy is learning that even though they can't see you, the crate is still a great place to be.

Once your puppy is totally happy with that stage, up the challenge by using anything suitable you have at home (a large cardboard box, a piece of furniture, your puppy's bed tipped on its side) to create a barrier that your puppy has to move round to be able to get inside the crate. You may need to help them out a little to begin with by luring them round the barrier with a piece of food and encouraging them to get in the crate. The more your puppy learns that there is lots of benefit in moving away from you and going inside the crate, the happier they will be spending time hanging out in there when you're not close by.

Continue to play with the crate door open and closed. Staying in the crate should be a choice, regardless of whether the door is open or closed.

Step 8: Add distractions

Can you or someone else calmly walk past your puppy's crate? Reinforce calmness. No interaction and no response is a good thing. Your aim is to get to the point where your puppy is able to spend time calmly in the crate while day-to-day distractions go on around them.

> **TIP:** Once you know that your puppy is happy being in the crate, pick times of the day when you know they are naturally sleepy or quiet, put the crate nearby and see if they choose to go in. When they do, close the door and post some food through the bars. You might find that your puppy goes to sleep. This is when you can start to build up to them being able to spend longer periods of time in their crate.

Boundary games

We're going to be talking a lot about boundaries in this section. We would define a boundary as a bed, a mat or even a shallow box. It can be anything that has clear edges or sides.

We love boundary games! Incorporating them into your puppy's life from the start will supercharge your success in so many ways and will also help your calmness training.

They teach your puppy to happily go to a bed or defined area and to stay there and chill out until you say it's time to do something else.

Rewarding your puppy for staying within a boundary – on a bed, mat or blanket – in a calm way promotes self-control and gives your puppy a super-safe zone to chill out, whatever is going on in the household.

When your puppy learns to love staying within a boundary, that area becomes an anchor that helps them to settle and embrace calmness. Boundary games can form a valuable part of your management strategies for a settled household, so teaching your puppy now will reap many rewards in the future. They can be introduced at any time following the same process even with a slightly older puppy.

You'll find playing boundary games will help avoid struggles as your puppy gets older, such as:

- Counter-surfing – this is when a dog stands on their back legs and jumps up to grab objects or food from the kitchen worktops.
- Jumping up on visitors.
- Chasing household cats or pets.
- Barking at the door or the window.
- Being unsettled in the car.
- Jumping, nipping or chasing excited children.

Creating your boundary

To make it as easy as possible for your puppy to understand the rules of the game, create a clear boundary. We like to use a bed that's slightly raised off the floor on legs, but use whatever you have available – a dog bed with sides, a sturdy shallow box, a mat or even a towel. If you're using a flat surface, the thicker the better – you want to create a surface that your puppy can clearly step onto. The aim is to train your puppy to stay within this boundary.

Introducing the boundary

Step 1: Start with your puppy on the floor next to the boundary. If they hop straight onto it, reward them with a few pieces of food placed inside too. If you find they need a little encouragement, popping some food onto the boundaried area should help them figure out where the best deal is. Reward any interaction at all – just like you did with the crate. Break it down into tiny steps if needed. If your puppy looks at the boundary – reward them! If they move towards it – reward!

Step 2: Once your puppy is happily within the boundary, throw a small piece of food onto the floor outside it so they jump out of the boundary, then see if they hop back in. Like their crate, you want them to see this area as a place of value – somewhere they want to spend time. Be generous with your puppy's food reward when they choose to be within the boundary. It can help to place your pieces of food within it rather than feeding them directly to your puppy so they start to value the area. You're not asking your puppy to get within the boundary area at this point. You want them to figure out that the boundary is a place of value – a tropical island where they can hang out and relax – and you want it to be their choice.

Step 3: Alternate between placing food on the boundary to reward your puppy's choice to hop onto the boundary, and onto the floor, so that they're practising jumping on and off.

132

Step 4: At this point, you are going to add a release word, just like you did with the crate. Say your chosen word (again, any word is OK as long as you're consistent, but it will help your puppy if you use the same word you used to bring them out of the crate). A second or two after you give the verbal release cue, throw a piece of food for your puppy to follow, so they start to pair the word with jumping off the boundary. When you say the release cue, there should be a pause before you throw a piece of food for your puppy to follow. The pause is key so that your puppy is learning to listen out for your verbal cue – which is permission to leave the boundary. Throwing the food is just there to help them out to begin with. This is really important for your puppy to understand so, as you continue to work on their boundary games and start to incorporate these into your daily life, your puppy is able to stay within their boundary even in the face of distractions, unless you give them permission to go and interact with that distraction.

Step 5: As your puppy gets more confident in hopping onto the boundary, say your release word and then throw the food a little way from the bed in different directions – as if you were working around a clock face. Each time your puppy hops back on, reward that choice and then throw the next piece in a slightly different direction (always close to the bed) – and reward them for hopping back on. This keeps them flexible.

Step 6: Randomise when you give the release cue so that your puppy never quite knows when it will happen. Sometimes say it almost immediately, other times delay it as you feed them for staying on the bed.

Please release me!

Examples of release cues:

- Free
- Break
- Release
- Go
- All done
- Done
- OK
- Your puppy's name
- Easy
- Finished.

TIP: You want your puppy to LOVE the release cue. The more they do, the longer they will wait to hear it.

Step 7: You might find your puppy is a bit like a jack-in-the-box – jumping straight on and off the bed – so your next aim is to keep them on there a little longer. Start to build duration by placing several pieces of food on the bed, one after another, to encourage your puppy to stay on the boundary for longer periods of time before you release them. Make sure their body is calm and quiet. If they are too fidgety and are having a difficult time, you may want to speed up how often you deliver that reinforcement (feed more often) while keeping your movements slow and steady. Gradually, you can lengthen the delay between rewards. Don't always make it harder or be too predictable though. Sometimes, delay the reinforcement for 5 or 10 seconds before you deliver that food, then make it a bit easier again.

Step 8: To help build up how long your puppy will stay on the bed, fiddle about with the food in your hands. We know this sounds odd, yet it's a gamechanger. Moving the food from hand to hand slows your puppy down a little and teaches them to do NOTHING! The anticipation of that food being delivered is all part of the reward experience, and your puppy will come to understand that food isn't going to rain down on them constantly whenever they are on the bed. If they stay put, or are at least more still than usual, then definitely reward them for their awesome choices. Those moments of stillness might be few and far between at first, but spot and reward them and they will become more frequent. Watch for moments where your puppy drops into a sit or a down while they're on the bed. If this happens naturally, reward it with some calmly delivered food.

Step 9: Once your puppy values the boundary, you can begin to test them a little. Try dropping some food on the ground beside the bed. If they stay put, reward them. You can also try to introduce a little bit of distraction to the game by standing up, moving around, jiggling about, sitting down and being unpredictable. Do they still stay on the boundary? Super! Reward that.

Don't expect to work through all these stages in your first session. As with all our games, it's not about the length of time that you play. Remember, our motto is 'a fun time, not a long time', and this is especially important for puppies, who will naturally have shorter attention spans. Spend a few minutes on each session then take a breather and come back to it later. Short, regular sessions will get your puppy used to being within a boundary.

Also, remember always to give the release cue so that your puppy learns to wait for permission to leave their boundary.

TIP: Keep it varied

The key to your puppy learning the concept of boundaries is being able to transfer this learning from one boundary to another. Make sure you don't do all your boundary games sessions using the same bed, in the same corner of the same room or standing facing your puppy from the same angle. Think about all the different things you could use as boundaries once your puppy understands the basics. That might include mats, dog beds, chairs, towels, crates or even tree stumps in your garden. Be creative and have fun!

As soon as you have built that valued area and your puppy actively wants to stay on the boundary, mix it up. You might take the same boundary to different locations or use objects that are already in the environment. This is key to the success of your boundary games.

TIP: Watch out for action prompting

Throughout all of these earlier steps, it's very normal and natural that some puppies will start to 'action prompt'. You might notice your puppy shift their weight, throw a leg out to the side, whine or wag their tail while practising what we call 'fake calm' – we discussed this in more detail in chapter 8. This is their way of attempting to get you to reward them with food.

It's very easy to fall into the habit of reinforcing their action-prompting games. Often, it's not intentional – their action simply prompts us! They whine, we think we aren't reinforcing enough and we reinforce them . . . which leads to more whining. Or they shift their weight, they kick out a paw, maybe they move their shoulders a bit, and because they choose stillness just after (or just before), we reinforce. Work with what you're seeing. If you think your puppy is having a genuinely hard time staying on the boundary, it's important to recognise that and speed up your rate of reinforcement, then gradually decrease it again to avoid action prompting.

Delaying the reinforcement until your puppy is truly still can also be a gamechanger. Ultimately, if you are consistent, the action prompting will begin to fade away.

Troubleshooting

Boundary games have many levels, and the ultimate aim will be to transition these seamlessly into your everyday life. Not only will this grow and promote calmness at home, it will build other skills that your puppy is going to find invaluable throughout their lifetime.

Don't feed too fast

One of the most common struggles with boundary games is not being able to move beyond the stage where your puppy will only stay on the boundary while they are constantly being fed. We often find that people successfully train the basics of boundaries but get stuck at the stage of crazy rapid-fire feeding.

It can be easy to find yourself standing really close to the boundary, firing food onto the bed to keep your puppy from jumping off, only to discover that the energy has actually gone up instead. Your puppy is probably even less likely to stay on the boundary at this point! You and your puppy are both getting more and more manic and the boundary is becoming less and less calm.

If this happens, slow everything right down and increase the amount of time between feeding them. Deliver the food more slowly by first moving it from one hand to the other or move further away from the boundary so you have to walk towards it to feed them.

You need your puppy to learn that, sometimes, they hang out calmly on a boundary, and that's a cool place to be! It's just something they do. It's not a high-energy training session.

This will take time, and keep the following in mind when you and your puppy are learning boundary games.

Reward strategies

The way you deliver your food rewards will make a huge difference to your success. Remember, your aim is for your puppy to learn to embrace calmness **on** their boundary – not bounce on and off it like a trampoline!

If you find your puppy is wearing boundary disco pants – perhaps they are standing up on the boundary, spinning around on it or leaning over the edge – feed calmly towards the back of the boundary so they drop back in order to get that food. Understanding how to slow your puppy down is likely to be key to progressing your boundaries.

Combine Mouse Game (page 118) with moving food between your hands and Aeroplane Game (page 111) feeding strategies discussed earlier to cultivate less animation on the boundary and add a level of stillness and calmness.

Make it part of your day

Weave boundary games into your daily life. Making dinner? Why not settle your puppy on a boundary in the kitchen and occasionally drop a piece of food onto their bed while they hang out calmly with you. Sending some emails? Why not pop your puppy on a boundary while you sit at your desk and reward their choice to hang out calmly with you while your full attention isn't on them?

This teaches your puppy that spending time on a boundary while you move around and get on with your normal activities is a great option that gets rewarded. It is also incompatible with counter-surfing (see page 291), and keeps your puppy out of harm's way if you happen to drop something on the floor that they shouldn't be snaffling.

Crates and boundary games are such an integral part of your puppy's training. Many owners see the crate as something they will only use when their dog is a puppy, but we value crates so much that we keep them throughout our dogs' lives. Even when they are fully mature, our dogs still sleep in crates and we use them daily in the car and the house for rest and sleep.

With boundary games, you are never done. This is a skill that will benefit from constantly being topped up and reinforced. Even our most experienced dogs, who truly LOVE their boundaries, will catch us out on occasion.

Remember that your ultimate aim is for your puppy to learn that the boundary is a cool place to hang out and relax, ignore whatever else might be going on in the environment, and stay there until you give them a cue to do something else. That might feel a long way off at the moment, but building these foundational layers and getting the basics right will supercharge your success in the long run. Your puppy will be a boundary games superstar in no time.

CHAPTER 10
Key Concepts: Optimism

Another key concept that you want your puppy to develop is optimism. Just like humans, some dogs are born optimists, while others are more pessimistic by nature. If your puppy is naturally optimistic, whenever they come across something new or slightly strange, they will assume it to be something good rather than something to worry about.

If we told you that we had to take our dog Poppy to the vet to get her growth measured, how you interpret that statement will depend on how naturally optimistic or pessimistic you are. You might assume Poppy is a growing puppy. You might hear that statement and think Poppy is very overweight and needs to go on a diet. Or if you're very pessimistic, you might take that to mean Poppy has a large tumour and we're going to the vet to see how long she's got left to live.

In the same way, your puppy's natural optimism or pessimism will influence the way they interpret all the information and experiences life throws at them.

Levels of optimism can vary between dog breeds too, so your puppy's breed may have some influence on their natural outlook. For example, Border Collies have been bred to notice every little detail and to spot when something is out of the ordinary, so as puppies they're likely to need a lot of support and reassurance to teach them that novelty is nothing to worry about. Not all puppies read the 'breed manual' though! You'll find more variation within a breed, and even within a litter, than you will across breeds. Every puppy is unique, which is why working with your individual puppy is so important.

In the first few days and weeks that they're with you, your puppy is going to be exposed to lots of new situations. This could be the first time they hear certain noises such as a car door slamming or a firework, meet a new dog or see traffic on a busy road. Conventional dog training says that you need to expose your puppy to as many of these new situations as you can within a small but crucial 'socialisation period' and reassure them that these things are OK. In reality, all that does is overwhelm your puppy and puts pressure on you as an owner to get your dog out there and work through a long list of different types of experiences. More importantly, the more you expose your puppy to, the more chance there is that they're going to have a bad experience or get scared or worried by something.

Instead, you want to train your puppy to be optimistic so they are not worried about new and novel events when they do encounter them. This means they can cope with any situation life unexpectedly presents them with and know instinctively that it's OK.

> ## Tom's story: Keep calm – it's a camel!
>
> A few years ago, Tom took two of his young dogs, Lava, a standard poodle, and Thistle, a miniature dachshund, to a country show in Devon. As they approached a certain area, they could hear lots of other dogs barking. Tom assumed they would come around the corner to find a cow or a tractor, but was surprised instead to come face to face with three camels! All the other dogs who found themselves confronted by that unexpected sight were barking and pretty alarmed by that novelty. However, despite the fact that they'd never seen a camel in their lives, Lava and Thistle remained calm. They were totally cool with this unexpected turn of events, because as well as being trained to be calm, they'd been trained to be optimists.

Socialisation

You can't possibly predict every scenario that you'll face with your puppy or tick off every possible experience they might have over the course of their lifetime. Optimism is the greatest gift we can give our dogs as it not only prepares them for anything on your socialisation checklist, but it also prepares them for the events you never even knew were coming – even camels!

An additional challenge with the more conventional approach to socialisation is that one bad experience for a dog far outweighs a hundred good ones. And if you're repeatedly putting your puppy into new and novel situations, that bad experience is bound to come along at some point.

If your puppy gets spooked by a sudden noise, you might think the very best thing you can do is expose them to more noises so they get used to them. Or they have a bad experience with another dog, so the temptation might be to make them meet as many other dogs as possible so they have lots of positive experiences. In reality, if you do this it's likely at least one of those experiences is going to be a bad one too. Not only that, your puppy's bucket may be overflowing so they will be less resilient and able to deal with novelty. Instead, give your puppy a few days off with minimal exposure and play some optimism and calmness games at home.

A few scary or negative experiences can very quickly shape a puppy's view of the world and make them pretty pessimistic.

When we understand this, it's clear how important it is to be careful about what we expose our puppies to and what experiences we allow them to have. Try and avoid putting your puppy in situations that are too much for them. By focusing on the quality of the experiences your puppy has rather than trying to fit in a certain number of experiences, you can make sure those experiences are positive ones.

Training for the situation versus training in the situation

Our belief is that training and preparing FOR those unexpected situations by building a foundation of optimism sets your puppy up for the most success.

Training IN the situation only sets your puppy up for failure, because they are unprepared and don't yet have the skills or knowledge to know how to deal with and respond to, new situations or experiences.

Consider the difference between these two approaches . . .

Training in the situation

You take your puppy for their first walk but they quickly start pulling towards home or are frozen to the spot because they are so terrified of the noises and unfamiliar sights around them. Instead of seeing this as your puppy needing to build their skills away from the situation, you keep taking your puppy out and trying to persuade them that the environment isn't really that terrifying. This makes your puppy more fearful and walks become increasingly challenging and less fun for both of you.

Training for the situation

You want to be able to take your puppy on walks and you know from observing their reactions at home that they will be worried and overwhelmed experiencing all the new things they might encounter. To prepare, you play games at home that focus on growing their confidence and optimism, so when they do go out into the world and experience a new sound or situation, they don't view it as anything to worry about.

By teaching them to see novelty as nothing to worry about, when they encounter real-life situations, they will be a rock star!

How can I tell if my puppy's an optimist or a pessimist?

Playing games is a good indicator of your puppy's personality. We often say that how your dog plays a game is how they play life. You'll quickly see if your puppy approaches the games you are going to play optimistically or more warily and cautiously. If your puppy is more of a pessimist, you might need to take things a little more slowly in order to build their confidence and flex that optimism muscle. Observe how they respond to the optimism games in this chapter.

Signs of a pessimist

New puppy owners sometimes assume their puppy is going to be naturally confident and happy all of the time. The reality is that puppies can find life pretty overwhelming. Every event that happens in your puppy's world is new and potentially scary or worrying. A fearful puppy might not show that in an obvious or expected way such as trembling or whining. So how do you know if your puppy is unsure?

Puppies have three coping strategies when they're feeling pessimistic: fight, flight or fool around.

When presented with novelty or something unexpected, a puppy who is unsure might bark or growl in an attempt to make that scary thing go away (fight). Alternatively, they might back away or try to hide (flight). Some puppies show they are uncomfortable with a situation by appearing overenthusiastic or excited (fool around). Your puppy might become wriggly and jumpy, or wee on the floor. Don't assume that means your puppy is excited; it could also mean that they're worried. It's similar with humans – when nervous or worried about meeting someone new, some people appear very over the top. They might be unable to stop talking, say something inappropriate or withdraw completely.

While you're getting to know your puppy and learning about their natural strengths, as well as those areas and skills that need a little more input, err on the side of caution and reassure your puppy through every new experience.

Signs of an optimist

You can tell if your puppy is more of an optimist because when novel events happen, there is no discernible change in their behaviour or energy. The ideal response you should be looking for in your puppy is no response at all!

Just as you don't want your puppy to be scared by novelty, neither do you want them to be especially excited. You want them to be curious about their environment and have the confidence to explore it, without those novel events being a big deal. Instead, you want your puppy to be able to carry on with their business, unfazed by life's camels!

Tom's story: A bowl half empty

When I was working in the world of dog behaviour research, there was a test that we did to determine whether a dog was an optimist or a pessimist. Two food bowls were put in opposite corners of a room. In one corner, the bowl always contained food. In the other corner, the bowl was always empty.

Each time, the dogs would typically head enthusiastically towards the bowl whenever it was in the corner where they had learned it contained food. Whenever the bowl was placed in the other corner, the more pessimistic dogs in the study took longer and longer to head towards it, or stopped going to it altogether, while the more optimistic dogs kept checking it out just in case!

The bowls were then moved to different positions between the two corners. What we found was that even if the bowl containing food had moved just 10 cm from its original spot, the more pessimistic dogs stopped checking it out because their natural pessimism was telling them that there would no longer be food in that bowl now it had moved towards the corner where the bowl was always empty. The more optimistic dogs still headed straight to that bowl.

What this research study went on to show us was that this optimistic versus pessimistic attitude has a direct correlation with certain behaviour struggles. The dogs that performed more pessimistically in the bowl test were more likely to have separation struggles, for example. This only emphasised to me the importance of building optimism in your puppy, as it will prevent behaviour struggles further down the line. If you've got an optimistic puppy, the chances are you will have a well-behaved, happy dog.

Games to grow optimism

These games will encourage your puppy to develop an optimistic attitude.

NOISE BOX

This game is played with a cardboard box, an empty child's paddling pool, a laundry basket or any small container that your puppy can step in and out of easily and safely. Make sure you only use items that are safe for your puppy and supervise this game while they are playing.

Step 1: Use some of your puppy's daily food allowance to encourage them to climb in and out of the box.

Step 2: Once they're happily hopping in and out, add some novelty/something unexpected to the box. Items such as plastic bottles (filled with coins or kibble to add difficulty, and securely closed of course), noisy paper and baking trays are great for this game because they will make noise as your puppy is finding all that yummy food.

Step 3: Allow your puppy to keep exploring while you scatter more food into the box. Pairing all the novelty of objects that move and make noise with a tasty reward is going to hugely boost their confidence because your puppy is hearing and experiencing something new and unexpected while getting a positive outcome (that tasty dinner!).

Step 4: Vary the box and its contents as often as you can. It's a great way to use your recycling and any packaging that arrives at your house.

TIP: If your puppy shows they are worried by moving away, backing off, barking or choosing not to get involved, go back a stage and try to develop their confidence gradually. Remember this is a game to grow their confidence, not to worry them.

NOVELTY SURPRISE PARTY

Have you ever noticed your puppy startle at a perfectly normal household object simply because it's been left somewhere different? Or maybe they've been a little spooked by an unusual object on a walk. Some puppies take novelty in their stride, while others can find it a little more challenging. You can grow calmness and confidence around novel items by scattering some of your puppy's daily food around these items for them to explore. You're going to throw your puppy a Novelty Surprise Party!

Step 1: Start out with a single novel item such as an umbrella or a bucket (any household item that your puppy isn't used to seeing), placed on the floor when your puppy is out of the room. Work at a distance that your puppy is comfortable with so you don't worry them. You're aiming to pair that novelty with a positive outcome (yummy food).

Step 2: Scatter some of your puppy's daily food on the floor around the novel items as your puppy explores, or deliver pieces of food as they check out the novelty.

Step 3: Set up your Novelty Surprise Party in different

locations and with different objects to keep the learning fresh each time you play.

Step 4: Can you add a noisy item to the party? Perhaps a baby toy that makes sounds or has lights and movement? Is your puppy cool with that or does it worry them? Adding different items can be a great way of introducing this kind of novelty to your puppy in a positive way.

KNOCK 'EM OVER

This is a confidence hero game especially for dogs who are sensitive to noises, because it teaches your puppy that they can control the noise as well as being able to control changes in their environment.

Step 1: Using an object that you have at home, such as a plastic milk carton from your recycling, a water bottle or a flask, start by rewarding your puppy for any interaction with that object. Make sure you don't choose an object that is going to scare them.

Step 2: As your puppy becomes more confident interacting with your item, try to encourage them to knock the object over. They might do this with their paws or their nose. Reward them when they do!

Step 3: Keep the game fresh by picking a different or more difficult object. That might be something bigger, noisier or generally a little different.

Step 4: You can change or increase the noise an item makes when your puppy knocks it over by thinking about the surface you are playing on (carpet versus hard/tiled floors), the material the object is made of (plastic versus metal) and by adding items to the object (you could fill it with kibble or gravel so that it rattles as it falls).

DMT - DISTRACTION, MARK, TREAT

There will be occasions, especially in those early days and weeks when you first bring your puppy home, that you can't avoid unexpected noises and situations that could potentially worry your puppy. That might be the doorbell ringing for the first time, the post arriving or the sound of next door's lawn mower. Remember, everything is going to be new and novel and potentially alarming to your puppy. So how do you help your puppy cope with the things that day-to-day life throws at them and view them through a lens of optimism?

The answer is something we call DMT – Distraction, Mark, Treat. With DMT, whenever novel events (Distractions) happen, you tell your puppy that you have noticed them too by using a calmly conditioned verbal marker (Mark) and following up with a reward (Treat). In this way, you are essentially saying to your puppy that you've noticed that weird, unusual or potentially scary thing too and that it's not something they need to worry about or be excited by.

Imagine you were in a supermarket and someone tapped you on the shoulder. What would you think? You might assume you've forgotten something or that you've dropped your wallet or accidentally taken someone else's trolley. Instead, the person who tapped you on the shoulder gives you a £10 note. You find that a little weird, but carry on walking. The person taps you on the shoulder again, so you assume they're probably going to take the £10 off you because they mistook you for someone else, but instead they give you another one. They keep doing this and, before long, you start to anticipate the tap on the shoulder and see it as something good.

That's effectively what DMT is. You recognise those unexpected moments or situations (what we call 'novelty') and follow them up with a calmly delivered, positive outcome so your puppy starts to assume them to be something good.

We always joke that when pessimistic dogs hear fireworks, they immediately think the fireworks are aiming at them, whereas when the optimists of the dog world hear fireworks, they assume it's their birthday and a celebration is happening just for them.

When you build optimism in your puppy, the cool thing is it exists even when you're not in the picture. Your dog will go through life being optimistic.

At first, you will use DMT a lot with your puppy, as every sound or situation is new and novel. As you build their confidence and optimism around novel events and sounds, you will need to support them less – and when something does come along that could cause your puppy concern, you will already have created such a strong pairing between your marker word and a positive outcome that your puppy should look to you, reassured that there is no need to be worried.

Even before vaccinations when you're still carrying your puppy around, you can be feeding them bits of food as they're experiencing the world.

How to DMT

In order to communicate to your puppy that all the distractions of the world are nothing to worry about, you first need to teach your puppy the significance of your marker word. A marker is a word that communicates to your puppy that a positive event is about to come their way. It's a way of saying to your puppy that they have done something right and here is their reward. It's different to a verbal cue, which is a command. If you use your verbal cue, you are telling your puppy to do something.

For DMT, we like to use the word 'nice', said in a long drawn-out way ('niiiiice'), which makes sure we're saying it calmly and positively. Other examples of markers are 'good' or 'yes!'. Your marker is followed by a treat. When first learning DMT, the treat will normally be some of your puppy's daily food allowance, delivered calmly, so your puppy learns to associate your marker word with a calm, positive outcome.

- The first step is to teach your puppy your marker. Say your marker word ('niiiiice') and follow up by feeding them a piece of their daily food. Repeat this until your puppy hears that magic word and knows that a positive outcome (some yummy food) is going to follow it. At first, do this at home in a non-distracting environment. As soon as your puppy starts to respond to the marker and knows there's food coming, you can start to pair your marker word with distractions.

- Start with easy distractions, not things your puppy is obviously worried by, such as someone closing a door upstairs or walking across a room, a bird flying across the sky or a twig falling from a tree. The aim is to pair your marker word with distractions and novelty and tell your puppy that those things are OK, not something to worry about. This helps to create an optimistic and calm dog.

- You can use DMT for anything from a major event like someone arriving at your house to something as minor as the phone ringing. It becomes a way of life for your puppy. It's really important to pair your marker word with all distractions, not just things your puppy is concerned about. Otherwise, your marker can accidentally become a signal to your puppy that there is something they need to get worried about.

- One of the big questions that we get asked is what to do if your puppy is already reacting to a distraction by barking. If you DMT at this point, aren't you going to be rewarding the barking? Here's the thing. That behaviour is motivated by an emotion your puppy is feeling (probably fear or over-excitement, or sometimes frustration). The aim of DMT is to change your puppy's emotional response to things that worry them. You can think of it this way: imagine if you don't like spiders but we cover you in them and then we feed you cake. You're not going to be more worried the next time you see a spider because you got cake. What you're likely to think instead is that maybe spiders aren't such a bad deal, if you get cake whenever they appear.

Optimism is a feeling of hope and confidence about the future. For your puppy, this means they will always expect the best outcome from the world and the people around them. An optimistic dog isn't worried when something new or novel appears in front of them. They can adjust to new situations and bounce back when things go wrong.

Optimism is not only an essential skill for your puppy to learn to navigate life, it's good for their emotional well-being. An optimistic puppy is a puppy who is less likely to have behavioural issues in the future. They will go through life confident, calm and happy and, as an owner, that's the greatest gift that you can give them.

CHAPTER 11
Key Concepts: Proximity

From early on, you want your puppy to see you as the centre of all things fun and rewarding. Proximity is all about teaching your puppy that there are benefits to staying close to you. To develop proximity means to grow a reward zone, a space or a bubble around you, where your puppy wants to stay. Instilling value in proximity essentially means that your puppy WANTS to hang out with you.

Pulling on a lead when you're on walks won't be an issue because your puppy will choose to stay close. Recall won't be a battle because your puppy will understand that coming back is the very best deal. When your puppy is off lead, they will choose to hang out nearby and check back in with you without you having to call them back all the time. Proximity truly is power!

Imagine a series of circles radiating outwards, with you in the centre. Each circle represents a distance from you. Your puppy will spend the most time in the circle that represents the most value. Without input, most dogs don't naturally enjoy staying close. The world is exciting and full of distractions, so they tend to gravitate to the outer circles where they have opportunities to meet other dogs, find exciting things to sniff, chase birds or wildlife or snaffle a half-eaten hamburger that someone has dropped in the park.

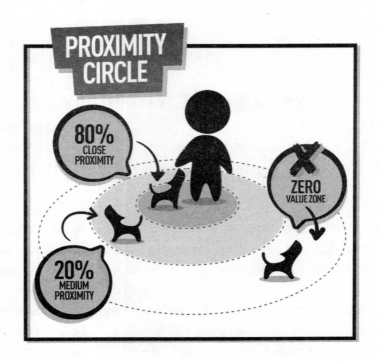

As owners, we often accidentally reinforce this. If you send your puppy into the distance by throwing a ball away from you over and over again, you can be sure they are learning that fun and value are way out there, far, far away from you! You can still play fetch with your puppy, but it's best to wait until they have at least a baseline understanding of proximity. If you play fetch with a dog who has learned the value of proximity, as soon as they get the ball then their default reaction is to bring it straight back to you because they want to be close to you.

Dogs will stay where the value is. If you were always to reward your dog in a particular square metre of a room, you would find that if you watched your dog on CCTV, even when you weren't there they would still spend most of their time in or around that area.

Putting value into proximity isn't about stopping your puppy from being able to explore and enjoy being a dog. As we discussed in chapter 10, you don't want your puppy to be scared of the world. Instead, it's about teaching your puppy that, however much excitement is 'out there', there is way more to be said for staying close to you. Proximity says to your puppy, when you're not sure what to do, here's the best place. It means that when your puppy is choosing between you and something else, such as an unknown dog in the distance, they are more likely to choose you than wandering off. They'll want to hang out with you because you're the coolest thing in the world!

Zoning out

When considering how to build this concept, we like to think of it in terms of proximity zones.

- **The central area**, a 1-metre radius around you that we call the close proximity zone, is where you want your puppy to be most of the time. This is the zone of loose-lead walking, of checking in and staying close on walks. When you think about where you put value and fun (with your puppy's daily food allowance, with your reward experiences and through your games), aim to put 80 per cent of that value in close proximity.

- **The second area**, the medium proximity zone, is where your puppy is no more than 10 metres away from you. Your puppy is able to mooch and explore and have freedom to enjoy being a dog, but they are going in the same direction as you, you can still clearly see them and they are still responsive to you. When you are teaching your puppy proximity, aim to put 20 per cent of the value in this zone.

• **The outer area**, where your dog is further than 10 metres away from you, is the zero-value zone. You don't ever want your puppy to spend time in this zone! Puppies who spend most of their time in this zone turn into dogs who run off on walks and go too far away from you. If this is you right now, don't worry! Games will transform this struggle too – there's always a game for that (in fact, there are lots).

How to grow proximity in your puppy

You guessed it! The best way to teach your puppy that the value is in being close to you is by playing games.

PROXIMITY ZONE

The aim of this game is to get your puppy mirroring, shadowing and following you and to reward them for being close to you. This communicates very clearly to them that the best deal comes from staying close.

Start off somewhere you know your puppy is going to be successful. A room of your house without too many other distractions is likely to be a good choice to begin with.

Playing this game both on and off lead (or attaching a lightweight line to your puppy's collar or harness) will also give you the foundations of loose-lead walking. Alternate between letting the line trail on the floor and holding it loosely. You are looking to see that your puppy is choosing you regardless of whether you are holding the line or letting it trail.

Step 1: Begin by simply moving around. As your puppy mirrors and follows you, feed them a piece of food to show them that coming close to you and following your movements is an awesome choice.

Step 2: At times, your puppy might leave you to check out something else that has caught their attention. If this happens, don't panic. Your puppy is figuring out where the value is. Keep moving around and when they re-enter the close proximity zone, feed, feed, feed to show them what a great decision they made! All these little choices are creating a history of your puppy choosing you over other distractions and options they could consider, which will ultimately translate to your puppy picking you over the squirrel or the dog on the other side of the park.

Step 3: Once your puppy has got the hang of the game, vary your movement. Take a couple of steps to the side and see if your puppy will follow you. Reward them for choosing to come in close again. You might move away a little faster. Do they still hunt you down?

Step 4: You'll hopefully get to a point where your puppy almost won't leave your side and you struggle to get away from them even if you try.

PROXIMITY VORTEX

You want your puppy to understand that the environment is a cool place to be and is not something they need to be scared of – but you should always trump that. This game is basically saying to your puppy, 'You can have vegetables out there, but cake with me!' They're always going to choose cake, right?

Step 1: Have low-value food in one hand and higher-value food in the other. Your choice of food will depend on your individual puppy. One puppy's cake is another puppy's cucumber! For the majority of dogs, low-value food tends to be kibble or vegetables like broccoli or carrot and high-value food is something like cooked liver, chicken or ham.

Step 2: Throw one piece of lower-value food a little distance away from you for your puppy to locate.

Step 3: When your puppy comes back to you, reward that choice with the higher-value food from your hand.

Step 4: Repeat. Throw the lower-value food out and when they eat it and come back to you, feed them the higher-value food in close proximity. This reinforces the point that it's almost a bad deal to go away from you, because you are where the high value is.

Step 5: Once you've mastered this game in your house and garden, you can start to play in other more challenging environments. When you move up a level, attach a lightweight puppy line to keep your puppy safe and make sure they stay on task even if there are distractions. You can leave the line trailing on the floor, but you have that safety net if you need to take hold of the line at any point during the game.

FUNder

The next three games – FUNder, Tornado and Typhoon – are all great ways to help build proximity and teach your puppy that if they come in close, they get to go out into the environment again.

These games communicate the message that the world is great, but you are even better fun – and that your puppy gets to experience the world through you!

Tom and Lauren both own Border Collies who have been bred for many generations to stay at a distance from people. No amount of simply feeding them close is ever going to be enough to make them think proximity is great, but games like this can be so powerful. All of a sudden, we can't get rid of them! They want to come close so we can send them out again.

Step 1: Start the game by throwing a piece of food and see if your puppy will chase it. You may need to warm up with a few rounds of this.

Step 2: Once your puppy is engaged with chasing the food, throw a piece between your legs so they're running through your legs to get the food.

Step 3: Turn around to face your puppy and throw another piece of food through your legs for them to chase in the opposite direction. Again, they should be running through your legs to get to the food.

Step 4: Every few repetitions, vary the picture by touching their collar and feeding them, or clipping on the lead and feeding them. This teaches your puppy that coming in close and being touched or having the lead clipped on isn't a bad deal, and doesn't always signal an end to the fun.

Step 5: Begin another game of FUNder . . .

TORNADO

Step 1: Throw one piece of food away from you so that your puppy follows it, eats it and bounces back to you.

Step 2: Have another piece of food ready and, as your puppy runs towards you, use that piece of food to lead them around your body, as you turn in a half circle.

Step 3: Release the piece of food forward across the floor to send your puppy back out again.

Step 4: Repeat!

TYPHOON

This is slightly trickier to play than Tornado but it's high on the fun factor scale.

Step 1: Throw one piece of food out for your puppy to follow. They're going to eat it and come back to you like they did in Tornado.

Step 2: As your puppy heads back towards you, reach between your legs from behind, holding another piece of food so you can lead your puppy through your legs from front to back and around one leg before releasing that piece of food forwards to send them back out.

Step 3: Make sure you play this one in both directions (around both legs) to keep you and your puppy flexible.

THE WANGER

Many of you will have one of those 'ChuckIt!' throwers that you might use to launch balls (and ultimately value) away from you into infinity and beyond! We like to call it a 'wanger'. Here at Absolute Dogs, we wouldn't recommend using a wanger when you are trying to teach your puppy proximity. But if you do have one, this is an alternative and much cooler way to use it that will bring the focus back to you, as well as putting lots of value into proximity.

Step 1: Pop a piece of food into the cup of the wanger.

Step 2: Allow your puppy to take the food out of the cup so they understand that yummy food is inside.

Step 3: Repeat this a few times to build the value for the wanger.

Step 4: Refill again, and now raise the cup of the wanger just above your puppy's head to create beautiful upward focus. When they look up, lower the wanger so your puppy can take the food from the cup. Your timing is going to be important here. Some puppies quickly learn that bouncing up at the wanger is a faster way to access the contents, as the food gets knocked out of the cup and lands on the floor. Your aim is to keep your puppy's paws on the ground, so using some wetter food that is less easily bounced out of the cup can help discourage this and keep the game a little calmer.

Step 5: Once your puppy gets the idea that the wanger holds value, and good value at that, you can start to walk with it. We bet your puppy will follow you and keep the upward focus.

TIP: **With all these games, you want to keep your sessions short. A few minutes at a time is all you need to play for, especially with higher-energy games. Remember, it's about a fun time, not a long time! Keep that in mind and you can't go wrong.**

Location, location, location

Once your puppy is comfortable with the games, and is staying close to you consistently at home and in the garden, take them to practise proximity in different locations. You want your puppy to stay in the close proximity zone, regardless of what the temptations are in their environment.

At first, this can be somewhere there are distant distractions, such as a quiet corner of a park or the countryside, where there might be the occasional cyclist or person passing far away. Then play the games somewhere there are closer distractions, such as in a park close to a playground, near a footpath or somewhere where there's a road in the distance.

We love taking our puppies to industrial estates, retail parks or grassy areas of service stations and playing some proximity games with them on a lead. Choose any quiet area, safely away from traffic, where people are busy doing something else in the background and, if there are other dogs around, they are likely to be on a lead so they are unlikely to run up to your puppy.

This is all about getting your puppy used to being out in public and exposing them to different distractions, sights and sounds they might see on a walk but in a gradual way, while learning to value staying close.

Make sure you're playing those games in lots of different environments and teaching your puppy that the very best fun is always with you, regardless of what other options might be available. Be sure to spot opportunities to reinforce good decisions to hang out in proximity too!

Safety first

Seek advice from your vet about your puppy's vaccinations and when you'll be able to venture out into the world. Depending on where you live, it might be safe to drive or carry your puppy to different locations before they are fully vaccinated, in order to play games such as DMT or Proximity Vortex and get them used to different distractions before going for a walk. This will very much depend on your local area and the places you might be going to with your puppy, so do check with your vet to be sure that you're keeping your puppy safe.

Proximity before walks

In chapter 12, we're going to be looking at taking your puppy on their first walk. It's a good idea for your puppy to have played these proximity games before you do this. Many puppies quickly get the hang of them, and it might only take two or three days for your puppy to master them.

Proximity is an essential skill for stress-free walks. Before you consider heading out on a walk, you should ask yourself this question: if you dropped your puppy's lead, where would they go?

If you know for sure that your puppy would run off, it might be worth asking yourself whether they are really ready to be walked or whether you need to spend more time growing that love of proximity. You want to see that if you were to drop that lead, your puppy would stay close and not change their behaviour. Once they value proximity, you have a solid foundation for heading out on adventures together.

CHAPTER 12
First Walks

The one thing that most new owners are desperate to do when they get a new puppy is to take it out for a walk. Firstly, don't be in a rush to head out with them. There's so much you can be doing in those first few weeks to prepare your puppy for the big wide world. Your main emphasis should be on growing calmness, optimism and proximity by playing the games that we've shown you in the previous chapters. It's also a good idea to get your puppy used to being on a lead at home first before you take them out for a walk. Walk them around the garden or play games while they're on a lead or a lightweight puppy line.

When you do eventually head out, think of your walks as an extension of the games and skills you've been growing at home rather than having a particular destination in mind or thinking a walk should simply be about walking in a straight line from one point to another. Look at a walk as layers that you build up gradually – so at first you don't have to go far or go anywhere very noisy or busy with lots of distractions.

Above all, just because your puppy is able to go for a walk doesn't mean you are obligated to take them, if they're not ready. If your puppy is struggling with calmness, if they have shown you they are a little pessimistic and wary of novelty, or if they don't yet know the value of proximity, your first walk might not go the way you want it to and it won't be enjoyable for either you or your puppy. Remember the power of rehearsal and the importance of safeguarding your puppy from experiences that might dent their optimistic sparkle. Don't be in a rush to put them in situations they aren't ready for and don't yet have the skills to cope with. There are so many other ways to exercise your puppy that don't involve taking them for a traditional walk.

Workouts without walks

Conventional dog training would have us believe that the purpose of a walk is to exercise your dog to tire them out so that they are calm the rest of the time. As you will already know from chapter 8, that's a myth. The more you walk your puppy, the more energy they will have. Depending on the size of their bucket, walks could also be a huge bucket filler, which means the more often your puppy goes out for a walk, the worse their behaviour will potentially become. Your puppy will find it harder to relax, switch off and access that all-important calmness.

Here are some other ways for your puppy to exercise:

- Play short sessions of food chasing games where you toss food for your puppy to chase.
- Play with your puppy for short periods of time. Always mix high-energy games with calmer activities like boundary

games to make sure your puppy doesn't get overstimulated. For more information about toys and how to play with your puppy, see chapter 5.

- Once your puppy understands the idea of following food in your hand, you can use food to lure them into different positions. Holding food just in front of your puppy's nose, encourage them to follow that food as you lure them into a sitting position, or a down, or in a right or left spin. This isn't about teaching those behaviours, so you don't need to use any words or ask your puppy to 'sit' or 'down'. It's more about helping your puppy move their body in different ways, which is great for building confidence while also encouraging body awareness and working plenty of muscle groups. Not only does this help prevent injuries, it's a great alternative to a walk.

- Play games that work your puppy's brain. Believe it or not, mental exercise can be more exhausting than physical exercise for puppies. A good option is playing search games in the house and garden. Encouraging your puppy to sniff out pieces of food uses their nose, brain and body.

- Set up a balance path for your puppy. This is a great way to build optimism and confidence around new surfaces and textures, as well as being awesome for body awareness, so it's another brilliant alternative to a walk. Use a variety of items (any safe household items that aren't too high for your puppy to climb onto, such as cushions from the sofa, a folded raincoat or a towel) to build a 'path' for your puppy to navigate. Use different heights, textures and surfaces that are safe and appropriate for your puppy's size. It can help to bait the path with bits of food to keep them moving at a nice slow pace.

Speed can often indicate lack of confidence around the different surfaces, as your puppy tries to get across as quickly as possible. If it seems too hard, switch up your items. As with every game, it should be fun for you and your puppy. Now you've ditched the bowl, your puppy can earn some of their daily food allowance by navigating your balance path, meaning you have great fun together, grow your relationship and work on lots of key concepts all at once. Winner winner chicken dinner!

> **TIP: Keep exercise sessions short, then give your puppy a break by giving them a passive calming activity like a Kong or a long-lasting chew.**

How to have a fantastic first walk

When you think that your puppy is ready for their first walk, here are some tips to set you up for success.

1. Game first, walk later
Before the walk, play a few repetitions of some of the proximity games you have learned from chapter 11. This will remind your puppy that you are the best deal and will help make sure their focus is on you from the start. Keep the energy nice and low. You don't want your puppy's bucket to be overflowing with excitement before you even leave the house.

2. Start as you mean to go on

All walks with a puppy should be training walks, meant to instil the behaviour you'd like to see in them as an adult dog. Stay well within your puppy's limits on walks to avoid stressful situations.

3. Keep it short and sweet

Set yourself and your puppy up for success by keeping your first walk short – even 5 minutes is absolutely OK. Always go for quality over quantity. It's less about how long you walk for and more about what you do on that walk and what your puppy rehearses. Realistically, your puppy isn't going to be able to cope with 30 minutes of loose-lead walking, play games in the park and then sit nicely while you have a 30-minute chat with your neighbour at the end of the walk. Initial walks should be short so that success is guaranteed. Gradually increase or reduce the distance, depending on how your puppy gets on. Ten yards down your street and back is a success if your puppy remains calm, focused and only makes great choices, so go home and celebrate! Walks are a skill to grow gradually, not one where we throw a puppy into the deep end. Take your time and remember you are challenging conventional thinking, so do ensure that you are ready to politely thank anyone who wants to question what you are doing. You'll reap the rewards!

4. Game on

A walk is just an extension of what you're already doing at home with your puppy, so bring your game playing to your walks. As you're walking along, play Proximity Zone (see page 160) with your puppy and reward them for staying close to you. A to B (see page 261) is another great game to get skilled at yourself before walking your dog. This game can act like a get-out-of-jail-free card – it's a really key skill! You'll also need to use DMT frequently to support your puppy and build their optimism around all the new noises and experiences they encounter. You might go through a large chunk of your puppy's daily food allowance on your first short walk and that's absolutely fine.

5. Avoid busy places

At first, try and avoid walking your puppy in busy environments where there is a lot going on. Even going onto the street outside your house will be a lot for your puppy to process with traffic, people and other dogs. We see so many puppies being pulled around country fairs or shopping centres and it's too overwhelming for them. Is there somewhere you can walk your puppy where there are people and other dogs but not traffic as well? For example, you could walk your new dog in a quiet woodland, a moorland, a quiet cove or beach or even the supermarket car park for some training games. There are so many options. Build things up slowly for your puppy if you can.

6. It doesn't have to be daily

Be aware that the first walk is going to be very bucket filling for your puppy and they might need a day or two off afterwards. They will have experienced so many new things and it's a lot for them to process. Puppies don't need to be walked daily providing they are getting that mental and physical stimulation in other ways.

7. Ditch the walk

We've all seen it before – a new puppy sitting on the pavement, refusing to move, with their desperate owner trying to drag them along. We know it's because they're not optimistic, they're worried and they don't see the value in proximity, so they are overwhelmed by the whole experience and don't understand why their owner expects them to follow them. If at any point you feel your walks are more of a struggle than fun, take a break from them. It doesn't mean forever, but you don't want your puppy to keep practising this behaviour. Work on proximity and calmness at home through games and then return to your walks when you know your puppy can handle it. Puppies progress at different rates and some won't be ready for daily walks for a while. Here at Absolute Dogs we often ditch the walks, and while we always want to get to the stage of more walking, we also know that a lifetime of adventures awaits our dogs, and that therefore getting it right is imperative.

Lose the lead

We know it might sound scary, but where it's safe to do so, it's good to start practising letting your puppy off lead right from these early days. Your puppy's eyesight isn't properly developed yet, which means they won't be able to see distractions in the distance. Young puppies generally choose to stay close, so this is a brilliant time to put lots of value into teaching your puppy that hanging out with you is the very best option, regardless of whether they are on or off lead. Find a safe, secure location away from busy roads and other dogs who might come and interrupt your game, attach a lightweight long line to your puppy and play some fun games. (You can get suitable puppy lines from the Absolute Dogs website.) Begin by holding the line and once you're sure your puppy is fully engaged with you, drop the line and let it trail on the floor. The line acts like a safety net that you can easily pick up if you need to stop your puppy from running off, interrupt a less desirable choice or intercept them to keep them safe. Reward your puppy for any unprompted check-ins and for staying close and keep them engaged by playing games the entire time they're off the lead so they don't rehearse anything except awesome proximity and great choices. See chapter 20 for more on being able to let your puppy off lead confidently.

Games to help prepare your puppy for walks

Although you might be desperate to take your new puppy for a walk, many dogs struggle at first. So it's good to be prepared and play some games that encourage them to stay close to you and get them used to some of the basics before you head out on your first adventure together.

HARNESS AND COLLAR SHAPING

It's easy to assume your puppy will automatically be OK with the idea of wearing a collar and harness, but not every puppy naturally embraces this. The majority of dogs *will* be happy putting their head in a harness and having it clipped around their body but some dogs find this scary or even punishing. If your puppy's bucket has filled before you've even headed out of the door for your walk because you've had to wrestle them into their walking equipment, their ability to cope with the potential novelty they're going to come across on that walk, to interact appropriately with other dogs and even to walk calmly by your side is going to be compromised. To avoid this happening, you're going to teach your puppy to enjoy having their harness and collar put on by making it into a game.

Depending on the style of harness you have selected, your puppy may have to push their head though quite a small opening, or you may have the option of clipping the harness around their neck like you do with their collar. Either way, this is a great confidence-building game and one to start playing as early on as possible, so that by the time you're ready to start heading out for walks your puppy is wearing their walking equipment like a superhero cape!

Step 1: Begin with your puppy's harness or collar on the loosest possible setting. It can help to start with something bigger so if you have a larger collar or harness that your puppy is yet to grow into, you could use that for this game. Hold the harness/collar in your hands in front of your puppy and begin by rewarding them with some of their daily food allowance for interacting with it in whatever way they like. They might nose it or dive right in and push their head straight through. Whatever your puppy offers, feed them. Depending on how your puppy approaches the game, you might need to start by simply rewarding them for being around the equipment.

If your puppy seems nervous around the collar or harness and is reluctant to put their head through, don't worry. Be creative and try playing this game using something that you can tie into a larger loop instead. This could be anything from the belt of a dressing gown to your puppy's lead.

Step 2: Each time your puppy interacts with the harness/ collar, pop it behind your back to reset your puppy for another go. Throwing a piece of food away from you for your puppy to follow keeps the pressure low.

Step 3: As your puppy's confidence grows, hold food in a way that encourages your puppy to push their head through the harness loop. When they do, feed!

Step 4: As your puppy gets used to putting their head through the loop, make sure the way you lure them with food is less obvious. If you hold the food further away from the loop, will your puppy still put their head through? Make sure to reward their choice and show them what a great job they are doing.

Step 5: Over time, as your puppy becomes more comfortable with the game, you can gradually make the loop smaller and smaller, always checking your puppy is still happy to put their head through. Be mindful that some puppies will become a little more cautious when the loop is small enough to touch sensitive ears, while others will embrace the challenge with gusto.

Step 6: Practise this until your puppy is happy and willingly putting their head into the loop of the harness on the setting they will need for heading out and about. At this point, you can progress to doing up the clips of the harness. Some puppies will find this more challenging than pushing their head through the loop because the sound of those clips close to their body can be pretty alarming. Reward them lots at each stage and take it at your puppy's pace.

Step 7: Once your puppy is comfortable having their harness clipped on, play some games. Games involving movement will help create a positive association with wearing the harness and help your puppy understand that their walking equipment isn't something they need to feel inhibited by.

MAGIC HAND

This game is one of our favourites. It helps your puppy to understand there is value in staying close to you on a walk, it's great for upward focus and can be a brilliant strategy for getting your puppy's undivided attention as you move past distractions.

To play this game, your puppy will need to be able to catch, so you're going to practise that first. Some puppies do struggle to master catch so don't be disheartened if this takes a little while. It takes coordination, so very young puppies may find this particularly challenging. Keep persevering and when your puppy is catching like a pro, you can progress to Magic Hand.

Magic Hand prerequisite: catch

Step 1: Start with food that's easy for your puppy to see and easy for you to handle.

Step 2: Stand facing your puppy, and gently throw a piece of food towards them. Reinforce their effort. If they try and catch, tell them what a great job they did. If they drop it, don't worry.

Step 3: Keep practising. Short, fun sessions are best. You might find it helps to give your puppy a 'Ready . . .' cue before you throw, so they anticipate the food and are ready to try and catch. As your puppy begins to catch more consistently, vary your position. If your puppy can catch food thrown towards them, can they also catch food dropped from above?

Step 4: You can practise catch with toys too, so they get used to catching different sized things.

Magic Hand

This game takes your puppy's food catching to the next level. The aim of the game is to drop food between the fingers of your upturned hand for your puppy to catch. It's a brilliant one for teaching and reinforcing all the concepts your puppy needs to learn for loose-lead walking and for hanging out in proximity, because in order to catch the food they need to be by your side.

Your upturned hand itself eventually becomes a magic, supercharged cue (even if there's no food in there!).

Step 1: To start teaching Magic Hand, have some high-value food – something your puppy will enjoy and want to catch. Before you even begin working with your puppy, practise the mechanics yourself. With your palm open and turned upwards, put a piece of food into the middle of it. Now, using your thumb, push the piece of food towards your fingers. Open your fingers and let the piece of food fall through the gap. Have a few tries so you become adept at dropping food, a piece at a time, through your fingers, with your palm upturned.

Step 2: Now you're ready for your puppy to join the game. Begin by holding some food in your closed fist and see if your puppy can stand under your hand. Feed them for standing under your hand close to your side to put lots of value in that position.

Step 3: At this point you can begin to drop food through your fingers, a piece at a time, for your puppy to catch. You are aiming to keep your puppy standing right under your upturned hand and to catch the food as it falls between your fingers.

Step 4: Once your puppy is a pro at catching the food that's dropping from your magic hand, and you're a pro at dropping it so your puppy can catch it, you can add in movement. You want your puppy to be attuned and responsive to you. The ultimate aim is for your puppy to match and mirror you, to follow your movements and be aware of where you are in the environment. Start with very subtle moves. You're not aiming to go straight from static catching to a proficient 'heel work to music' routine. Can you lean slightly forward and see that your puppy can match your movement? Can you lean back and see the same? Don't be in a rush to get to this stage. It can be a challenge even for older dogs. Gradually add more movement as your puppy shows they are ready.

Step 5: You will know your puppy sees amazing value in your magic hand when you have no food, and you still have that same upward focus. Your hand has become the magic cue!

TIP: Don't underestimate the amount of focus and concentration that goes into this game. Make sure you don't overdo it. Short sessions are always best.

MIGHTY MIDDLE

Mighty Middle is a super proximity game and a brilliant way to help your puppy learn to value coming in close. Get into the habit of playing this at the end of your walks. It can boost your puppy's recall and make it much easier to encourage them to come close at the end of a walk so that you can pop the lead back on without a battle to try and capture them.

Step 1: Start with your puppy facing you and use a piece of food to lure them round the side of one leg, behind your back and between your legs. Feed them as they stand between your legs, facing forwards.

Step 2: Repeat this several times, making sure you bring your puppy around from both sides and into the middle – and each time feed them in this position to reinforce the value of that spot between your legs.

Step 3: Once they've got the hang of that, you can start to make the lure slightly less obvious. As your puppy learns that the middle is a valued position, you have to do much less work to help them back into position each time. Watch your puppy start to seek out that position. Reward! Bonus! Wow!

Step 4: Aim to keep your puppy standing because Mighty Middle is a foundation for many more games involving movement (it's much harder if your puppy learns to sit in the middle position).

Help - Dog approaching!

You're out walking your puppy for the first time and suddenly you see another dog coming towards you on the pavement. Do you allow your puppy to interact with them? Traditional dog training would suggest you should seek out other dogs to teach your puppy how to behave and interact, but we strongly believe, especially with a young puppy, there is much more value in teaching them to walk calmly past other dogs at first. This way, you safeguard your puppy's optimism and avoid interactions that might not necessarily be positive experiences for them. If another dog is running towards your puppy, pick your puppy up or play Mighty Middle and feed them. If the other dog doesn't look as if it's going to approach you, carry on walking and feed your puppy to reward them for staying close and not reacting as the other dog goes past.

If an interaction is unavoidable

First of all, don't panic! Try and make it a short but positive experience. Don't let it go on for too long (ideally no more than three seconds) or allow your puppy to get too excitable, as that's when things can quickly go wrong. It's OK to pick your puppy up, remove them from the situation and walk away. Be your puppy's best advocate.

This is why it's good to have practised games in places where your puppy has got used to seeing dogs at a distance before your first walk. If you know that your puppy is totally cool, calm and collected about seeing other dogs from afar, it probably means that a close interaction is going to be OK. Your aim is for a calm

183

interaction and then to reward your puppy for moving away. We dive into dog-dog interactions in much more detail in chapter 17.

Don't be a slave to the routine

In chapter 8, we talked about the importance of ditching the routine in all aspects of your puppy's life. Dogs are masters of prediction, so chances are your puppy will be quick to learn that when they see you put your coat on, pick up their lead and open the door, you're heading out for a walk. This prediction and antici-pation can quickly fill your puppy's bucket and make your walks challenging. Have you already begun to notice that your puppy gets excited and starts to dance around your legs at the prospect of a walk? Or perhaps they bark and run about so it's hard for you to get their harness on and attach their lead. Is your puppy really in the best frame of mind to start a walk where they're going to face even more stimulation? If you start a walk with your puppy in a state of excitement, any triggers that you meet when you're out are more likely to create a reaction. Your puppy is so much more likely to be responsive to you rather than reactive to the environment if their arousal levels have not been elevated by the same predictable actions that always lead to a walk.

Simple changes here can make a big difference. Work out the beginning stages of your prediction chain and vary them, or do them at different times as part of a different activity. You might feel a little crazy, but that's OK! The key is to avoid having a set routine and to be intentional about minimising any predictors of a walk that are going to fill your puppy's bucket.

Strategy 1: Variety and unpredictability

The first way in which you can avoid predictability is to be deliberate about ditching your routine around when your puppy heads out for a walk.

- Different times of the day.
- Different locations.
- Vary your route and the length of time you are out.
- Sniffy walks, training walks, no-rules walks.
- Multi-dog household – vary which dogs walk together.
- Ditch the walk for a day and play games at home.

Strategy 2: Avoid creating predictors

In addition to being unpredictable about when your puppy gets a walk, you can also be proactive about ensuring that certain actions or activities don't become predictors of a walk. Vary the things you do before you head out on a walk – don't always follow the same order of getting the lead out, putting your shoes on etc.

- Open a door and close it again.
- Put your jacket on, sit down and read a magazine.
- Put your puppy's lead on, then play some calm boundary games in the house.
- Pick up your puppy's lead or harness throughout the day and then put it down again.
- Pick up your keys then make some toast.

By eliminating any predictability, you remove anticipation, and your puppy will head out on their adventures with you in a much better headspace and with a much emptier bucket.

When walks go wrong

At first, your puppy's walks aren't always going to be a walk in the park! Things can, and will, go wrong. The main thing is, keep calm, try not to get stressed, and make sure that your puppy is safe. Calmly pick your dog up (if you are able) and carry them home. Ditch the walks for the next 72 hours to allow your puppy's bucket to empty fully. Instead, play games focusing on calmness, optimism and proximity and before you know it, the next time you go for a walk it will be stress-free for both you and your puppy. What we say at Absolute Dogs is: be more Lara Croft! Your dog needs you to strut and stick your chest out proudly: you've got this.

CHAPTER 13

Home Alone

'When can I leave my puppy home alone for the first time? And when I do, how do I make sure that they are OK and not anxious at being left?' These are questions that we get asked time and time again by so many owners. Here at Absolute Dogs, we like to start as we mean to go on, as much as we can, and we have a process that ensures being left alone is just part of normal life. Saying that, puppies don't arrrive knowing that being left alone for periods of time is a good thing. Depending on where and how your puppy started life, they may not have had any opportunity to learn this before you brought them home. Some puppies will take this in their stride. Others will struggle and will need more support to learn that spending time separated from you, and ultimately being able to relax at home when you need to go out, is OK.

Owners often worry that if they have taught their puppy proximity and they have learned that staying close to them is a good thing, won't their dog then struggle to spend time away from them? However, you will find that if you work on both of these concepts at the same time, your puppy will develop context. They will come to understand that if they are in a crate or on a bed then it's not about being close to you. But if they are out on a walk with you, then it is.

If you're discovering that your puppy is struggling to be separated from you, this can quickly become challenging. If they cry when you walk out of a room, find being contained in a safe space such as a puppy pen or crate worrying or upsetting and want to go everywhere with you (even the bathroom), knowing how to help them choose calm, contented independence without causing stress can feel overwhelming.

When a puppy is tiny and wants to follow you everywhere, it can be easy to allow this – either because it seems the easiest and kindest option, or because you just love hanging out with your adorable new puppy (who wouldn't?!).

However, as your puppy grows and matures, there are many reasons why it's going to be in their best interests to be able to spend some time alone happily. These might include:

- Safe space and time to relax away from other dogs, other pets or young children.
- As part of your management strategies to limit your puppy's choices and keep them safe.
- To ensure they sleep well, which will help grow calmness and limit challenging puppy behaviours that are often the result of lack of sleep and a full bucket.
- To prepare your puppy for vet visits, groomers or other environments where being separated from you will be necessary – most likely in a crate.
- To help with toilet training by limiting access to areas of the house where you don't want accidents.
- To allow you to go out, for shopping, work or other activities that are not suitable for your puppy.

Your goal as a new puppy owner is to teach your puppy that spending periods of time alone is OK and something they can learn to embrace. In fact, you can tackle separation at home.

We like to think of separation as a pyramid.

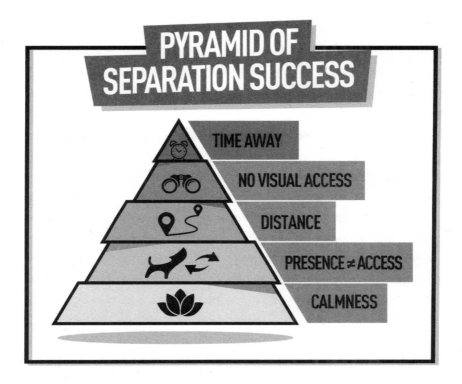

LAYER ONE: Calmness

At the base of this pyramid, there needs to be a foundation of calmness. If your puppy struggles to be calm when you are with them, you can't expect them to be calm without you there. Calmness is where it all starts.

LAYER TWO: Presence ≠ access

This is the next layer and perhaps the one that most people forget. What do we mean by this? When you're at home, does your puppy have access to you whenever they want? If they do, when you come to leave the house that becomes a huge deal for them.

The typical approach that owners learn is to leave the house for a short time and then come back and check on their puppy. It is all very regimented – on day one, leave the house for 5 minutes and come back. On day two, build up to 10 minutes. But this approach skips an essential step, which is being separated from your puppy when you're at home.

You don't want your puppy to get their disco pants on and be ready to party every time they see you. You want them to be able to lounge about in their pyjamas, be calm in your presence and accept your comings and goings as a non-event.

Yes, the Absolute Dogs approach is all about you and your puppy having a great relationship. You want your puppy to see the value in proximity and be secure in knowing that you are going to meet their needs and spend time with them. But they also have to understand that your presence doesn't automatically mean access to you all the time. With more and more people working from home, teaching puppies that presence ≠ (doesn't mean/equal) access is especially important.

Being able to handle 'alone time' is crucial to your dog's mental well-being, whether that's being downstairs while you shower or having a snooze in their crate while you make dinner.

Containing your puppy in a crate, pen or room when they're alone is also a matter of safety. Your puppy might struggle with this to begin with. Don't expect to just shut your puppy in a crate or separate room and that they will automatically be OK with that.

There are three other layers to consider when building your puppy's understanding of 'presence ≠ access', which need to be solid before you leave your puppy home alone: distance, visual access and time away.

LAYER THREE: Distance

While your puppy is learning, our mantra is 'Stay close, visit often'. You might start off in the same room as your puppy's crate or just on the other side of a baby gate so they still have the reassurance of your presence but they can't actually get to you. To begin with, try not to move around too much, which is likely to make it harder for your puppy to remove their attention from you and settle in for a nap. Read a book or check your emails. Your aim is to be physically there but not to be reactive or responsive to your dog. As your puppy gets more experienced and shows they can handle the physical barrier, add some 'purposeless movement' (stand up, sit down again, move about with no specific intention or purpose), which will help your puppy learn that your movement is not important either. All this builds towards a picture of being able to leave your puppy alone.

When first introducing the idea of distance, think about how far away from your puppy you are. If you stand or sit too close to the crate or baby gate, there's a chance that your puppy will want to interact with you. This can increase your puppy's energy and anticipation, which can make it very hard for them to disengage from you and settle. However, if you add too much distance, this can also cause your puppy to struggle and might be too much, too soon. Work with what you're seeing and don't make it too challenging too quickly.

BOUNDARY DISENGAGEMENT GAME

This is a great game for teaching your puppy that there is value in moving away from you. The game is played using a boundary.

Step 1: Start by feeding your puppy several pieces of food on their bed or boundary. Put lots of value within the boundary.

Step 2: Now move a little distance away and pretend to place a piece of food on the floor. Call your puppy off the boundary to get the imaginary food. They'll probably look at you like you've gone a bit crazy ('Where's the food, human?'). That's OK! Throw a few pieces of food back onto the boundary behind them.

Step 3: Your puppy should move away from where you're standing to get back on the bed and find that food you've just thrown. If they're a bit slow to work out the game, throw a few more pieces of food on the bed so you're really clearly spelling out to your puppy where the value is (in this context, away from you!).

Step 4: Repeat the steps of the game, gradually moving further away from the boundary. Your puppy is learning that there is value in moving away from you towards their boundary.

LAYER FOUR: No visual access

In order to be able to leave your puppy home alone, you need them to be happy even when they can't see you.

You may discover your puppy finds it much easier to settle when separated from you by a physical barrier if they can still see you – or you might find they actually settle more easily if they have no visual access.

If your puppy is having a hard time whenever you go out of sight, you can start to introduce this idea without ever leaving the room by using visual obstructions. This might be as simple as putting your chair somewhere their view of you is obstructed, or covering their crate with a blanket so they can't see out through the bars. You're still there, but they can no longer see you.

Giving them a passive calming activity (see chapter 8 for more information) can help them settle and see this as a good deal. As you move towards being able to leave your puppy home alone, you can also use passive calming activities before you leave and when you get back to help keep your puppy in a calm, settled, positive frame of mind.

Once your puppy seems able to settle with you in the same room, try leaving the room. You might go into the kitchen and make a cup of tea for a few minutes and then come back. Is your puppy still settled or did they whine the moment they sensed you'd left?

If your puppy is struggling, build more value in the area you're leaving them in before making it harder by leaving the room. Try giving them a long-lasting chew or a Kong to encourage them to be calm.

When you start adding visual barriers, you may need to make your separation sessions shorter again to begin with. Figure out what your puppy is able to manage so that you are setting them up for successful learning.

CARDBOARD CHAOS

This is a great confidence booster to play with a puppy of any age and is also a brilliant way of introducing visual barriers in the context of a fun, rewarding game. The aim of the game is for your puppy to forage some food from inside cardboard boxes, breaking visual contact with you as they move around. Start with a single shallow box so that they don't feel overwhelmed and nothing too big if your puppy is still very small. If you find that it's too easy, you can add more boxes at the next session.

Step 1: Scatter the food inside and around the box before you introduce your puppy to the cardboard.

Step 2: Observe how your puppy responds to movement beneath their feet, the sounds of the box as they explore and how resilient they are when faced with a challenge or novelty.

Step 3: Increase the challenge based on how confidently your puppy explores the chaos. You want your puppy to sniff the box, push it, get on it or in it. Add larger cardboard box so your puppy has to break their line of sight with you for longer in order to seek out that tasty dinner. Are they happy and confident breaking visual access?

Step 4: If your puppy is playing confidently, step out of the room momentarily. Does your puppy continue foraging, or does your absence worry them? Work at your puppy's pace based on what you're seeing when they play.

LAYER FIVE: Time away

The final part of the pyramid to think about is time away or adding duration. If you've got all the building blocks in place – you've grown calmness, you've taught your puppy that your presence ≠ access, and they're cool being at a distance away from you and visual obstruction – duration will be the easy bit. However, it will be the hardest bit if you don't get those other things in place first.

Don't become predictable

While working on teaching your puppy the value of 'presence ≠ access' and growing their understanding that spending periods of the day separated from you isn't a big deal, don't make your training sessions predictable.

Ditching the routine will be really important here. If your puppy is already worried about being left alone, predicting that you are going out, or that a certain time of the day means they are going to be shut in a puppy pen or crate, will be filling their bucket just as much as the actual time alone.

By staying flexible and unpredictable, you can help to eliminate all this extra stress. If your puppy never quite knows what is next and their day isn't built around a set routine, they are more likely to choose calmness, which helps keep their bucket empty.

It can be easy to become predictable – especially if you have commitments and schedules that can't be changed all that much. This is especially true with a puppy, because your day is going to have an element of routine dictated by toilet training and making sure your puppy has adequate sleep.

Remember – the goal of ditching the routine is to make exciting or worrisome events unpredictable and uneventful, as a way of eliminating any exaggerated emotions, guarding optimism and focusing on calmness instead. Building this into your day (see chapter 8 for suggestions on how to do this), every day, even when there are certain unavoidable rhythms and flows to that day, can be a true gamechanger for you and your puppy.

Work towards being able to put your puppy behind a baby gate or a puppy pen or in a crate at different times of the day, give them a long-lasting chew and then carry on with your business.

PURPOSELESS MOVEMENT

As well as learning that your presence is important, puppies can very quickly learn that your movement is important, which can be another factor in separation struggles.

Have you ever noticed your puppy studying you? Perhaps they seem to be snoozing soundly, but the minute you get up from your seat or cross a room, they are under your feet, or right behind you. Every move you make, they're watching you!

Dogs can very quickly learn which of your movements are predictors of you leaving the house or leaving the room to go and use the bathroom. If your puppy is looking for any sign that you might be leaving and is getting worried at the prospect of being home alone (or downstairs alone), it might be tempting to try to fool them into thinking you are still there by sneaking out of a back door or even a window. This is not the right approach!

The very last thing you want to do if your puppy is worried about being left is to cause them to think they missed a sign that you were about to leave. This will increase their vigilance. Your movement will become something they pay even more attention to. Instead, you want your movement to be of no consequence to your puppy at all.

Whether you are moving to another room, or leaving the house, this should be none of your puppy's concern. It also means not saying goodbye or hello to your dog when you leave or arrive back home.

How often do you stand up or move about for absolutely no reason? Probably very rarely, unless you happen to be having one of those scatterbrain days where you can't remember what you were doing! As a general rule, we tend to be lazy (or you might prefer to call it 'efficient'!). We get up to answer the phone, or because there is someone at the door, or because we need to move to a different room. If every move you make has some significance, it's no wonder your puppy will see your movement as important. You need to stop your movement being a predictor of something happening.

With your puppy securely in their crate, you are going to add what we call 'purposeless movement'. The rules of the game are simple. Move for no reason!

- Get up and sit down again.
- Walk towards a door, come back and sit down.
- Go out of the room and come back in again.

Aim to look as natural as possible. Your puppy will know the difference! As well as teaching your puppy a valuable lesson, you will get a good workout into every day.

Over time, your movement will become less important and will trigger less arousal. Your puppy's bucket will fill less, their awareness of your movement will be reduced and leaving them will become much easier.

How to work out if your puppy is ready to be left home alone

- When you stand up or move suddenly, what is your puppy's reaction?
- When you go to walk out the front door, what does your puppy's behaviour look like?
- How often do you find your puppy underfoot or waiting nearby, no matter what task you're doing?
- How deeply does your puppy sleep? What can take place around them without their sleep being disturbed?
- Can you pick up their lead without changing their behaviour?
- Can you leave one room and go into another?
- Can you pick up your keys, wallet and shoes without any noticeable changes in your puppy's behaviour?
- Do they ever put themselves into a different room to relax where you are not present?

If you're seeing indications that your puppy is finding any of these scenarios hard, you need to work through all the layers of the pyramid before you can expect your puppy to be OK without you being there.

Before you leave your dog

There are a few additional considerations that are going to be important for making sure your puppy has the best chance of staying settled and relaxed when leave them home alone for periods of time.

Meet your puppy's needs

If your puppy is hungry, thirsty, too warm, too cold or needs the toilet, it's going to be very difficult for them to settle. That's before you even add in the aspect of them being home alone.

To set your puppy up for success, you need to make sure that each of their needs is met. Make sure they've had a drink and have enough food in their tummy that they're going to be comfortable, but not so much that they'll need to go to the toilet again imminently. Give them ample time to relieve themselves before you head out and be mindful of how often they need to go to the toilet. If your puppy currently needs to be taken outside every hour, then at this point it wouldn't be fair to leave the house for any longer.

Make sure the temperature is OK before you leave too. If you've ever been stuck somewhere too hot or too cold, you'll know how quickly you become uncomfortable.

Leaving your puppy for longer

You've played some crate games and you know that your puppy is happy being in the crate. You've sat and read a book next to your puppy's crate and you've introduced the concept of a visual barrier. You've also varied the length of time that you spend away from them within the house – it could be anything from 5 minutes to 50. Ideally, what has started happening in these scenarios is that your puppy has settled and eventually gone to sleep.

If your puppy is able to hang out happily in their crate for an hour while you empty the dishwasher and cook dinner, then you can probably leave the house for an hour and be confident they will be OK.

Make your comings and goings a non-event

If you want your puppy to understand that being left alone for periods of time isn't a big deal, you, as an owner, have to keep your side of the bargain. Even though your puppy is super cute, don't make a fuss when you get back from being out of the house. All this does is add excitement to your arrival home, which makes it more important. If you coming home is an emotional reunion for your puppy, then logically, you going out will become an emotional event too. Ideally, you want to be able to come home and not immediately greet your puppy or let them straight out of their crate. You want your comings and goings to become a non-event. The idea of having dogs that get excited and run to greet you when you come home may seem lovely, but the very best scenario is coming into the house and for everything to be calm. This is a really good indication that your puppy has been content while you've been gone and unworried by your absence.

How do I know if my puppy's not OK with being home alone?

- Are they able to eat in your absence? If not, this can be a sign they are worried about being left.
- Is your puppy happy to have a drink while you're not there? Always take note of how much water is in their bowl so you can tell if they've drunk anything while you've not been there. Drips on the floor around the water bowl can be another good indication that your puppy has had a drink.
- If your puppy isn't already lying down settled when you return, is their bed or sleeping spot warm from where they've recently got up?
- Ask your neighbours whether there has been any barking or whining while you've been away from the house.
- Whining when you leave or greeting you excessively when you return are indicators that all may not be calm and relaxed while you're away.
- Are you finding any chewed items or any other damage to your home when you return? Even something like a chewed toy can be a sign that your puppy isn't happy being left home alone.

> **TIP: One thing that's really useful for seeing if your puppy is calm and happy when you leave the house is leaving your phone or tablet camera on record when you go out. This is a great way of cutting out the detective work. If you are only going a very short distance away, you could also use a baby monitor to check that your puppy is settled. Puppy cams are also useful, but we don't recommend the ones that you can talk to your puppy through. Imagine your poor dog's confusion if they can hear you but they can't see you.**
>
> If your puppy is struggling, go back a stage of the separation pyramid. It is important that your dog doesn't have the chance to practise being anxious when you leave, so when possible try not to have to leave your puppy home alone until you know that they are calm, settled and can cope. Even if your puppy rocks it, remember to keep topping up on that optimism, keep that bucket as empty as possible and continue working on the idea that presence ≠ access at home. Being inside the crate should feel normal.

Help! I need to leave my puppy before they are ready

If you absolutely have to leave your puppy home alone before they are ready, consider asking a friend or family member to stay with them (if your puppy is comfortable with that). Pet sitters and dog walkers are other options that might help you out in the short term while you're working on your puppy's ability to handle time alone.

If there is no option other than to leave your puppy alone for a short period of time, choose somewhere well away from any visual access to the outside world, or anything that is going to trigger heightened levels of arousal or anxiety. Leaving a radio playing, or some calming classical music (we've found that reggae is a good option for some dogs!), can help mask any external sounds and increase the chances of your puppy being able to relax.

Leaving your puppy home alone can feel daunting at first but it all hinges on them learning that skill of separation. Once they have learned that your presence ≠ access, they will come to see time alone as a good thing and something that both you and your puppy will enjoy. It will give you both the opportunity to empty your buckets and makes the time you do spend together even more awesome. As an owner, it gives you true freedom. You know that you can leave your house spontaneously without it becoming a military operation and that your puppy will be absolutely fine with it. In fact, they will relish some 'alone time' and see it as an opportunity to rest and recharge.

CHAPTER 14

How to Stop Mouthing, Biting and Nipping

Ouch! A puppy's teeth hurt! It can be really disheartening and frustrating when your puppy suddenly turns into a furry piranha who nips and bites and pulls at your clothes. Milk teeth are only small but they are thin and sharp and can easily break the skin. That first time your puppy tries to grab at you or latches onto your ankle with their teeth can be pretty alarming. You might start to wonder what you've let yourself in for. Before we dive too deeply into why your puppy is biting and how to overcome this very common puppy struggle, the first thing to remember is that this behaviour is completely normal. Your puppy isn't being aggressive and nipping or biting are not a sign of more worrying behaviours to come. This is your puppy navigating a normal part of puppy-hood, and with the right strategies it is something you can, and will, overcome.

Biting is exploring

Puppies are curious and like to explore the world around them. They do that primarily with their mouths. What does it feel like? How does it taste? Is it soft or hard? You are part of your puppy's new world, so it makes sense that this exploration will often be directed at you. Your body, especially your hands, are prime targets!

Your puppy might also be teething. Between the ages of 12 and 24 weeks, your puppy loses 28 milk teeth and 42 new adult teeth start to replace them. Can you imagine growing 42 teeth in such a short period of time? Consider how uncomfortable and irritating that might be! Teething can contribute greatly to their mouthing and biting behaviour. Timing varies by breed; some dogs will only teethe for 2 or 3 weeks and some smaller breeds can hold on to their baby teeth a little longer, but by 7–8 months most pups will have traded their first set of chompers for permanent adult teeth. It is important to be patient and kind throughout this process. Your puppy doesn't understand what is happening and is responding to the discomfort in the only way they know how.

So, now you know puppy biting is normal. But what do you do in those moments when your sweet, adorable puppy turns into a land shark?

There are two really important things to consider if you want to inspire great choices in your puppy and reduce inappropriate mouthing.

Preventing rehearsal

Our approach is always about setting your puppy up for success by arranging their environment in a way that limits their opportunities to make inappropriate choices – we call this management. As we've covered extensively, your puppy will do more of what they rehearse, so limiting your puppy's chances to practise biting is really important.

It can be really easy to accidentally reinforce your puppy's biting without even realising. If your puppy's mouth finds your hand, or your sleeve, or the leg of your trousers, you might instinctively yelp and pull away. After all, those teeth are sharp and they hurt! You may even have been told to do that as a way of mimicking what your puppy's mum or littermates might have done. What that actually does is add animation and energy to the situation, which your puppy will find hugely rewarding. If you have young children who naturally shriek and run if they find your puppy nipping at their ankles, the situation can quickly escalate. To your puppy, that's a great game, and one they'll want to repeat.

The important thing is to be aware of this and be intentional about how you react when your puppy does bite. It's your job to inspire great choices in your puppy and, when they do bite, to direct them to more appropriate choices – and to do that really calmly. If you give your puppy an outcome that increases the excitement and energy, you will quickly enter a vicious cycle of reinforcing that biting.

If your puppy bites, calmly interrupting them by lifting them up or taking hold of their collar or puppy line and gently stroking them is a great way of stopping that biting without adding arousal.

You don't want your puppy to think this is a big deal. It should be soothing for your puppy – not scary or intimidating.

We'll come back to strategies in more detail below as we take a look at the various possible causes of your puppy's biting behaviour.

Why is your puppy biting?

1. Lack of sleep

Your puppy needs 17–20 hours of sleep a day, so the answer to most puppy struggles is often a little more nap time, a little less adventure. We've all seen a toddler having a meltdown in the park or the supermarket. That child might be having a meltdown because they're not getting their own way; they might have seen a chocolate bar they want or a new toy they can't live without. These frustrations might be the tipping point of their behaviour, yet the reality is they would be more tolerant and less frustrated had they not missed their nap.

We understand that you want to spend as much time as possible with this adorable new family member. Perhaps you're working and you feel guilty that your puppy isn't getting every bit of your attention, so you condense a lot of fun into your mornings, evenings or lunch breaks. Don't worry! Your puppy is growing constantly and they need the sleep. If your puppy is growling, biting, grabbing at you and at things around them, it's a very good indication that they are overstimulated, and desperately need a nap to reset their tolerance meter. Rest is truly the golden answer to most puppy struggles.

How can you encourage more naps?

Make sure your puppy has a quiet, calm place to relax that won't disturb the quality of their sleep. You'll notice that your puppy will resist nap time more as they get a little older. This isn't because they need less sleep, but because the world has become more stimulating and they're having a harder time settling and tuning things out. This is why having a smaller space such as a crate, a puppy pen or puppy-proofed area of confinement is essential to your puppy's success. Covering your puppy's crate with a blanket can also help to drown out or block the distractions in the environment that might be preventing that golden sleep from happening. For more information about crates, see chapter 9.

2. Too much freedom

Another cause of a puppy biting is too much freedom, meaning too much access to you and their environment. This can be information overload for a puppy. Your puppy is just a baby and has no idea how to coexist with you and what your rules and expectations are. Every single second that they're awake, they're learning, absorbing and taking in everything around them as information. When your puppy has too much freedom and is exposed to too much, too soon, they can easily feel overwhelmed and overstimulated. Too much freedom and access to you provides more opportunities for your puppy to make poor decisions. Of course your puppy should have access to you. They are part of your family. However, when they're overstimulated, giving them an opportunity to relax and settle away from you can prevent those less appropriate choices.

This is especially important to be aware of if you have young children. As we covered in chapter 3, babies and young children are 'novelty machines' – they make noise, they move unexpect-edly and they cry, all of which can be very worrying or exciting for a young puppy. Limiting the amount of time your puppy and children spend together is so important to help your puppy make great choices and prevent any opportunities for biting and nipping that, for younger children, can quickly take the shine off the excitement of having a puppy. Check out chapter 3 for everything you need to make sure you get the foundations right for an amazing relationship that will blossom as your children and puppy grow up together.

3. Excitement or frustration

When a puppy's behaviour is over the top, the most logical solution can sometimes be the wrong one. If you have a hyperactive puppy that zooms around, full of energy, you might assume that they need more exercise, yet the reality (as you'll know from chapter 8) is that the side effect of keeping going, going, going until they crash is more stamina and longer periods of craziness, because your puppy is getting really good at rehearsing chaos! The answer to this is always, first and foremost, calmness.

Of course, that doesn't mean your puppy shouldn't be provided with plenty of opportunities for exercise and mental stimulation. It's just important to consider what is appropriate – particularly if you have a puppy whose Energizer Bunny personality means they resist calmness and tend towards over-arousal, frustration and – as a result – nipping and biting.

Mental enrichment
You can help stop your puppy feeling frustrated or bored by offering

them some mental enrichment. This is all about providing your puppy with an opportunity to problem-solve and give their brain a workout. It can come in many forms, including:

- Games that encourage your puppy to use their nose.
- Games that encourage thought, such as learning how to put two paws on a box.
- Games that grow calmness – see chapter 8.
- Stuffable food toys such as Kongs and bones.

There are many ways to encourage mental enrichment so it's important that you choose games that encourage a calm and settled body. If you pick lots of fast-paced, intense games (which, we have to admit, are really fun!), it could escalate your puppy's biting and nipping.

The Aeroplane Game for slow feeding, which we showed you in chapter 8, is also a good one to try and will help calm your puppy when they are frustrated or overexcited.

4. Nothing appropriate to chew

Does your puppy have access to chews they enjoy? If you want to channel your puppy's biting and chewing towards appropriate items, giving them access to long-lasting chews is really important. Chewing is one way in which your puppy might choose to self-soothe, particularly during that painful teething period, and you will find that inappropriate biting and chewing is greatly reduced.

Chewing/biting options
In chapter 4, we looked at some great options for long-lasting

chews. Observe your puppy to see what textures they prefer and be aware that as they grow and move through the teething process, their preferences are likely to change.

It's good to have a selection of chews that you alternate every few days. This helps to keep things interesting for your puppy and means they are less likely to disregard them in favour of having a good chew on the nearest table leg, your skirting board or your ankles.

5. Defence

When you have a new puppy, it is natural for everyone to want to meet them, but it's important to remember that your puppy might easily be overwhelmed by all this attention. Not every puppy enjoys being handled. Dogs can't tell you when they're starting to feel worried or aren't enjoying an experience, so it's up to you to be your puppy's best advocate and to not knowingly put them in a situation where they feel they have no other choice but to defend themselves.

Biting as a form of defence can happen if a puppy has been overhandled, or if their collar has been grabbed too frequently to manage them when they've made less appropriate choices. Putting a lightweight line on your puppy and letting it trail is a great way of preventing this ever becoming an issue. It allows you to casually step on the line if you need to interrupt your puppy or step in before they get into trouble or mischief. Use the line as and when you feel you need to.

Your puppy may also choose to bite or snap if they feel cornered, put into a crate when they aren't comfortable with confinement or if someone surprises or startles them by touching or trying to move them unexpectedly. Be careful not to overwhelm your puppy or put them in situations where they feel uncomfortable.

There are several games you can play to teach your puppy that being handled is OK. See chapter 16 for more suggestions.

HAND OVER HEAD, RELAX

This is a super game for puppies that have a difficult time with handling.

Step 1: With your puppy in a calm, relaxed state of mind, begin by simply moving your hand towards them. If they are able to acknowledge your hand by calmly looking at it, let them know that was a great response by marking ('Good', 'Yes') and rewarding with a piece of their daily food. If you discover your puppy is especially wary of approaching hands, you might need to start with a very subtle hand movement by your side, or a twitch of your fingers, marking and rewarding that to build up a positive association.

Step 2: As your puppy becomes more comfortable, aim to move your hand so that the palm is facing down and over your puppy (as if you were going to stroke them gently). Begin with your hand really high and continue to mark and reward.

Step 3: Gradually, offer your hand closer. If your puppy struggles at any point and tries to step back, you've progressed too quickly.

This may take multiple sessions, and that's OK. The aim is that your puppy embraces the idea that hands moving towards them, around them and ultimately touching them are not invasive or scary. Remember to do this calmly, coolly and confidently. Your dog can sense your intentions and it's really important to get this right.

What to do if your puppy bites

If you implement all the strategies that we've given you in this chapter and help your puppy to embrace calmness and learn the value of disengagement and self-control (see chapter 22), you should find that instances of biting and nipping are few and far between. However, there might still be times where it does happen, so you need to prepare for how you're going to deal with it in the moment.

Let them nap
This is the number one way to handle those occasions when your puppy's bitey side comes out. In those moments, your puppy is probably feeling frustrated, overwhelmed, overstimulated and tired, so give them the opportunity to have a nap. Also, remember to make sure they have enough rest time each day to help them avoid doing it again in the future.

Don't react
If your puppy nips, mouths or bites, you might instinctively yelp and pull away. Remember to try not to react in a way that increases

the arousal, the energy or the excitement. Instead, calmly interrupt and direct your puppy towards something more appropriate.

Redirect

There might be situations where you are able to direct your puppy's biting from something inappropriate (your hands or clothes) to something appropriate (a toy or long-lasting chew). By calmly switching your puppy away from an activity that you don't want them to rehearse (biting you) to one you do, you are reinforcing that more appropriate choice and making it more likely to happen again in the future. You can also use this as a great opportunity to practise disengagement (we will delve more deeply into this concept in chapter 22). After redirecting your puppy onto something appropriate, and providing they don't go right back to mouthing and biting you, reward that choice by calmly delivering a few pieces of food. At this point, you could also try some hand-feeding. What your puppy will then learn is that food comes from hands and hands are not food!

End play

If biting happens during play, your puppy may simply be enjoying a social opportunity with you without understanding the situtation. If your puppy is able to be redirected onto the toy, then carry on playing (remembering to keep your play sessions nice and short – a fun time, not a long time). Choosing toys with longer handles gives you a safety layer, especially while those puppy teeth are so sharp. This makes it less likely that your puppy will accidentally bite your hand if they mis-grab the toy.

Toy play can quickly increase arousal though, so watch for signs that your puppy is tipping over into that headspace where their bucket is a little too full. If they carry on biting or your hands seem to become the target, remove them to a safe, calm space and give them a long-lasting chew, scatter feed or try an appropriate passive calming activity to bring those arousal levels back down. Remember to stay calm. Your puppy is learning, and you are the calm and kind educator leading their journey. Stay cool! Biting is a normal part of puppy development. See your dog as a worthy apprentice and you'll stay in the best learning space.

ATTENTION NOISE

One of the questions we get asked often by puppy owners is how to stop their puppy in the moment from doing things they don't want them to be doing. Perhaps they start chewing on your sofa or a chair leg or steal your shoe or a pair of socks. What can you do in that moment to stop that in-appropriate behaviour?

That's where an Attention Noise comes in.

The purpose of this game is to grow a positive association with a sound or word, which you can then use to interrupt less desirable decisions and redirect to great ones.

Step 1: With your puppy ready for games (not overly excited), throw one piece of food a little distance away from you for your puppy to go and find. Don't throw it too far, other-wise you'll lose the momentum of the game as your puppy snuffles out the treat or finds something else to do.

Step 2: Just as your puppy finishes the food, make your Attention Noise. This can be any short, fun sound that will come naturally when you need it – try a beep, a chirp or even a kissing noise. Whatever noise or sound you choose, it should be made in a way that doesn't imply punishment or disappointment but grabs your puppy's attention in a positive way.

Step 3: When your puppy turns to look at you in response to the sound, mark ('Good', 'Yes') and then reward them with another piece of their food allowance.

Step 4: Repeat this a few times so your puppy learns that orienting to you when they hear your Attention Noise is a great deal.

Step 5: Play lots of short sessions to keep the learning fun.

Attention Noise in action

A typical scenario might go like this:

Your puppy is noticeably getting excited and showing signs that they might start biting.

Use your Attention Noise to redirect their focus. Because you've played this game many times, your puppy will stop what they're doing and look up expectantly.

Verbally praise them and then scatter a few pieces of food on the floor. This rewards their choice not to bite, directs their attention to something more appropriate and also brings their arousal level down by giving them an activity (sniffing) that is naturally calming.

Redirect to an appropriate toy (if that works for your puppy) or move them to their safe space with a Kong or other calming activity.

When is the biting going to stop?

Good question! As long as you set your puppy up for success and limit opportunities for your puppy to rehearse inappropriate biting, a puppy will typically stop biting as they finish teething and head towards adolescence.

During this time, the more you invest in calmness and grow your puppy's skills of disengagement and their ability to regulate their own arousal levels, the more easily this phase of your puppy's development will pass.

CHAPTER 15
Travelling with Your Puppy

Being able to travel with your puppy – whether that's visiting friends and family, heading out for walks further afield, taking them with you when you go on holiday or to routine vet and grooming appointments – is likely to be an important part of life with your new furry family member. Establishing great foundations and making sure your puppy is happy with all the novelty associated with travelling is something to start working on as early as possible.

The car

Every dog is likely to need to travel in a car or other vehicle at some point in their life. Get your puppy used to being in the car right from the very beginning so that it doesn't become a big deal. If possible, try and introduce the vehicle into your training from early on.

The way you introduce this experience will mean the difference between travel success and more challenging journeys.

Having a dog who is happy to spend time in your vehicle and can travel in a calm, relaxed way will make any journeys much more pleasant and enjoyable. It will avoid car travel becoming something that fills your puppy's bucket.

When it comes to taking your puppy in the car, your main aim is to make it into a non-event. You want a car journey to be totally boring. Absolutely nothing to see here!

Build positive associations

You want your puppy's introduction to your car to be gentle and positive. Every interaction your puppy has with your vehicle in their early life should be paired with some of their daily food allowance. Your aim should be for your puppy to learn to be happy getting in and out of the car and comfortable inside the vehicle with whatever set-up you have – whether that's a crate in the back of your car or in the boot space, custom crates fitted into a larger vehicle or another arrangement that works for you.

You also want your puppy to learn that the car is somewhere to hang out calmly. As you discovered in chapter 8, dogs are brilliant at predicting. If your puppy learns early on to associate your vehicle with trips to certain places, this can quickly mean that journeys become stressful or exciting just because they have paired being in the car with that destination.

There might be places your puppy finds worrying, such as the vet, or places your puppy finds hugely exciting – perhaps particular walking locations or visits to the beach. Either way, if the vehicle and the journey become a predictor of a specific destination or experience, your puppy's bucket will fill before they even arrive, car travel will become a high-arousal event and calmness in the car will be a challenge.

Journeys with a dog who is stressed and unsettled, or where

the anticipation of a destination means immediate over-arousal, barking, whining and chaos when you are in traffic or the moment you stop, are not only stressful, they are potentially dangerous if your puppy becomes a distraction while you're driving. Just as importantly, they mean your puppy is stressed, either during that journey or when you arrive. Walks won't start off well if your puppy's bucket is already full from a stressful car journey – so their choices are likely to be less appropriate. Their ability to deal with novelty will be impacted, their interactions with other dogs you come across may be less robust, they are more likely to pull on the lead, less likely to be responsive and less able to hang out calmly in proximity. Getting car travel right really does matter.

Safety first

Wherever possible, we'd encourage you to use a crate for vehicle travel. Having your puppy secured in a suitable travel crate is the very best option for keeping everyone safe.

If your car is unable to accommodate a crate, a crash-tested safety harness is another option to consider. Never ever travel with a puppy or dog of any age loose in the vehicle.

Think about using covers and screens to limit visual access too. This will not only help manage what your puppy can see, but what people looking in can see too. Having a puppy in full view of passers-by when you're out and about or when your vehicle is parked isn't necessarily a wise choice.

Finally, don't ever leave your dog alone in the car for long periods of time unattended. Dogs can become overheated very quickly inside cars, so don't take the risk.

Game on outside

The very early stages of getting your puppy happy with being in the car are not necessarily going to involve getting into it at all. Allow your puppy to explore the area around your car while it is safely parked and away from the road. Scatter a little of their dinner on the ground or feed them to create a positive association with your vehicle.

Game on inside

Once you've played games outside the car, start playing games in the car. Encourage your puppy to explore inside while your car is parked. Check to make sure they're happy getting in and out (lift them while they are too small to jump safely), as well as happy to explore the seats, footwells and other areas. Reward and encourage them with pieces of food. Put their open crate inside the car and see if they are interested in going into it.

At this stage, your puppy should be free to explore without any pressure. If their body language shows you they're not comfortable getting into their crate, work on this independently of the car first. You don't want your puppy to feel trapped or pressured. Everything about these early introductions should be positive and rewarding, while remembering that you ultimately need your puppy to understand the car is a calm, relaxing space to be.

Look out for the point at which your puppy is moving as confidently in the car as they move on the ground. Don't start asking for stillness and calmness until your puppy is showing they are confident. Only once you've reached this point should you begin to introduce small journeys.

Ditching the routine around car journeys

Being intentional about what associations your puppy learns to have with the car from the outset will give you the very best foundations for stress-free journeys and make travelling with your pup a pleasure. See chapter 8 for other ways you can ditch the routine.

- Try and mix up car journeys, interspersing boring destinations with exciting ones. Making the majority of your journeys uneventful and pretty boring to begin with will help your puppy see the car as just somewhere else they hang out and relax.

- It can help to get a friend or family member to join you on some of your car journeys so that they can feed your puppy through all the new and unusual noises and pair all that novelty with a positive outcome. It's easy to forget how many strange sounds, smells and movements a car makes – think doors opening and closing, the ignition turning on and off, the boot slamming, the handbrake going on and off, indicators, traffic sounds, motion and the smells of things you might pass along the way.

- Avoid making the same trip in the car at the same time every day. Where routine journeys are unavoidable (school runs are a good example), try to leave a little extra time whenever you are able to detour from your usual route or stop somewhere along the way so you can sit and reward your puppy for being calm.

- Ditch any routine with the vehicle itself too. The car should be an extension of your home and garden when it comes to training and doesn't have to mean you're going somewhere. Sometimes, you and your puppy might get in the car and get straight out again! At other times, you might sit in the driveway and read a book or answer some emails while your puppy hangs out calmly in their car crate with a long-lasting chew. Pop your puppy in the car with a Kong while you tidy the boot, and then get them out again and go back inside.

- If you know there are destinations that get your puppy particularly excited or scared (they may quickly learn to associate trips to the vet with worrying outcomes, for example), drive there but then drive away again, or drive there, get out of the car, play some games and then drive home again. That way, the anticipated outcome isn't always the one that actually happens.

Tom's story: Bet and the telltale

When my Border Collie Bet was younger, she used to squeak any time I put my car's handbrake on. I quickly realised that I only used the handbrake when we were at our destination, so she had learned to pair the handbrake with getting out of the car and doing something. I live in the middle of the countryside, so I rarely get stuck in traffic jams. Typically, my handbrake isn't used until I want to park the car. To overcome Bet's squeaking, I had to make a conscious effort to use the handbrake at every set of traffic lights, but even then there are only about three sets near where I live, so I also started pulling up briefly in front of a shop or petrol station, putting the handbrake on and then setting off again. Thankfully, it all helped to break that association for Bet and the squeaking stopped.

> **TIP: Could it be car sickness?**
>
> Nausea can be a big struggle for some puppies at first, which means they may dislike going in the car. In 99.9 per cent of cases, this tends to resolve itself in a matter of days or weeks. If it doesn't, then your puppy is likely to be feeling nauseous because they are scared of the car, so revisit all of the steps above.

Taking your puppy on long journeys

If you are frequent travellers like us, it's important to get your puppy used to long car journeys quite quickly.

- Make sure you stop when needed for a drink – this can be as much as every hour with a puppy, but when they are settled our young dogs can go 2–3 hours between stops, so you need to be guided by what's working. Give your puppy chance to stretch their legs and go to the toilet.

- If you start to sense that your puppy is getting worried or noticing a little too much of what is going on outside the car, make a stop and give them a long-lasting chew or a Kong (or ask a passenger to do so). These are a great way to help your puppy tune out particular events or embrace calmness and to disengage from whatever is happening outside your car windows.

- If you're travelling with someone and your puppy is unsettled, get your passenger to post some of your dog's daily food allowance through the bars in their crate. Or your passenger could simply sit next to the puppy – sometimes, all a pup needs is to know someone is close by.

Fear of cars and car-chasing struggles

Of course, cars and other vehicles aren't just something your puppy is going to come across in the context of travelling. Depending on where you live, vehicles can be a regular feature on your walks, and something your puppy is very likely to encounter in day-to-day life as you go out and about.

From quite early on, you may discover your puppy will bark and lunge at cars or try and chase them. This is often a struggle for herding breeds, who are naturally very stimulated by movement, but can be true of any breed, depending on their personality.

Other puppies find cars intimidating or scary. You might discover your puppy is very fearful of cars and traffic noises. If this is the case, you need to first build up their optimism and confidence away from situations in which they are going to encounter traffic.

Some puppies react in a much more active way to things that worry them, so it is not unusual for a puppy who is terrified of the noise and movement of cars to lunge towards them in an effort to appear scary and make the cars go away. Because those cars keep moving, your puppy thinks their 'go away' behaviour of lunging and barking has worked, and will continue rehearsing this unless you step in and show them a more appropriate way to respond to scary things. This should always be done by building their skills outside of situations that they are not yet ready to deal with. Make sure you check out chapters 17 and 22, which introduce the concept of disengagement, if you're noticing this type of reaction when your puppy encounters things that worry them.

Going on holiday with your puppy

Depending on your holiday plans, it's great to take your puppy away with you if you can. It's good for your puppy to have the challenge of a new environment.

If your puppy has grown the skills they need at home, then going to stay somewhere new for a few days provides a chance for you to consolidate that learning. It will help your puppy transfer all those super skills you have been growing at home to other environments. And even if they haven't got all the skills yet, rock and roll, that's life, and it's worth having a go as long as you're able to put in place some management strategies (such as a crate in a quiet room, for example).

If you plan to travel with your puppy, think about all the frameworks you're going to take with you.

- Keep their toileting routine the same.
- Use your calmness strategies (see chapter 8) to show your puppy that the hotel, holiday accommodation or a friend's house is a place of calmness too.
- DMT any new sights, sounds or experiences and be sure to protect your puppy's optimism, be mindful of their bucket, and provide input where needed to help them make the very best choices. See chapter 10 to learn how to DMT.
- Provide lots of opportunities for long-lasting chews, Kongs and other calming activities to help your puppy settle.
- Playing optimism-building games in new environments is a lovely way to help your puppy feel comfortable somewhere less familiar. Whenever you take your games somewhere

new, start again from the beginning as if your puppy has never played before. That will mean you set them up for success and – even better – will mean your puppy feels like a winner! Because your puppy has played a game at home first, you are giving them easy wins with things they already know.

- Think about what you take along that will give your puppy enough familiarity to help them settle somewhere new. A crate will make sure your puppy has somewhere to sleep and keep them contained when necessary. A boundary is another great option for helping your puppy relax somewhere less familiar. Bring along their bedding or a favourite blanket.

Get all that right and, rather than being a bucket filler, your car can become a place where your dog has learned to chill out, relax and empty their bucket. Journeys and being away from home will be a pleasure. You will have much greater freedom to enjoy travelling with your puppy and will find you have a dog who is a lifelong travel companion.

CHAPTER 16
Caring for Your Puppy

Welcoming a puppy into your home is incredibly rewarding, yet it comes with many responsibilities. From grooming and dental care to overall health and well-being, as your puppy's guardian you are responsible for every aspect of their care. Over the course of their lifetime, your puppy will need to visit the vet for routine appointments and vaccinations. Depending on your puppy's coat, they may require regular trips to the groomer.

By growing their optimism and confidence and putting value into calmness, you've already given your puppy some awesome foundations when it comes to handling all those novel experiences. So what else can you do to give your puppy the very best chance of taking those things in their stride?

As with all our puppy foundations, this starts at home, and is something that is grown and inspired through games.

Get your puppy used to being handled

Not every puppy will naturally be comfortable being touched or handled, whether that's being stroked, picked up or lightly restrained either by you or a vet or groomer. Yet over the course of your dog's life, there are situations in which a level of handling is going to be necessary, whether that's during those routine trips to the vet or groomer, or even for something as simple as being able to put their lead or harness on and off with minimal stress. While you may have a puppy who loves to be cuddled, stroked and petted on their own terms, it might be a whole different story when it comes to the handling that is required for grooming or vet visits. For some puppies, handling can cause huge concern and quickly become something they actively avoid and dislike.

Depending on your puppy's personality, you may need to build their confidence in this area. This goes hand in hand with your puppy seeing the value in proximity and learning that being close to you is a good deal.

Building your puppy's optimism and confidence being touched and handled in a positive, pressure-free way from the very beginning of their life with you will set them up for success. It will help make any situations where they need to be handled as stress-free as possible for all involved. We truly believe this is a valuable thing to invest some time and patience in. Not only for your puppy, but also for anyone else who may need to handle your dog throughout their lifetime.

There are so many games you can play to boost the value your puppy places in being close and help them find joy in being touched, handled and groomed. If you've not played Go Commando yet, it's a great one to start with. You can find it on page 91.

You can grow your puppy's tolerance of being handled by playing the games that follow little and often. They will build up their desire to be close and stay close to you as well as boost their confidence with being touched and handled all over their body.

Combining proximity and touching games with your puppy will encourage a level of permission to be stroked, picked up or lightly restrained.

Whenever you are playing these games, be sure to observe your puppy for any signs and signals that they aren't comfortable. Watch how they move and notice if they back off if the pressure becomes too much. Your aim is to make handling a non-event and something your puppy will allow you to perform when necessary.

The value of Mighty Middle for handling

Back in chapter 12 we introduced you to one of our all-time favourite games, Mighty Middle. Once your puppy knows and likes Mighty Middle, you can use it to build value for being touched and handled. The reason this works so well is that it gives your puppy a very clear option to leave if they start to feel uncomfortable at any point during the game. While your puppy remains in the Middle, they are giving their consent for the game to continue. If at any point they pop out from between your legs, you know they were uncomfortable with what you were doing. Remember – that's just information that you need to build their optimism and confidence more gradually and that the value they see in proximity may need boosting too.

MIDDLE + GENTLE TOUCH

This is a great place to start because it is similar to stroking, which your puppy may already enjoy. It's a good idea to begin with whichever part of your puppy's body they are most comfortable with you touching. This will probably be their shoulder area, back or around the hips.

Step 1: Invite your puppy into the Middle.

Step 2: Stroke them lightly, reinforce with a calm verbal marker ('Nice', 'Good' or whatever comes most naturally) and feed, to pair being touched with a positive outcome.

Step 3: Release your puppy from the Middle by throwing a piece of food ahead of you for them to go and find, and wait to see if they come back willingly into the Middle position to continue the game. This 'pressure release' is really important and gives your puppy the option of re-engaging in the game or showing you they have had enough.

Step 4: As you continue to play, all you are asking of your puppy is that they remain in the Middle and allow you to continue stroking, marking and feeding. Remember, your puppy should be free to leave at any point if they start to feel uncomfortable. If they do, it's a sign that you have done too much or gone too fast.

Step 5: Over the course of a number of sessions, working at your puppy's pace, move on to other areas. You might stroke their chest or run your hands down one leg. Can you lift a leg and hold your puppy's paw without any sign that they are uncomfortable? Remember to feed generously to make this a great experience, and be sure your puppy is participating willingly at each step. You will find your puppy is much more sensitive about being touched in some places than others, so go slower in these areas.

Step 6: Taking it at your puppy's pace, and remembering those all-important pressure releases as part of short, positive sessions, work up to being able to stroke and touch every part of your puppy's body.

Incorporating touch into your play sessions

Another great way to create a positive association with being touched is by incorporating it into your play sessions.

Can you gently touch your puppy in various places as you play? Perhaps you touch a paw, run a hand down their side or give a firm but gentle stroke over the head.

Bear in mind that touch can add arousal and excitement, so putting your hands on your puppy during a high-energy game of tug is going to create a very different picture from some gentle calming touch incorporated into a game of Mouse or while you and your puppy are working on some boundary games.

Grooming your puppy

Whether it's brushing, washing or clipping nails, grooming is a necessary part of life for a dog. Some dogs, such as curly-coated breeds, need regular grooming to avoid becoming matted. Dogs with long hair often need to be trimmed around the face area so they can see and even short-haired, smooth-coated dogs will benefit from regular brushing.

Grooming will not only ensure your puppy looks and smells fab, it's important for overall well-being too. When you're grooming your puppy, it's a good opportunity for you to have your hands on them and work out what your dog's 'normal' is. It's also a great way to spot any lumps or bumps on their skin and coat as well as noticing if they feel uncomfortable being touched or moved in a certain way. If you do notice anything unusual, please speak to your vet about it.

Unless you are an experienced home groomer you will probably want to take your puppy to a professional, so seek their advice about how often your puppy needs to be groomed to keep their particular coat in tip-top condition.

How to make grooming a happy experience

For grooming to be safe and stress-free for both you and your puppy, you need your puppy to be able to calmly stand still for periods of time. A dog who fidgets or wriggles is much harder to groom, and you or the groomer will risk a slip of the scissors or clippers, which at best will give your dog a dodgy hairdo and at worst could cause injury. Stillness does not come naturally to a lot of puppies and as they grow up, they may need more than a hygiene trim or introductory session with the groomer.

It is much easier for your puppy to feel confident about something if they are moving! We often make early grooming experiences disempowering by focusing on stillness too soon. Instead, focus on your puppy moving confidently in the grooming environment (e.g. on the table) to boost their optimism!

With your puppy's confidence and optimism soaring, you can then revisit chapter 8 for a refresher on building calmness. Two great games for this are Mouse Game (see page 118) and Aeroplane Feeding (see page 111).

Preparing your puppy for the groomer's

It's easy to understand why some dogs are terrified of going to the groomer. Imagine being lifted onto a table and suddenly finding that an unfamiliar object is swooping towards your body, vibrating and making a very loud noise. A trip to the groomer can feel daunting for both you and your puppy but if you put in some prep, it is possible to make it pleasant and stress-free.

There are so many new things your puppy is going to experience, including:

- Handling – often by a stranger or someone who is not part of your puppy's everyday circle of humans.
- Bathing (not all dogs naturally enjoy water).
- Trimming and cutting of hair (meaning the need to hold still and maintain positions while sharp implements are close to their body).
- Noise – clippers and hairdryers all make loud noises.
- Vibrations – clippers not only make noise, they also vibrate close to your dog's body.
- Ears – a grooming session might include cleaning and hair-trimming.
- Nail care – using clippers or a grinder.

234

That's a lot for your puppy to take in and can quickly fill their bucket, but there are things you can do to prepare them for all these experiences.

Confidence around grooming equipment

Notice how your puppy responds to other noises they might hear at home. Are they concerned about the sound of the vacuum cleaner, the tumble dryer or the food processor? Do they bark or leave the room when you use certain appliances?

There are lots of super-fun games you can play with your puppy to help them grow optimism in the face of novel sounds.

Revisit Noise Box (see page 149) and Knock 'Em Over (see page 151). These games build confidence and optimism around noises and novelty, and teach your puppy that noises mean fun and food!

DMT and grooming equipment

One great strategy is to incorporate noises into your training, and show your puppy that the weird and wonderful sounds aren't cause for concern. You can use the same strategy to teach your puppy that the various pieces of equipment they may come across as part of a grooming session are not inherently scary. Use DMT to teach your puppy that the noise of a hairdryer or clippers, or even the sight of a hairbrush, is nothing to be concerned about.

You might simply have a grooming brush or a set of clippers (turned off to begin with) nearby and pair the presence of those items with your verbal marker and some tasty food. The idea here is not to present the items to your puppy in a way that is going to alarm them. You want to create a calm, positive pairing and show your puppy these items are not scary. Once they are OK with seeing these items, turn them on for a few seconds. Again, pair this with your marker and some more food.

Another option is to play them the sounds. There are lots of audio resources available (check YouTube and Spotify) where you can find recordings of clippers or hairdryers. Play them at very low volume while your puppy is busy with a passive calming activity and DMT the sound. Remember that dogs have hearing that is many times more sensitive than ours, so your puppy will hear a recording played on low volume much more acutely than you will. If it sounds quiet to you, turn it down even further.

Make being brushed a great experience

As well as getting your puppy comfortable being handled, teaching them that being brushed is a positive experience is really valuable from early on. A daily battle with a puppy who learns to dislike being brushed can be a huge withdrawal from your relationship bank account.

Lick mats can be really useful here, particularly if your puppy is happy to lick away while you brush, but remember that your aim is to create a positive experience of being brushed – not to use food as a way of trapping your puppy. You don't ever want your puppy to feel conflicted (i.e. 'I want the food, but I don't want to be here').

Giving your puppy a bath

You don't need to bathe your puppy regularly because it dries out the natural oils in their skin, but inevitably you are going to have to bathe them at some point. There's nothing some dogs love more than a roll in fox poo or a giant muddy puddle! They will also be bathed when they go to the groomer so you do want to get them used to being in water. Some dogs love water but for many dogs the experience is altogether less enticing and some will actively avoid bath time. Coercing your puppy into the bath or shower, getting covered in muddy water and coming out of the experience with both you and your dog feeling stressed is not pleasant.

Don't worry! As always, there's a game for that . . .

WATER CONFIDENCE

For this game, you need a low-sided plastic container (children's paddling pools and sandpits work really well, but anything low-sided that is appropriate for your puppy to safely climb in and out of will do). Make sure the surface isn't slippery by using a non-slip bathmat or similar, which will help your puppy feel more secure.

Step 1: Begin by rewarding your puppy for any interaction with the empty, dry container by giving them some of their daily food allowance. How confident is your puppy getting in and, just as importantly, getting out again?

Keep in mind that you will be adding water, so make sure your puppy is confident but in a controlled way. You don't want them launching themselves like a missile into the container, because when there is water in there, that could be dangerous.

Step 2: Toss a few pieces of your puppy's daily food allowance in and see if they are happy to climb in to get them. If they are less confident, mark and reward any time they look at the container or move towards it. Throwing a few pieces of food away from the container will help keep the pressure low and give your puppy opportunities to reset and try again.

Step 3: Once your puppy is happily climbing in and out of the container, you can start to introduce water. Start off with a few centimetres at first so just their paws are covered. Are they still happy to climb in and out? Add a favourite (waterproof) toy or use your puppy's daily food allowance to create positive associations and reinforce this as a good experience.

Step 4: It's important to take this at your puppy's pace. Even a millimetre of water might initially be too much for some dogs, whereas others will be splashing around in joyful abandon. Do be mindful of safety whenever your puppy is playing in water, whether they are fishing a favourite toy out of the water or bobbing for kibble. You don't want them to swallow too much water. Play safely!

Step 5: As your puppy gets more confident, you can increase the amount of water in the container – initially when your puppy has stepped out, but perhaps also while they are standing in there (remember, you ultimately want them to be comfortable with the idea of being showered or bathed).

TIP: Super important – remember your puppy should always have the choice to leave.

Depending on the time of year and whether you have outside space, hosepipes and sprinklers can be another fun way of growing your puppy's confidence around water – particularly water that squirts or moves in different directions.

All the same rules apply here – you are creating a fun experience that your dog is choosing to engage with. Firing water at your puppy from a hosepipe isn't an appropriate way to teach confidence and optimism around water.

Take it slowly and don't rush your pup. Getting the foundations right is key.

Clipping your puppy's nails

Even if you opt to use a professional groomer, it can be useful to be able to clip your puppy's nails at home. Nail-trimming can be a stressful experience for many dogs, so getting your puppy used to having their feet being handled will help make them more comfortable. Regular nail maintenance is more than cosmetic. Unhealthy nails can cause pain, so keeping them in tip-top condition will keep your puppy comfortable and prevent any avoidable issues.

Your puppy's nail consists of the living pink quick and the hard outer material called the shell. The quick supplies blood to the nail and runs through the nail's core. Your puppy's nails will wear down naturally if you make sure they get regular walks on pavements or harder surfaces, but you may still find you need to clip them from time to time.

Done correctly, this shouldn't cause any discomfort. Clip them a bit too short and you'll catch the quick, which is uncomfortable and will probably cause the nails to bleed.

Clipper or a grinder?

Human nail clippers are ideal for puppies. You can nip off the sharp ends and quickly get your pup used to nail clipping.

As your puppy grows up and their claws become thicker and tougher, you may find it easier to use a grinder. Whatever you choose to use, ask an expert to demonstrate so you know you're using it correctly, and make sure you spend time getting your dog fully comfortable with the experience.

As soon as you bring your puppy home, get them used to having their paws touched and comfortable with you examining their claws. Often owners will only do this when they need to clip their dog's nails, but it is important that your puppy is happy being handled in this way first and understands that it's a positive experience. Get them used to the sensation of you picking up their paws without any clipping at first, by gently picking up each paw, handling each claw individually and rewarding your puppy (with some of their daily food allowance). Remember the importance of allowing your puppy the option of leaving if they have had enough.

- Examine and wiggle their toes. Touch their pads and hold the foot gently but firmly.
- Let them examine the nail clippers.
- Touch the clippers to their toes and nails.
- Lift both the front and back feet.
- Build duration and get them in a comfortable position while you examine and fiddle with their feet. Remember, you're looking for progress, not perfection.

How to trim your puppy's nails

When trimming your puppy's nails, your aim is to shorten the nail so that it doesn't curve over and touch the ground when your puppy is standing. The best way is to make two cuts, as illustrated below. The first cut should trim the excess length within approximately 2 millimetres of the quick. The second cut should trim the nail in three places, blunting the shell to minimise sharp edges and make sure that the quick recedes and stays short.

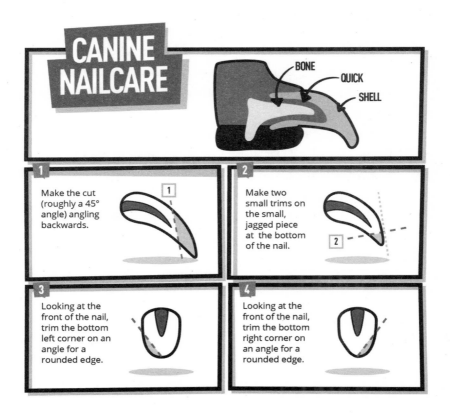

CANINE NAILCARE

BONE
QUICK
SHELL

1 Make the cut (roughly a 45° angle) angling backwards.

2 Make two small trims on the small, jagged piece at the bottom of the nail.

3 Looking at the front of the nail, trim the bottom left corner on an angle for a rounded edge.

4 Looking at the front of the nail, trim the bottom right corner on an angle for a rounded edge.

If you accidentally cut into the quick, the claw will bleed and your puppy is likely to let you know that it hurt. Don't panic. Applying gentle pressure should stop the bleeding pretty quickly. Make sure you top up your relationship bank account with lots of positive interactions. You might want to give your puppy a passive calming activity and a bit of bucket-emptying time.

Tips to make nail clipping easier

- Don't make it a big event. Use your puppy's daily food to reward calmness and stay calm yourself.
- Clip one or two claws in a session and do it over a few days. If you try and do all of your puppy's claws at once, there's more of a risk of your puppy getting annoyed, impatient or uncomfortable.
- If you're using nail clippers, make sure that they're sharp. If the blade of the clipper is blunt, it will squeeze the nail, which can hurt your puppy.
- If your puppy has a black claw, it can be hard to spot the quick. You can sometimes spot it by looking down the centre of the nail. If not, trim your puppy's nails little and often.

Perfect paws

Some things to look out for when you're checking your puppy's feet:

Nails
- Are they too long? If they are sharp or you hear them tapping on the floor when your puppy walks, they are probably too long.
- Are they cracked, split or missing?

Pads
- Are they cracked, cut or worn?
- Are there any foreign objects in or between the pads?

Toes
- Can you touch their toes without any discomfort?
- Are you able to move them around without any discomfort?
- Is there any noticeable swelling or hot spots?

Webbing between the toes
- Is the skin between the toes free from dirt or knots?
- Is the area free from grass seeds that can pierce your puppy's skin?

TWO PAWS ON AND PAW TARGETING

For true nail-trimming success, you need your puppy to be happy and confident allowing you to handle their paws. Teaching your puppy to give a paw is a great way to make this into a game and inject some fun into the experience.

Step 1: The first step is to teach your puppy to put their front paws on an object. We call this Two Paws On. Start with something large and flat (a book, a yoga block or a small box), placed on the floor. Begin by rewarding any interaction at all – even just a glance at the object. Expect a little more effort each time until they are putting their front feet on it (one or both!). Feed generously when they place feet on the object and then throw a piece of food away from the object so they can reset and try again. As your puppy begins to understand the game, you can move to smaller and smaller objects.

Step 2: When your puppy starts to show real understanding of Two Paws On smaller targets, you can then begin luring single paws onto your targets. Reward for every small movement towards the final behaviour and begin to ask them to hold the position for longer once your puppy starts offering a single paw on your target.

Step 3: Once your puppy clearly understands Two Paws On and is able to place a single paw on your object, you can take the next step by teaching your dog to move their paws from one target to another.

Step 4: Begin to take your target item in your hand and raise it from the ground, asking your puppy to target the raised object. Reward for any attempt your puppy makes, and reward BIG when they successfully get it – both with food and verbal praise.

Step 5: When your puppy is successfully targeting the object in your hand, it's time to transfer their target to your hand. Do a few practise sessions with the target in your hand, then hide the target and offer your empty hand in the same position. As soon as your puppy targets your hand with their paw, mark and reward. Play little and often until your puppy is consistently targeting your hand and you can begin to build in some real duration. Make sure you alternate between paws to boost your puppy's flexibility.

As well as teaching your puppy to offer a paw and be comfortable having it handled, this is a pretty cool trick to show your friends!

Other sensitive areas

Whenever you're working with your puppy to help them learn to be comfortable being handled, remember to make it fun and be led by your puppy's actions. Build up that relationship bank account to get the most from your puppy. If you get these awesome foundations in place while your puppy is little, you are much less likely to have a battle to bathe, groom or handle your dog as they grow and mature.

Ears

Ears are a sensitive area for many dogs. As part of a full groom, your puppy is likely to need to have their ears brushed, and the hair inside them may need trimming, so it's good to get them comfortable with their ears being handled from early on.

Using all the handling techniques above, start by teaching your puppy to be comfortable having their ears gently stroked. Once your puppy is happy with that, see if you can lift an ear and let it fall again, or move it backwards and forwards gently. Observe your puppy and don't be tempted to rush.

> **TIP: At some point in your puppy's life they are going to need ear or eye drops, so get them used to this early on. Periodically, when we're handling our own dogs, we use a small plastic bottle and pretend to put in some eye drops, or lift up an ear and pretend to put in some ear drops, all while they're enjoying some of their daily food allowance. This is a great, low-pressure, stress-free way of getting your puppy used to these experiences in advance, so they are already comfortable with the idea if you ever need to do it for real.**

Teeth

As you know from chapter 14, puppies have 28 sharp milk teeth they love to explore the world with, and which are typically replaced by 42 adult teeth by the time they're 8 months of age (sometimes sooner).

Get your puppy used to dental care

Just as it is for humans, looking after your dog's teeth is vital to keep those pearly whites in good condition and to prevent dental disease. Plaque builds up on a dog's teeth within 12 hours of cleaning, so daily efforts to remove plaque are vital to keep those teeth healthy. This can take a variety of forms. Long-lasting chews, playing with tug toys and a dental supplement (such as our own A-OK9 Plaque-K9) added to food are all options you can explore.

There are so many games you can play with your puppy that will prepare them for when their adult teeth come through and that daily brushing or dental regime becomes so essential.

DENTAL HANDLING

This is a really effective game to play that will truly prepare your puppy for regular dental care when they are older. Keep in mind that it might take some time for your puppy to feel completely comfortable having your hands around their face, so take it slowly and keep your sessions fun, positive and pressure-free. Use some of your puppy's daily food allowance to build a positive association with each step, and don't expect to work through all the steps in your first session.

Step 1: Start by cupping your puppy's lower jaw in one hand. Pair this with some of your puppy's daily food allowance to make sure it's a positive experience, especially if your puppy is a little wary.

Step 2: Now use your other hand to cup the top of their muzzle/bridge of their nose and cover their eyes.

Step 3: With the hand that is on top of your puppy's head, use your fingers to pull their lips up to examine their teeth, doing this on both the left and right side, until you're able to see all their teeth.

TOOTHBRUSH TARGETING

This game empowers your puppy and gives them control over how close they are to the toothbrush. The idea is to present the toothbrush to your puppy and reward them for moving towards it, looking at it, or interacting with it in any way.

Step 1: Hold out the toothbrush to your puppy.

Step 2: Whenever your puppy shows any attempt to interact with the toothbrush (that might be sniffing it, looking at it, bopping it with their nose, or anything else your puppy offers, except attempting to grab it with their teeth), use your verbal marker to tell your puppy they made an awesome choice!

Step 3: Remove the toothbrush from sight and reward your puppy with some of their daily food allowance, so you can reset for another go.

Step 4: Add a small amount of your puppy's toothpaste to the brush and repeat the earlier steps. You can also break this up further by letting your puppy lick a small amount of the toothpaste off your finger first. It helps if your puppy enjoys the taste, so you might need to try a few brands before you hit on one your puppy is happy to taste. Moving the brush away from your puppy rather than towards them can increase their motivation to seek it out, and make sure they are willingly participating in the game.

OBJECT HOLD

Teaching your puppy to hold an object firmly between their teeth can give them something to focus on while you brush their teeth. This means their teeth are easily accessible with a simple lip lift (like you practised in the Dental Handling game above), which makes brushing much easier.

Taking your puppy to the vet

Vet visits can be really stressful for both you and your puppy, especially if your puppy's early experiences of the vet happen to be negative or unpleasant ones. But there is a lot you can do to prepare yourself and your puppy for regular vet visits and check-ups.

Top tips for stress-free vet visits

- When you first get your puppy, it's worth booking an introductory appointment with your vet. This is an opportunity

249

for your pup to experience the sights, sounds and smells of the clinic and meet the vet. Ideally, you want to avoid your puppy's first visit being for something they may find traumatic or unpleasant, such as a vaccination, which can easily impact how they feel about vet visits from that point onwards. If your puppy isn't vaccinated, carry them into the clinic – don't put them down on the floor or let them interact with other dogs.

- Ditch the routine before a vet visit. Before taking your puppy in the car and setting off to the vet, consider the steps you'll take and make sure you don't do the same preparations each time so that your puppy predicts what's to come.

- The temptation is to sit in the waiting room and show everyone how cute your puppy is, but waiting rooms can be very noisy and chaotic and full of stressed animals and their owners. Why put your puppy through that if you don't have to? Instead of heading straight into the vet's, wait in the car or outside. It's much more relaxing and comfortable for you and your puppy. You can call reception to tell them that you've arrived. Ask them to ring you or even wave out of the window when they want you to come in. Alternatively, bring someone else with you who can go into the clinic and wait on your behalf.

- Before you go into the vet's, let your puppy stretch their legs and give them the opportunity to go to the toilet while you wait.

- Use any time you do have to spend in the waiting room playing some proximity or optimism games with your puppy. Mighty Middle or Two Feet On can be great options.

- In the consulting room, if it's safe to do so, put your puppy on the examination table rather than on the floor. The surface is non-slip and that way the vet and vet nurse are beside your puppy and not looming over them. This is also a great way of taking control of your puppy's instinct to predict. If your puppy is examined or treated on the floor, there's a risk they could develop a negative association with people approaching them, which could affect them in all sorts of ways in day-to-day life. If your puppy develops a bad association with being on a table, that situation doesn't regularly occur in day-to-day life so will be much easier to deal with.

- Try and see the same couple of vets so you can develop a good, open and honest relationship with them. If you see them regularly, they will get to know you and your puppy.
- Aim to give your vet clear, specific information. If you're visiting because your puppy is unwell, keep a diary or make notes: when they were sick, how many times, what colour the vomit was, or when they started limping. This helps to take any guesswork out of it for your vet.
- If your puppy is ill or has an injury, it can sometimes help to take a video or a clear photo to show your vet. If your puppy has a limp, a video of them moving will help your vet clearly see the problem, even if your puppy manages to conceal it when you arrive. If your puppy has a rash, a picture can be really helpful. The vet will still need to see your puppy, but coming prepared means they have good, clear information before your puppy has even got on the table to be examined.
- Take some of your puppy's daily food allowance with you and use it during their appointment. As the vet is examining

your puppy, you can be feeding them to make the experience as positive as possible.

- Remember, you are your dog's expert so don't be afraid to make suggestions to your vet. Lauren's dog recently had to go for an X-ray but there was going to be a short wait for the machine to be ready. Instead of leaving her dog at the clinic and coming back for her later, with all the added stress of being separated, Lauren asked if she could take her outside to wait instead. They came back inside 10 minutes later and the X-ray was done quickly, with minimal stress. Don't feel bad or like you are being difficult by making suggestions. You know your dog best and more often than not, your vet will be happy to oblige.

- After your appointment, don't hang around in reception with your puppy. Providing it is safe to do so, take them back to the car and get them settled. Then you can return to reception and pay your bill and pick up any medication or information. Give your puppy a passive calming activity in the car to help them decompress.

- Ditch the routine on the way home from the clinic. Depending on what your puppy's appointment was for and how they are feeling, don't always go home immediately after a visit to the vet. Do some chores or take your puppy for a walk (being mindful a walk might not be the best option if they have had a bucket-filling visit).

- When you arrive back home, let your puppy rest in the car for a few minutes, if safe. Set your puppy up with a passive calming activity, such as a food-filled toy or lick mat upon entering your house. Let them relax and empty their bucket.

Games to help your puppy cope with vet visits

HOLD ME HERE

This is a great game to get your puppy used to being handled and can be used if your dog needs an injection or a tail lift for a temperature check. Listening to the heart with a stethoscope can also be made easier if your puppy knows this game. Lots of short sessions will help your puppy feel comfortable being gently restrained, which is a great foundation for the handling they may need to be comfortable with at the vet's.

Step 1: Encourage your puppy to come in close so they are standing with their side leaning against your legs (you can use food to lure them into position). You need to be able to reach over their back to their opposite side. While your puppy is in this position, you are going to be feeding them with one hand and gently restraining them with the other.

Step 2: With your puppy in position, place a gentle hand near their neck, while you feed them from your free hand.

Step 3: Throw a piece of food forward to release your puppy from position then invite them back for another go.

Step 4: Repeat, but this time place your hand at the point right between your puppy's thigh and stomach. Again, feed while you gently restrain, then throw a piece of food forward so your puppy gets that all-important pressure release.

THE SCRUFF GAME

Your puppy's scruff is the loose skin at the back of their neck. This is the most common place for injections to go, so getting your puppy comfortable having their scruff handled will make this much less scary when it needs to happen.

Step 1: Place one hand on the back of your puppy's neck while feeding generously from your other hand.

Step 2: Build up slowly to the point where you can lift that loose skin on the back of your puppy's neck and hold it gently between your fingers, again pairing this with food being delivered from your other hand.

Step 3: Once your puppy is completely comfortable, holding your puppy's scruff in one hand while briefly touching the scruff with a finger of your opposite hand (a gentle poke) can get your puppy familiar with the sensation of pressure on that scruff. This will make a needle much less worrying when it happens for real. Feed your puppy to create positive associations with each step of the process.

Going to see the vet or taking your puppy to be groomed are probably never going to be events that your puppy will look forward to but for any responsible owner, they are an integral part of caring for your dog. If you prepare your puppy for the situation and play games that boost their calmness and optimism and get them used to being handled and examined, then a trip to the vet or groomer will become as stress-free and comfortable as possible for both you and your dog. Because you've prepared your puppy and they are calm and can tolerate being touched and examined, the process will run more smoothly and will be over sooner. Your vet will be able to record more information, administer medications, give advice and even reduce your visit times. It's a sign of a brilliant owner that you have helped prepare your puppy for those moments when invasiveness into their physical space cannot be avoided in order to keep them happy and healthy. And finally, we can't emphasise enough that you are your dog's best advocate when it comes to their care. If something is advised, you don't need to make that decision immediately – you have time, so don't be rushed into a decision and absolutely ensure you think for your dog, not just to please whoever is advising you.

SECTION TWO

Superstar

(13-24 weeks and beyond)

CHAPTER 17
Interacting with Other Dogs

As a brand-new puppy owner, you'll probably be keen to make sure your puppy gets out and about as soon as possible and has the opportunity to meet other dogs. Popular culture often reinforces the idea that every dog should be sociable and friendly and enjoy spending time with other dogs. The conventional approach to dog training says that puppies must meet and interact with other dogs as much as possible while they are young. The thinking behind this approach is that we have to teach our puppies how to socialise – and that this must be done as early on as possible in that critical 'socialisation period'.

In reality, puppies arrive on this planet knowing how to interact with other dogs. As humans, it is actually pretty presumptuous of us to assume that we need to teach our dogs how to communicate in their own language.

However, some dogs, much like some people, struggle with certain parts of the conversation because they don't naturally have all the skills needed for appropriate interactions with other dogs. Think about a human who finds social interactions a little challenging. Perhaps they know how a conversation should flow, but when they find themselves face to face with a stranger, that conversation is awkward because they're nervous or anxious, or they find themselves unable to get away because they're not sure how to end the conversation politely. It's the same for our dogs. While all dogs have a hardwired interaction chain that enables them to have appropriate conversations, some lack the skills to progress from one step in that interaction chain to the next, and so those interactions become awkward or inappropriate.

Dog–dog interactions are easily one of the top struggles that owners come to us with, and bad experiences early on can really set your puppy up for challenges later in life. So what is the right approach when it comes to allowing your puppy to interact with other dogs? How do you safeguard your puppy against negative experiences and skill them up to have great conversations when they do encounter other dogs?

Learning to be 'dog neutral'

The truth is that dogs don't need to play and interact with every other dog they meet when out and about. In fact, there is much more benefit in teaching your puppy how to be what we like to call 'dog neutral'.

There is no question that dogs can learn from other dogs. Some dogs can provide you with a really brilliant buddy for your puppy – a doggy pal who can guide them along the right path and help them make the very best choices. However, the idea that forced socialisation is good for our dogs is often misguided. Do we make the best decisions when we're anxious and uncomfortable and feeling like we're being forced into a situation? No, and neither do our dogs.

Dogs are domesticated animals, so your household is their family. There's no desperate need for your puppy to socialise with other dogs. They are not missing out because you're not organising doggy dates or taking them to puppy parties. You don't actively need to seek out a buddy for them. Much more important is teaching your puppy to be calm and optimistic in the environments they find themselves in and to disengage from situations they find both worrying and exciting. As your puppy goes through the world, they will inevitably meet other dogs. If you have skilled them up and prepared them for those situations, they will have the very best foundations with which to handle interactions and have appropriate conversations when they do happen. While we can't teach two dogs how to have a conversation, we can teach them the skills to implement a conversation they already know how to have.

A TO B

A to B is a really useful tool that you can practise and then use if you ever need to calmly and quickly get your puppy out of a tricky situation, such as an approaching dog that you know your puppy doesn't want to greet. It arms you with a strategy for getting yourself and your puppy out of situations they are not going to cope well with and means that you have a well-rehearsed technique to pull out of the bag, rather than panicking. This will give you the confidence to manage whatever situation you might be surprised by. At the same time, it teaches your puppy the concept of disengagement.

The handling techniques are important for two reasons: firstly, they allow you to have much more control when turning your puppy in the opposite direction so you can get them out of a tricky situation as smoothly as possible; secondly, they become a cue, so your puppy knows what to expect and moves with you rather than against you. This needs to be a really positive experience for your puppy, not a scary one. Over time, this should become a reflex response for both you and your puppy. We like to use a double-ended lead for this game (a lead with a clip at each end), attached to the front and back attachment points on a harness, or to a harness and collar – but you can adapt it to whatever walking equipment you have.

The goal is for your puppy to learn that just because they find something that is up ahead exciting or scary doesn't mean they have to interact with it. There's more value in ignoring it and actively moving away from it. You're teaching them that it's none of their business.

As the name suggests, the game is about getting your puppy from A to B. You do this by sliding your hand down the lead towards your puppy's harness (or collar), turning them 180 degrees away from the distraction, adding distance and feeding as you move away so that disengaging is a good deal. You do this slowly and gently as if you were turning a corner. Practise this at home first so your puppy knows exactly what's happening and they are keen to turn with you.

Step 1: When you first introduce the game to your puppy, make sure the focus is on getting them comfortable with your hand sliding down the lead towards them. Some puppies will be more wary of this than others, so watch for signs your puppy is uncomfortable and build up slowly. Slide one hand down the lead towards your puppy and feed from your other hand to create a positive pairing with that hand coming towards them.

Step 2: Build this up at your puppy's pace until you can slide your hand all the way down towards their body.

Step 3: Once your puppy is comfortable with this, slide your hand down the lead then turn yourself and your puppy 180 degrees and feed them as you keep walking.

Step 5: Aim to perfect this in both directions, so that you can turn into your puppy as well as being able to move them around your body as you both head off in the opposite direction.

This is a game to practise lots and lots at home without distractions before you try it in a situation where you need it.

GIVING IN TO LEAD PRESSURE

Dogs are hardwired with something called an opposition reflex. This means that whenever you apply pressure to the lead, your puppy will instinctively pull in the opposite direction, which quickly becomes a recipe for a dog who pulls on the lead. Now imagine a dog up ahead that you don't want your puppy to interact with. Your natural reaction will be to pull your puppy away, which will activate that opposition reflex and can hugely increase your puppy's frustration as you restrict their choices. Giving in to Lead Pressure works with your puppy's natural desire to pull and conditions a different response.

The aim is to get to the point where your puppy understands there is more value in keeping the lead loose than from straining and pulling forward – and for tension on the lead to be a cue to move towards you rather than to keep pulling away from you.

Step 1: With your puppy on the lead, apply some gentle pressure and then reward your puppy in the direction of the applied pressure (towards you).

Step 2: Do this several times, applying pressure to the lead from various directions and rewarding in the direction of the pressure as soon as you feel the tension leave the lead.

Step 3: Add a distraction ahead of your puppy (a piece of food on the ground or a toy) just out of reach. Your puppy might initially strain forward to get it. As soon as you feel that tension slacken, reward your puppy away from the distraction – and then occasionally let them access it for a double reward.

How the ideal interaction looks

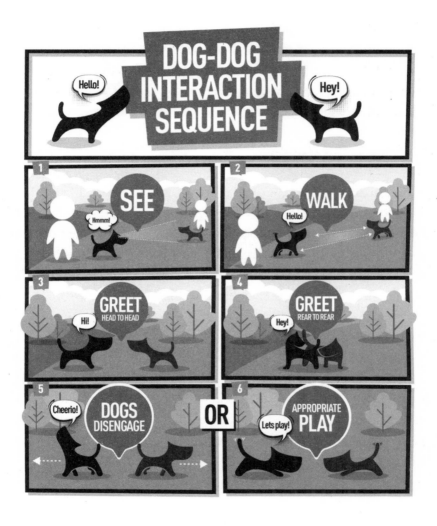

When two dogs meet, there is a natural chain of interaction that should take place. This is a sequence of steps that dogs should ideally follow every time they interact. Because this chain is hardwired, your puppy will instinctively know these steps. However, at every transition between one stage and the next in this interaction chain, there is the possibility that your puppy might get stuck. If your puppy lacks the skill of disengagement, they will struggle to leave one step behind and move on to the next.

It should look like this:

• **See/hear**

The first step of the chain is when your puppy hears, or more commonly, sees, another dog. The distance at which they become aware of an approaching dog will vary from one dog to another. If you observe your puppy, you will begin to recognise the point at which they notice another dog in the distance.

• **Approach**

The next step of the interaction chain is the approach. This is where a dog can first start to struggle. They might be feeling really scared or excited as another dog approaches them or they approach another dog. You want to make sure that your dog is really comfortable with the approach – sometimes feeding them through it can help.

• **Head to head**

After the approach, dogs will naturally greet nose to nose. This should be a brief sniff of each other's faces.

- **Rear to rear aka the bum sniff**

After a friendly nose-to-nose greeting, dogs should move to the rear and have a little sniff of each other's bottoms.

- **Play or move on**

In an appropriate greeting chain, your puppy should then either engage in well-mannered play, or move on completely (disengage from the other dog and carry on with what they were doing before the other dog appeared). It's as if they're saying: 'OK cool, I've met you and now I'm moving on.'

The tricky part of the chain

Many dogs get stuck on the nose-to-nose part of the interaction chain and find themselves unable to move to the rear. This mounting pressure can create tension, which often leads to an inappropriate interaction such as humping, mouthing, barging, rough play or even biting and nipping. If your puppy is put in situations where they repeatedly practise getting 'stuck' at this point, there is a much greater chance of a negative interaction. Not every dog they meet is going to tolerate having a puppy hovering around their face or have the skills to disengage from that conversation and move on. Even if your puppy manages to avoid negative interactions, the more they practise getting stuck and feeling that mounting pressure and inability to move on, the more awkward their interactions with other dogs will become.

Tom's spaniel, Ketone, struggled with the nose-to-nose part of the chain when she was a puppy. Tom would notice a visible sigh of relief when he extracted her from these awkward greetings. If your dog gets stuck, you have several options. Either lead them away (if they're on a lead), interrupt them by doing an Attention Noise, recall them (see chapter 21 for more on this) or pick them up.

Understanding that your puppy may be struggling to progress to the next step of that greeting chain is so important when it comes to being your puppy's very best advocate. If your puppy doesn't know how to disengage, they are likely to put themselves into situations that they don't actually want to be in, including those awkward interactions with other dogs. This can happen even if they find other dogs worrying or scary. Once they have put themselves into that situation, they are unable to disengage, their stress levels increase, their fear increases, the situation escalates and it is at this point that they may have an inappropriate interaction – not because they want to, but because they don't know how to remove themselves from a situation they are worried about.

A broken interaction chain

As well as awkward conversations caused by a struggle with disengagement, a dog's interaction chain can also become broken as a result of bad experiences. Instead of an interaction with another dog ending in appropriate play or in the two dogs moving on, your puppy might find themselves faced with a dog whose own interaction chain is broken. This could lead to any number of less appropriate interactions – anything from humping, mouthing or barging and rough play to being barked at, nipped, snapped at or even worse. This is why safeguarding your puppy and being mindful of the interactions you allow to take place is so important.

Dogs do not like conflict situations, so if your puppy learns that interactions with other dogs lead to negative outcomes, they begin to anticipate and predict the pressure of an interaction well before it actually happens. Even if your puppy started out with a perfectly intact interaction chain, this anticipation of the negative interaction can mean they start to become worried much higher up the chain – perhaps as you approach another dog or even when you see another dog in the distance.

Observe your puppy when they are interacting with another dog. Remember, rehearsal is power – because whatever you let them practise is effectively what you are training. Try and identify any breaks in the chain. You might observe your puppy staring at another dog or lying down when they see another dog approaching. Both of these can indicate a struggle with one of those early parts of the chain, long before your puppy even comes close to the other dog. A dog who struggles to disengage from the bum sniff can show this by resting their chin or chest on another dog's back.

Alternatively, your puppy might be so excited by the idea of interacting with other dogs that the energy they bring to the conversation is entirely inappropriate and mismatched to the energy of the dog they are trying to greet. Again, this can create tension and conflict and cause your puppy's interaction chain to become damaged.

How to lay the foundations

So knowing all of this, what should you think about in order to give your puppy the best foundation to be able to interact successfully with other dogs?

Keep your distance

You can teach your puppy the skills of calmness, optimism and confidence around other dogs, as well as that crucial skill of dis-engagement, without ever getting close to another dog or putting your puppy in a potentially dangerous or volatile situation.

Is your puppy calm seeing other dogs who are 10 metres away? Can they focus on you even in the presence of another dog or do they struggle to ignore other dogs? Are they optimistic when they hear another dog bark or do you need to DMT that sound until they are? If you've got those skills in place, you've played games to encourage calmness, optimism and disengagement and your puppy is OK with seeing other dogs at a distance, then they are probably ready for closer interactions.

Be selective

In day-to-day life, your puppy is going to encounter other dogs but it's your job to be as selective as you can about the dogs that you choose for them to interact with. It's probably not going to be a good idea for your puppy to socialise with a dog that you don't know anything about while they're still learning about the world. The reality is that most dogs you come across are not dogs that you would want your puppy to be influenced by.

Be your puppy's advocate

Being your puppy's advocate is sometimes about saying no. When you get a puppy, friends can't wait to invite you on a walk with their dogs and you might find a whole dog-walking community in your local area. If you've got a question as to whether an inter-action between your puppy and another dog is going to go well, you probably should say no. We talk about being your puppy's best advocate in chapter 2.

Friends with influence

If you do choose to allow your puppy to socialise with other dogs, choose those dogs carefully. Your puppy will become the company that they keep. An older dog who is reliable, robust and can mind its own business can provide you with brilliant opportunities to teach and grow your less 'savvy' puppy. Look for a dog who will walk calmly with you and your puppy rather than spending the whole walk involved in crazy, free-for-all play or getting overexcited. Your puppy can quickly learn less desirable or inappropriate behaviour from dogs they interact or go on walks with. You might be working hard to teach your puppy the value of proximity and the desire to stay close, so if you take them for a walk with another dog who likes to race and chase and spend all its time in the distance, the influence of that dog is unlikely to grow your puppy in the right direction. Carefully consider what interactions you want your puppy to have.

Your puppy might not currently have the most seamless inter-action chain because they are still learning. A good-natured older dog is not only more likely to be able to handle that, they can also be a brilliant teacher.

Also consider the size of any other dog you choose to spend time with. If you've got a very small puppy, you're probably not going to go on a walk with a Great Dane who could accidentally inflict damage simply because of their size. Always ask yourself

271

the question: 'Is this experience growing my dog in the direction I want to grow them?'

APPROACH THEN LEAVE

This is a transformational game designed for dogs who have a break in their interaction chain. It works by beginning at the point of that predictable chain of hearing or seeing another dog, but finishing before the chain has played out. This removes the mounting pressure that dogs can feel if they have learned that interactions with other dogs don't always lead to positive outcomes. The more you play this game, the more your puppy comes to understand that seeing or approaching another dog does not mean that an inter-action is inevitable. It's a game you can play when you and your puppy are out and about on walks whenever you spot a dog up ahead.

Step 1: Whenever you see a dog in the distance, start to approach and as your puppy notices the other dog, turn and move away in the opposite direction. If your puppy needs a little extra encouragement, A to B is a great tool to add in here.

Step 2: As you move away, feed your puppy to reinforce the great choice they just made to disengage from the approaching dog.

Step 3: Vary how close you get to the oncoming dog before you turn and move away, depending on how easy or hard your puppy is finding it to disengage both their body and their mind from the other dog. If you discover that your puppy is very excited or worried by the idea of interacting with approaching dogs, play at a distance where they can remain calm and focused on you. It can be enough to take one or two steps towards the other dog and then turn and move in the opposite direction. Over time, you should be able to move closer and still see that your puppy is able to disengage from that approach and come away with you.

How to help your puppy interact

Grow their skills at home

Giving your puppy a foundation of calmness, playing games to build their optimism and growing their ability to disengage from things they find both exciting and worrying will give your puppy the very best foundations for having conversations with other dogs when they do encounter them.

What has happened before the interaction?

A lot of the success of a dog–dog interaction happens outside of the interaction itself. Sometimes the conversation your puppy is going to have with another dog has already gone wrong before that dog even appears, because your puppy is overexcited or over-stimulated. If we have a conversation with another human and we're already feeling anxious, stressed and frustrated then that

273

conversation is probably not going to go particularly well, because we've come into it in the wrong emotional state.

Your puppy's conversation with other dogs starts before they actually see each other. Does your puppy lose their mind when you pick up the lead to take them for a walk? Do they listen to you when you open the front door? All of these things are indicative of how that walk and any possible interactions are going to go.

Keep it brief
If an interaction with another dog is unavoidable, count to three, move your puppy on and reward them.

Help them out
If your puppy gets stuck in the interaction chain, help to move them on. Let's say your puppy gets to the nose and you know that they struggle to disengage from this point and move to the rear. Step in before they get stuck. Make an Attention Noise (see page 215) or call them over and offer them a piece of food to reinforce the value of moving away. The key is to help them out and coach them through the interaction by not letting them get stuck and by moving them on if needed. The cool thing is, if you've got a young puppy, they haven't had much rehearsal of this chain going wrong yet. Safeguard their interaction chain and their conversations will remain intact.

None of your business

Now you know what you're looking for from an interaction, you can create the picture you want and focus on the part of the chain that your puppy struggles with.

Your ultimate aim is to teach your puppy that other dogs are great and it's OK to check in with them but really they're none of their business. It's not about teaching your puppy to love other dogs. It's about teaching them that they're great at a distance.

How do you do this?

- Take some of your puppy's daily food allowance on your walk ready for whenever your puppy sees another dog.
- Feed your puppy some of the daily food allowance as you walk away from that dog.
- Your puppy thinks this is cool – every time they see another dog, they get rewarded for acknowledging that other dog, but then they move away rather than needing to greet any other dog they pass. At the same time, they get to have fun with you.

ORIENTATION GAME

Dogs can often find themselves wanting to interact with or react to things in the distance. This makes it very difficult to give your puppy freedom in distracting environments and know that they will bounce back to you if another dog appears up ahead. This game builds that reflex and desire to ping back to you, even in the face of distractions.

Step 1: Roll or throw a piece of food in one direction for your puppy to go and find.

Step 2: The moment they orient back towards you, let them know they did the best thing in the world, mark that moment with a word like 'Yes!' and throw another piece of food out for them to follow.

Step 3: Repeat, throwing the food in different directions and continuing to mark and reward that choice to orientate back towards you each time.

Step 4: Once you have the foundations of the game, add movement by playing while you walk or move around. Play both on and off lead, both inside and outside.

Other dogs are unpredictable and socialisation is all about preparing your puppy for the situation, rather than putting them in the situation and hoping for a positive outcome. Your puppy will now know the value of staying with you rather than running off to say hi to every dog they see. If an interaction is unavoidable, both you and they will know exactly what to do and as the best owner for your puppy, you will know to step in at any point that you can see they are struggling.

Some socialisation can be incredibly beneficial and we want you to experience joy in seeing your puppy interact with other dogs. Appropriate adult dogs that play infrequently and will ignore a puppy's overzealous attempts at interaction set great examples. They will help to teach your puppy that it's good to be calm and not get too overexcited. In fact, it's what the real world will expect from your puppy as they grow and mature.

CHAPTER 18
Greeting Guests and Visitors

Whether you live in a busy household with lots of people coming and going, or guests are a less frequent occurrence, your aim for your new puppy should be that visitors are a non-event that they can calmly ignore. Longer term, your aim may be to have your dog able to enjoy freedom to interact with your guests and hang out with them, but at first the reality may be very different.

Depending on your puppy's personality, the arrival of new people in your home might be hugely exciting and mean your puppy quickly gets overstimulated and starts making poor choices. Equally, for some puppies, interacting with lots of people that they are not familiar with can be a stressful experience.

When you first bring your puppy home, you'll probably find that everyone you know is desperate to meet them, but it's important to remember your puppy might easily be overwhelmed by all this attention. All that extra activity can be truly tiring and can add to your puppy's bucket. Remember, in chapter 2, we talked about being your puppy's advocate and learning to say no to situations that might not be in their best interests. The way they learn to feel about visitors and interact with them now is likely to set the course for the way they continue to react to visitors as they grow up. Remember – rehearsal is powerful!

When you're considering having visitors to your home, deciding what you want your puppy to be learning and how to set them up for success from the very start is really important, and something it's worth thinking about before you find yourself in the situation.

Think about all the events that are associated with having guests, many of which your puppy might be experiencing for the first time. Knocks on the door or the sound of the doorbell, unfamiliar voices, the extra noise of chatter, new smells, and more than likely an increase of energy and activity in your house. It's a lot for a young puppy to deal with.

So, how can you teach your puppy to consider people visiting your home a non-event? At this early stage, while everything is so new and your puppy's brain is like a sponge, limiting their choices and protecting their bucket is often best.

Dogs will do more of what they practise, so putting some management strategies in place will prevent your puppy from rehearsing undesirable behaviours, whether that's launching themselves at visitors, doing zoomies – zooming quickly around a room or across the laps of your guests – or learning to jump up for attention.

Make doors a dog-free zone

Setting your puppy up for visitor success starts way before your visitors even arrive. We've all been to people's houses where the owner is frantically restraining their dog to stop them from jumping up at you. Before your visitors are due to come, pop your puppy into a crate or pen so they are already calmly settled when you answer the door.

Your front (or back) door is an area of change, movement and activity – and consequently it's an area of high excitement for your puppy. This makes it much harder for them to make good decisions.

Keep your puppy away from arriving guests and delivery drivers by making sure that the door area is a dog-free zone. This will reduce the energy and activity around it and minimise opportunities for your puppy to jump up at visitors the minute they come through your door. This helps your guests enter the house or hand over parcels safely and calmly without having to deal with a leaping puppy. It also limits your puppy's access to open doorways and the potential dangers they could face if they were to escape in all the excitement of arriving guests.

The way you come into the house is something to consider too. However well you manage your set-up with visitors, your puppy is going to learn much more from those events that happen every day, so being conscious of what your puppy is rehearsing each and every time you or a family member comes home is a big part of the picture here too. In chapter 13 we looked at how coming and going from the house should be a non-event for your puppy. Jumping up can quickly become a struggle, so we're going to cover it in more detail below.

KNOCK KNOCK BED

Many dogs are quick to pair knocking on the door or the sound of a doorbell with the arrival of visitors. Mayhem often ensues, especially if they have also learned to bark or jump whenever they hear that sound. This can be a huge bucket filler for both you and your puppy, and means your puppy is much less likely to be in a calm frame of mind for making great choices and settling when guests do visit. This game will really turn that association on its head and create a triggered response to hearing a knock at the door that sees your puppy jump onto their bed and hang out there calmly until released. Play this lots, and over time you should see that the sound of knocking (or your doorbell) becomes a cue for your puppy to hop on the boundary. This is a super foundation for a dog who is able to hang out calmly on a boundary in the presence of visitors, and who doesn't rush towards your door any time someone knocks.

TIP: You need your puppy to have an understanding of boundary games before playing this game, so build some value for the boundary first. See chapter 9 for more information on this.

Step 1: Warm up with some basic boundary games, making sure your puppy is keen to hop on and knows their boundary is an area of high value.

Step 2: Once your puppy has plenty of desire for the boundary, call your puppy away from the bed and gently restrain them so they can't hop straight back on. You might hold their harness or collar, put a light hand on their chest, or, if your puppy is less comfortable with being restrained, use a puppy line.

Step 3: While your puppy is restrained, make a knocking sound on a wall or the floor (or play a recording of your doorbell) and immediately let go of your puppy.

Step 4: Your puppy should race to the bed because the desire for the boundary is so high from all the value you have previously put into Boundary Games. It's almost like a reflex. Reinforce that great choice by dropping a few pieces of food onto the bed.

Step 5: Think about the way you deliver the food and your own energy. Remember – if the sound of knocking is already a predictor of excitement for your puppy, you want to teach them that the very best option is to race to their boundary but then stay there calmly until released.

DOORWAY MANNERS

Doorways are a common struggle within a home because they're an area of anticipation and excitement. That prediction increases arousal and means dogs often learn to dash through doorways the moment a door is opened. For some dogs, putting a hand on the door handle is more than enough to increase arousal. Ditching the routine around all those predictors that fill your puppy's bucket will help overcome this struggle.

Step 1: Begin by placing your hand on the door handle and delivering a piece of your puppy's daily food away from the door. You're looking for a calm response.

Step 2: Build up to being able to open the door, while your puppy stays calmly where they are. If they immediately try and rush through the door, you've moved your game on too fast. As with the previous level, deliver a piece of food away from the door. You are teaching your puppy that the value is away from the door, not through it, which will stop them from rushing through.

Step 3: Incorporating boundary games can really help anchor your puppy somewhere they already value.

Step 4: Progress to being able to move calmly through the doorway with your puppy without them rushing ahead. Can you go through the doorway and head right back in, or send your puppy through by throwing a piece of food in one direction and then calling them back towards you?

Making the introduction

When visitors arrive, get them settled first before introducing your puppy. Those first few minutes when visitors arrive can often be a little chaotic as you greet them, take their coats and get them a drink. Do all of that while your puppy stays occupied in their pen or crate or behind a baby gate and doesn't have access to your guests. Then, once your visitors are settled and everything is calmer, you may decide it is appropriate to introduce your puppy to the room.

Boundaries are great for dogs, but they can be pretty useful for visitors too! Make sure your guests settle themselves somewhere comfortable before giving your puppy access. This will help prevent sudden movements that might startle your puppy or increase their excitement, and keep the energy low. Be particularly aware of how much energy young children can bring to the mix and consider whether allowing your puppy access is in everyone's best interests. For more information on puppies and children, see chapter 3.

Use a lead or a puppy line

Once you've decided to let your puppy interact, there are some ways you can ensure they make excellent choices.

If you think there is a chance they might jump up at your guests, a lead or puppy line can help. A lightweight puppy line can trail, so that if it all gets too much for your puppy, you can pick up the line and lead them away from the situation.

Let your puppy explore

Your puppy will be curious and will probably want to investigate your visitors. If they are calm, let them approach and have a sniff, giving them an opportunity to check out unfamiliar people in their own time and without any pressure.

Play a boundary game

After your puppy has had a calm sniff of the visitors, keeping them employed with a 'job' will allow them to make great choices and only rehearse appropriate, calm behaviour. Depending on how far along you are with boundary games, giving your puppy an opportunity to spend time in the same space as your visitors while playing some simple boundary games can be a great foundation for more responsibility and freedom as they grow and mature. Be super mindful of how much your puppy can handle and watch for signs their bucket is starting to fill or they're getting tired and overexcited.

Set up a gated community
While your puppy is young, the best option might be for them to be in a crate or puppy pen, well away from your visitors, with a long-lasting chew or Kong to help them tune out and chill around all that novelty.

For puppies who are inclined to think everything is their business and very much feel they should be involved, removing visual access by covering their crate or putting their puppy pen somewhere a little quieter can help them to tune out and settle.

Depending on how well your puppy is embracing the idea of 'presence ≠ access' (we explored this in more detail in chapter 13) and how easily they are able to settle away from you, you may have to start with the crate or pen close by. Be guided by what your puppy is able to handle.

Remember to notice and reward moments of calm and settled behaviour. This helps to create positive associations with all that novelty. Also, don't forget your puppy is still going to need plenty of opportunities to go outside for the toilet – possibly more so with all that excitement!

Jumping up

Jumping up is a very common puppy struggle, and one that can easily get rehearsed when your calm, well-managed home is suddenly full of visitors.

Even if your puppy is the tiniest, cutest little thing, bouncing up to head height to say hello when you come home, jumping all over your visitors or launching themselves at people that you meet on walks are not behaviours you want to unintentionally reinforce. It might seem sweet that your puppy gets excited to greet you when you arrive home, or to see new people visit, but it will be a different matter in 6 months' time when they're fully grown and potentially much bigger and stronger.

If jumping up isn't addressed while your dog is a puppy, it can turn your calm home into a place of complete chaos and mayhem. It can be dangerous too if there are young children or elderly relatives around who can easily be knocked over. We recently had a behaviour consult with a dog owner who hadn't been able to have visitors to her house for 8 years because her dog jumped up at everyone. Imagine that! Now is the time to nip jumping up in the bud if it's started to happen so it won't be an issue going forward. However, if your dog has already practised jumping up, there is always a way to transform the situation. Follow exactly the same same process, just be aware it might take slightly longer. Your management strategies (gated communities, keeping dogs on leads/lines and away from doorways) are going to be really important at first to help prevent more rehearsal while you're working on the situation.

So is there a way to teach your puppy to be less excited in the presence of people and to keep their paws firmly on the floor?

Absolutely! We have everything you need to turn this struggle into a strength for you and your puppy.

Why does my puppy jump up?

If you have a puppy who seems to have been born with springs in their paws, the key to transforming this bouncing is understanding what is motivating their jumping. Puppies who jump up are often expressing excitement. Your pup may also have discovered that jumping is a great way to get attention. Remember, dogs repeat behaviours that earn rewards, and few things are more rewarding than your attention. Other family members, visitors and strangers may all have unintentionally rewarded the jumping too. We all have that friend who loves dogs and doesn't mind being jumped on, even if we're trying really hard to teach our young dog calmer behaviours around people.

Your puppy might also need a little more input to help them embrace calmness as the best choice in situations that are exciting, as well as some help learning a little more self-control.

Disengagement – that ability to see value in moving away from things that are super exciting or worrying – will also help your puppy keep their paws on the floor. In the case of visitors arriving, jumping might be a sign that your puppy is actually nervous. As we discussed in the previous chapter, some dogs put themselves into situations they are unsure about simply because they don't yet have the skills to disengage and move away from things they find scary. We've had behaviour consults where dogs have jumped up onto a visitor's lap, the visitor has tried to stroke them and the dog has bitten them. Dogs don't like mystery, so if they're not sure how something is going to pan out, they will often put themselves into situations they're not confident with, simply in order to find out.

How to stop your puppy from jumping up

Don't panic if your puppy is already doing lots of jumping up – there's a game for that! The first thing we always encourage you to do is focus on what you DO want from your puppy rather than what you don't want. Not only is this more empowering, it helps you see solutions instead of just seeing the problem.

If your goal is a dog who greets people calmly and understands the very best option is keeping their paws on the ground, self-control, disengagement and calmness are the skills and concepts you want to inspire.

Paws on the ground

While you're helping your puppy see value in calm greetings and in keeping those paws firmly on the floor, limiting their opportunities to rehearse anything other than those awesome choices will really supercharge your progress.

To your puppy, shouting or squealing or even taking hold of their paws and pushing them off can be just as reinforcing as if you returned their over-exuberant greeting – even if your intention was to discourage the behaviour rather than reward it. Instead, place your hand on your puppy's collar and gently guide them to the ground. Stroke them and feed them for being on the ground or see if they choose to get on a boundary and if so, feed them there.

Consistency is key. Make sure other family members, visitors and strangers don't have opportunities to reward the jumping up, otherwise your puppy is going to end up very confused and conflicted about what's OK and what's not.

Let's play!

If you want to stop your puppy from jumping up, you need to be able to teach them an alternative behaviour that is incompatible with jumping – and put way more value in that choice than in the one your puppy was making.

FOUR PAWS ON THE FLOOR

How you want your puppy to greet people is ultimately up to you. The key is teaching them what to DO, rather than what NOT to do. A good starting point for a puppy is to encourage them to keep all four paws on the floor.

You can teach your puppy to do this when they greet people by placing some of their daily food allowance on the ground whenever they're around people they might otherwise jump up and greet (even you!).

The idea is to stop your puppy jumping by rewarding them before they can even think about leaving the ground. Your puppy will quickly start to understand that the value is on the ground and not up above.

First, work on this when it's just the two of you and you're alone. If your puppy finds being close to you so exciting that your presence alone is enough to prompt jumping, you'll know it's too soon to introduce the distraction of other people.

Step 1: With your puppy on a lead, begin by simply reinforcing the benefits of having all four of their paws on the floor by gently dropping some of their daily food allowance on the ground near your feet. This will help your puppy understand that there is value in containing that desire to bounce. Keep your body language and food delivery nice and calm so you don't add more excitement. If you have a very springy puppy, you're going to need to be quite speedy with your food to begin with so you don't give your puppy any window in which they can start bouncing again.

Step 2: As you continue to reward your puppy for having all four paws on the floor, you should begin to see moments of pause where they start to make a conscious decision to *keep* those paws on the floor. Mark and reward those moments to reinforce that choice – remembering to feed on the ground to communicate where the value is.

JUMPING UP AT OTHER PEOPLE

Once your puppy can be calm in your presence and keep their paws on the floor, you can use the game to teach them the same behaviour around other people. Over the course of a few sessions, you should find that this gets better and better, as your puppy practises keeping their paws on the floor around people. In time, your puppy will come to understand that four feet on the floor brings treats and reinforcement, while jumping up brings nothing.

It's best to start with someone your puppy is familiar with, but ideally not a person they find hugely exciting. This might be another member of your family or someone they see on a fairly regular basis. Ask the person to be as calm as possible. You want to set your puppy up for successful learning and not make it super hard for them. Remember that your aim is always to train for the situation, not in the situation – so this isn't a game to play with your puppy for the first time when they are already struggling to contain their bounce! If people coming and going creates a lot of energy and excitement in your puppy, wait for a degree of calmness before you start.

Step 1: With your puppy on a lead, throw one piece of food a little distance towards your visitor. You are looking for your puppy to move towards the food, eat it and then return to you for the next piece.

Step 2: Reward your puppy's choice to move away from the person by feeding them more of their daily food allowance – remembering to feed on the floor. This clearly spells out to your puppy the appropriate response to another person (disengage, remain calm and show some self-control by keeping your paws on the floor). If your puppy is more rewarded by attention, you can show them they made a great choice by calmly stroking them while they keep themselves grounded. Just make sure this doesn't set off more bouncing.

Step 3: Repeat these steps to build up a history of your puppy rehearsing what you do want.

Counter-surfing

Some puppies very quickly learn that the kitchen counter is a place where interesting and potentially yummy things can be found. Before this even becomes an issue, reward your puppy for keeping their paws on the ground any time they are in the kitchen or near surfaces where there might be food.

Setting your puppy up with a bed or boundary in the kitchen, away from the worktops and any temptation, will also set them up for success – see chapter 9 for more information on boundaries and how to use them. Reinforce the benefits of being in that area and your puppy will soon learn where the value is.

Rehearsal is powerful. This can work to your advantage if your puppy only ever rehearses great things. Tom's dogs would never even consider counter-surfing. You could leave a big juicy steak on the kitchen counter and they wouldn't give it a moment's thought – not because they wouldn't really, really love that steak, but because they have such a strong history of being rewarded for keeping their paws on the floor and staying on boundaries in the kitchen that food on the kitchen surfaces isn't even on their radar. That's pretty cool – and it's totally possible for your puppy to learn that too.

> **TIP: Scatter feeding**
>
> Scatter feeding (as discussed in chapter 4) is a great strategy to have for moments where jumping up does happen. If your house erupts into a barking, bouncing frenzy when you come home or visitors knock on the door, it can be hard to know what to do in that moment.

Scattering some of your puppy's daily food allowance on the floor can be a great option. While it may seem like you're rewarding the jumping, it's important to understand that if your puppy is already bouncing, they're not in the right headspace to learn more appropriate behaviour right at that moment.

Scattering food for your puppy to sniff out not only helps to keep those paws firmly on the floor, it reinforces calmness as the more appropriate emotional response – which will make a calm response much more likely the next time.

CHAPTER 19
The Language of Puppies

Barking! It's one of the most common struggles faced by dog owners, yet it can be one of the most damaging. Having a dog who barks excessively – whether that's at things they can see out of the window, at visitors, at the doorbell, or seemingly at every little noise (even ones you can't hear!) – can be hugely stressful. It can divide households, destroy family relationships and cause rifts with neighbours. We've known owners who have experienced such challenging situations with their dog's barking that the local authorities have become involved. It is also a sad reality that barking is one reason many dogs end up being rehomed.

Why do puppies and dogs bark?

The first thing to understand is that barking is your puppy's way of communicating in the language they know how to use.

Some dogs are more naturally inclined to bark than others. Certain breeds tend to be more vocal because barking is a trait that has been encouraged and promoted. That being said, barking is something that all dogs will do.

Barking can be frustrating. It can fill any human's bucket big time! If your puppy suddenly finds their voice, it can be easy to think they are being disobedient, stubborn, or giving you a hard time just because they can. You might come across the idea that a dog who barks is trying to be dominant.

In fact, none of those is ever true. That's great news, right? Your puppy is never trying to be difficult on purpose. Reminding yourself of that frequently as you work together to figure out rules and boundaries will help immensely in seeing things from your puppy's perspective. Understanding the WHY behind your puppy's barking can help you to be much more patient and understanding, and allow you to seek solutions rather than focus on the problem. Remember, your puppy is doing the best they can with the skills they currently have.

A form of communication

Whenever your puppy barks, they are experiencing an emotion. That might be:

- Excitement
- Fear
- Frustration.

Barking is one way your puppy has of communicating how they are feeling. You can't tell which emotion your puppy is experiencing simply by the fact that they are barking, but you can be certain they aren't in the best emotional space. There's more in this chapter on the emotions they might be experiencing. If your puppy is barking, you can bet their bucket is pretty full. Remember from chapter 8 – calmness is king!

If you find yourself faced with a barking struggle, the solution is never to try and silence your puppy. Instead, you need to consider what skills your puppy needs to grow and then play games that will reduce the barking by helping your puppy embrace more calmness and feel more optimistic about the world and less worried by novelty.

The barking will disappear if you can address the root causes. Alongside that, you need to limit opportunities your puppy has to practise barking.

Barking spreads like fire!

Just like any habit that you develop over time, such as biting your fingernails, the more you practise doing it, the more it becomes your default when you're excited, scared, bored or anxious. It's exactly the same for dogs. Remember, rehearsal is power. The more your puppy barks, the more they will do it.

Your puppy, your expectations

Knowing why your puppy is barking can help guide you to determine what expectations may be realistic for the dog in front of you, as well as what you are comfortable with as you navigate life and its many fun adventures together.

If you live alone or you are elderly, you might want your dog to let you know if there is something suspicious happening outside. Or you may prefer your puppy to be less vocal, especially if you are worried about noise levels and the impact on your neighbours.

When it comes to behaviour, it is important to be consistent in

295

your expectations. Some dogs are able to pick up on the context clues of a situation and learn only to bark in specific situations. There might be environments where barking is entirely appropriate. Some of our dogs bark gleefully round an agility course – but it's not something we would allow them to rehearse in everyday situations. However, it can often be difficult to communicate to your dog when barking is acceptable and when it isn't. If you don't mind barking when a delivery person arrives but don't want barking at visitors, your puppy may have a harder time discerning when it is appropriate and when it isn't.

It's often easier to simply say that you would either prefer they don't bark or that you don't mind if they do. Our choice is always for calm over loud.

Lauren's story: classic sounds

Lauren had never really had a truly vocal dog . . . until Classic arrived. Classic comes from a rather vocal herding breed and she certainly displayed those genetics and traits. In fact, she excelled at them. She barked, screamed, howled, shrieked, squealed and literally vocalised her frustration or excitement at any opportunity. Classic shocked everyone with her noises. All the strategies we share in this chapter are what Classic and the thousands of other dogs we've trained have taught us. Lauren can honestly say she no longer has a vocal dog in Classic: she is a calm, collected house dog and this is all down to Absolute Dogs games!

Translating your puppy's bark

Remember that all barking is an expression of an emotion your puppy is feeling. Let's delve into the different types of barking and how you can potentially identify them.

It's important to remember that you can't tell from your puppy's barking alone what emotion they are experiencing. You need to look at the whole picture.

Excitement

Barking that communicates your puppy is excited is often seen during play. If your puppy starts to bark during play, this can be a way of communicating their joy at the game. In this context, you may be totally cool with your puppy barking, although remember to be mindful of your puppy's bucket. Too much high-arousal play can quickly set the tone for the level of arousal your puppy chooses in other aspects of life too.

Frustration

Barking when you're playing games with your puppy can also indicate a degree of frustration, either because your puppy isn't clear what is expected, or because a desired outcome isn't forthcoming.

This type of barking can also be observed when your puppy is behind a barrier and access to something isn't immediate. You might already have experienced this in the context of crate training, or teaching your puppy the value of presence ≠ access. Feelings of frustration can also come about when a puppy who loves people and other dogs sees them and is desperate to access them. FOMO has kicked in! Rather than allowing your puppy to remain in that state of high arousal and frustration, which can easily flip into fear, it's important to build their skills and shape their brain to cope better with those situations, and avoid rehearsal in the meantime. Your puppy could also be frustrated because they're bored. Make sure your puppy is getting sufficient mental and physical stimulation – and enough sleep.

Fear

When a puppy is scared of something, they will typically choose either to get away from that thing or try to 'scare it away' by barking at it. This sort of barking (sometimes accompanied by whining or howling) can be also observed in puppies with separation struggles – see chapter 13 for more advice about how to get your puppy comfortable with being left home alone. Again, it's important not to let your puppy rehearse this emotional state and instead focus on games that build optimism and confidence and encourage calmness.

Action prompting

Barking for your attention, or demand barking, is a form of action prompting. If your puppy discovers they can bark in order to get you to do something – feed them, play with them, give them attention – you can accidentally reinforce the barking and actually make it more likely to happen again. Giving your puppy the specific outcome they want (usually something exciting) isn't the way to deal with this, but ignoring the barking is often not going to work either. If your puppy has their disco pants on ready for a party, ignoring them will often mean the demand barking will just escalate and get more demanding and more insistent. Instead, you're going to want to offer your puppy an alternative option that promotes calmness and helps them change into their pyjamas.

When thinking about not giving in to your puppy's demands, it's important to distinguish this from meeting your puppy's needs. You don't want your puppy to learn to feel powerless or helpless if you ignore their attempts to communicate a genuine need.

How do I reduce my puppy's barking?

The most important concepts to grow in your puppy to address any barking struggles are calmness and optimism.

Practise optimism regularly to keep your puppy feeling confident about the world around them – see chapter 10 for more ideas. As you already know from chapter 8, calmness is king! If your puppy is calm, they are not barking. What's really cool is that no matter whether your puppy is fearful or overexcited, growing their optimism and confidence, as well as establishing calmness as a default state, will combat your barking struggles and leave your puppy in a much better emotional state.

Management is also going to be really important. If you identify that your puppy is routinely barking out of the front window at people or other dogs passing by, limit their access to the window. Remember how powerful rehearsal is. You don't want your puppy to get better and better at barking because they get to practise it every time they see someone go past.

Being strategic about where your puppy gets to spend their time will not only limit their access to things they find worrying or exciting but will also help keep their bucket as empty as possible and give them the best chance of accessing their inner calmness.

'Non-event' training

No matter where the barking occurs, it is important to identify the triggers that prompt it. What is it in the environment that starts the barking?

Here are just some of the scenarios that might trigger your puppy to bark:

- Other dogs on walks.
- People on walks.
- Bags/moving objects you come across on walks.
- Unexpected noises.
- Other animals.
- Inanimate objects, particularly if they are in slightly unusual places – this could be anything from a wheelie bin on the road to pumpkins outside houses at Halloween.
- Things that have been moved to a different location from the one your puppy is accustomed to seeing them in – for example, if you have moved around your living room furniture.
- Seeing other dogs or people when in the car.
- Seeing other dogs or people on TV.
- Your own movement.
- Children running or moving quickly.

Using the power of DMT, which we introduced you to back in chapter 10, you can condition a more appropriate emotional response to any of these distractions – or to any other event your puppy finds exciting, scary or frustrating.

Without setting out to find these things, and only if they

naturally occur, reward your puppy for acknowledging them in the world around them and then moving on. No big party, no big fuss. They're no big deal. These are non-events.

In fact, try doing this BEFORE your puppy ever starts barking at anything. This will help prevent the behaviour from ever occurring and your puppy will feel more confident and safer in the environment. DMT is a no-pressure game where direct interaction with whatever it is in the environment is not required. Doing non-event training, where nothing really happens and your puppy gets to see that the world is cool at a distance, is a really important foundation layer of training for any puppy.

CRAZY LADY

This game might sound a little, well, crazy, but it really works. You are regularly going to practise saying 'hello' to no one! Yes, you heard us correctly. You will be saying 'hello' to thin air.

So what is the point of this game? As you know from chapter 8, dogs are born predicting and they often learn pretty early on that particular sounds or things we say predict specific events they find worrying or exciting. Those associations often become triggers for barking. This might be a greeting called out to someone you pass on a walk, the 'hello' you greet visitors with when they come to your door, or even the sound of you answering the phone. The game isn't just about saying 'hello' – it's about creating a calm, positive pairing with any sounds that tend to lead to barking. That could be anything from a knock on the door, the sound of your doorbell, even the jangling of a bell on a cat's collar.

Help your puppy see these noises as none of their business and nothing to get excited or worried about by making them happen randomly and teaching your puppy that they are non-events. The event they might be predicting isn't actually happening.

Play Crazy Lady while little else is going on in the environment. Observe your puppy to see their emotional response to each cue that they hear. You want to raise a confident optimist and this starts with games like this when no one is around. Pairing this game with boundary games (see chapter 9) can be very powerful. If you have more than one person at home, it's often helpful to have someone else create the sounds while you're playing the game. That way, you can focus completely on rewarding your puppy for a calm response, and it feels a little less staged.

Step 1: Begin when there are no other distractions happening. Say 'hi' or 'hello' or whatever your natural greeting to someone might be, and when your puppy gives no response, reward them with some of their daily food allowance. This can be a single piece fed directly to your puppy, or a few pieces scattered. If your puppy responds to your craziness by barking, you have started off too crazy! You're aiming to work at a level where your puppy doesn't react so that you can create that history of calm, positive associations with potential triggers of arousal and barking. If necessary, start with a whisper.

Step 2: Take the game out and about, to different rooms of your house and even on walks. Reward no response each time.

Step 3: Be unpredictable. Say 'hi', 'hello' or 'morning' when your puppy may least expect it.

Step 4: Begin to incorporate more distractions. If you have a doorbell, playing doorbell sounds and pairing no response with some of your puppy's daily food allowance can help reduce the chances that your puppy is going to learn to bark every time your doorbell goes. If people tend to knock on your door, randomly knock on walls, doors or floors and feed your puppy for no response. You might feel crazy, but it really does work!

SUCTION BOUNDARIES

Where your puppy spends their time is really important when it comes to opportunities for finding things to bark at. If they sit on the windowsill watching people and dogs go past, birds in your garden or next door's cat, there are many things they might decide are important.

However, if instead they learn to stay on a boundary away from all those distractions, opportunities for barking are going to be much fewer.

You don't need to have perfect boundaries to play this game, but it will help if your puppy has played the first few levels of boundary games and has learned that the boundary is a great place to be.

Step 1: With your puppy hanging out on their bed, remind them how cool the boundary is by delivering some of their daily food allowance.

Step 2: Release your puppy from their bed (use a verbal release word, pause, throw a piece of food) and then restrain them gently, either by placing a hand on their chest or by holding their collar or harness (like you did when playing Knock Knock Bed). Don't let them go very far from the boundary.

Step 3: When you let go, your puppy should return to the bed as if by suction. If they don't immediately hop back on, try throwing a piece of food onto the bed while you gently restrain. This should power them forward once you've let go! If you find your puppy gets a little excited by being restrained, that's OK – they need to be able to return to a bed as if by suction even when something exciting happens that they might be tempted to bark at. Chill them out a little by delivering some food calmly and slowly once they are back on the bed.

This game will form part of the bigger picture of teaching boundary games and weaving them into all aspects of your puppy's life. The end goal is that, wherever you are and whatever space you enter, boundaries have so much value that your puppy will seek them out and choose to hang out on them, rather than in places where they might make less appropriate (barky!) choices. Short sessions every day will make a huge difference.

Simple strategies for a bark-free household

- What emotion doesn't have barking as part of its repertoire? Calmness! If you can inspire and grow calmness then you're inspiring and growing a lack of noise. Build calmness by employing the Calmness Triad (see chapter 8). Ensure your puppy gets plenty of rest, time to relax through passive calming activities and is rewarded for being calm.

- Keep playing DMT to show your puppy that the world will present lots of novel situations for them to observe, but they are none of their business. This will help them to remain calm during unexpected events and barking no longer becomes their default behaviour.

- Grow your puppy's desire to remain on a boundary to prevent them from patrolling your house or garden looking for things to bark at. Boundaries also provide your puppy with a comfortable place to rest and get some calming sleep.

- Get your pooch to put their pyjamas on! If your dog becomes more barky when anticipating excitement, be ready to direct them to a calmer alternative such as a passive calming activity, a gentle lead walk or some boundary games. This way, you are showing them that absolutely nothing important is going to happen and disco pants are not required!

- Think about your puppy's bucket. Barking could simply be a sign that their bucket is full and they're just reacting to the world. As that bucket fills, you can bet the barking will get more frequent. On a typical week, identify the top ten things that are filling your puppy's bucket, and then think about what you could do to reduce those bucket fillers.

- Finally, listen to your puppy and try to understand why they are barking. It can be really helpful to keep a barking diary. What are the top ten situations in which your puppy practises barking on a daily or weekly basis? Understanding the triggers will help you minimise them through management of your environment and grow your puppy's skills to handle them in a quieter, calmer way.

CHAPTER 20
Off-lead freedom

Imagine a world where you have such an awesome relationship with your dog and such reliable trust and confidence in their behaviour that you really don't need a lead.

Off-lead freedom is one of those things that many people dream of. The reality can often be very different – day-to-day firefighting where your walks feel like a military operation: having to get prepared, worrying about what might be around the corner, constantly calling your dog back and trying to manage their choices. The truth is that off-lead freedom can't be achieved by taking all the responsibility on yourself as a dog owner. Instead, you need to equip your puppy from the outset with the skills they need to take some of that responsibility on themselves so that they can make great choices.

The prospect of letting your puppy off lead for the first time might feel daunting, but if you get those foundations right and inspire value in the right concepts, it really can be a joy.

Taking your dog off lead is a huge deal for so many owners and is often one of the biggest struggles they face. We understand how scary it can seem to a new puppy owner and we know it's something that many owners put off. However, please believe us when we say that taking your puppy off their lead can be straightforward. If you teach your puppy that being around you is the best option, right from the start, then being out in the environment really isn't such a big deal. Choose locations carefully – options include enclosed dog fields, the woods and the beach – but wherever you choose, pick a space where you have a lot of distance from others, not a place where other dogs or people can land on top of you. Also, think about spaces that are super safe, where your dog can't really run off, get spooked or get into trouble. These spaces are superb for early education. Take your dog's food supply and reward them for hanging around – some call this bribery, but we call it proximity and it's absolutely worth rewarding. Get all this right, and you'll find what we know to be true: having your dog off lead is one of the greatest joys of being a dog owner.

Retractable/extending leads

If you're nervous about taking your dog off lead, it can be tempting to think the answer is to get a retractable or extending lead. However, all this will do is effectively teach your puppy that if they pull to the end, they'll get more lead, which allows them to go a bit further away from you. This actually reinforces the idea that pulling away from you gives your puppy more of what they want – which is precisely the opposite of what you want them to be learning. It's going to create a future of pulling on the lead, which will be hugely frustrating for both you and your puppy when you're walking somewhere that you need calm, loose-lead walking on a shorter lead. Not only that, an extending lead does not give your puppy freedom to explore and make choices and show you that they have the right skills to be given that freedom. Rather than using a retractable lead, we encourage you to embrace the games that teach your puppy to be just as reliable and focused off lead as they are on lead.

What does off-lead freedom look like?

For us, off-lead freedom isn't about our dogs going far away from us into the distance. Even without a lead, our dogs will generally hang out close and walk with us or around us, because we've encouraged them to see so much value in proximity. If they ever do go slightly further, they will always check back in with us – so much so that we generally don't need to use recall, although we'll cover this in chapter 21. It is also about having a puppy that doesn't see you taking off their lead as a cue to run off excitedly into the distance.

Off-lead freedom starts with on-lead freedom

You will have played the proximity games that we talked about in chapter 11. Your puppy might already be really good at playing these games off lead at home and in your garden, but the transition to letting them off lead and playing those games out and about in parks or open spaces feels huge. It is a really big leap and there are actually a few important steps in between.

Most importantly, can you play the games on lead at home? You might not naturally think about this step. Most owners would rarely have their puppy on a lead at home, yet being able to play on lead will allow you to make that transition to new and more complex environments. In order to do that, your puppy needs to learn that games can be played both on and off lead. If your puppy only ever plays games off lead, you are creating a very specific picture of how those games should look. Try and play on lead for the first time somewhere new and your puppy's brain might just say 'no'!

Whenever you go somewhere new, you want to be able to do a 'temperature check' and be sure your puppy can still engage with you and play the games they are rocking at home in that new environment, where there is more to grab their attention. If they can't play games on lead, they aren't ready to play them off lead.

Practising your own mechanics of playing on lead as well as off lead at home is going to be really important too. If you attempt an energetic round of FUNder on lead for the first time in a field or on the beach, you might just discover that you and your puppy end up in a tangled heap as the lead wraps around your legs! Playing on lead can be a bit of an art, and you need to perfect this somewhere safe before you take your games on the road.

Once you've done that, take your puppy and play these games on lead out and about. Can your puppy be just as engaged and responsive as they are at home? If they can then that is a sign that you can progress it further.

Off lead in secure spaces

Once you are confident that your puppy is able to play games and remain engaged with you in a range of different environments on lead, it is time to consider taking that lead off.

Again, you are going to be playing games! Rehearsal is powerful and you want to be putting lots of value in proximity and engagement with you in those early sessions.

It's important to remember that your puppy's engagement with you and the value they see in hanging out close should not be contingent on whether the lead is on or off. If your puppy learns that lead off equals run off, then off-lead freedom is very quickly going to become a challenge. The big outdoors is full of opportunities, and your puppy needs to see that the best and most valuable opportunity is to stick with you.

A great way to go up a level and still set your puppy up for success is to take your games to secure spaces where you know your puppy is going to be safe if they happen to be tempted to stray a little too far. This will allow you to relax and focus on having fun with your puppy. You'll remember from chapter 11 that we encouraged you to build up a history of proximity and engagement in lower distraction environments first. The same is going to be true when it comes to letting your puppy off lead for the first time. Pick appropriate times and spaces before allowing them access to the big wide world.

Depending on where you live, enclosed fields, quiet beaches or even a friend's garden could all be good choices. You might consider open spaces where there is the option for your puppy to explore but not a lot that they can get into trouble with – no cyclists to chase, no other dogs that are going to surprise you if they appear around a corner suddenly, no children playing football to excite or scare your puppy. Open spaces mean you have ample time to assess any distractions that appear in the distance and see what choice your puppy might be going to make – and to be able to interrupt and call them back if necessary.

Think about what each environment might provide in the way of experiences. Beach walks on a sunny day with many other dogs that might run up to your puppy and interrupt your games are unlikely to be a great option while you're still building their skills and shaping that puppy brain.

If your puppy is particularly distracted by things that move, choosing a location that limits their chances of seeing other dogs racing in the distance, cars passing by, joggers and birds will be an important factor.

If you have a puppy who has already shown you they get easily distracted by a good sniff, take that into consideration when deciding where you are most likely to get successful engagement.

Lots of places now have secure dog-walking fields that you can hire just for your own dog. These can be a great option because they give you the security of knowing that your puppy is safe and you are able to relax. They tend to cost around £10–15 per hour.

Use a long line

When you're playing games with your puppy in an unsecured space like a park, it's a good idea to use a long line to begin with. This gives you a safety net if you need to rescue a situation by taking hold of the line and interrupting a less appropriate choice your puppy might be considering.

A long line should be left to trail on the ground. Treat your puppy as if they were off lead. If you find your puppy is heading off into the distance as you make a desperate grab for the end of the line, or you're walking around with the line taut as your puppy strains at the end, they are not ready for this level of responsibility and freedom. Pop the lead back on and build more value in proximity – revisit chapter 11 for more information on how to enourage your puppy to stay close to you.

Lead off, game on!

The games below are all about encouraging the concept of proximity, irrespective of whether your puppy is on or off lead, which will allow you the opportunity for increased off-lead freedom. The aim is to build your puppy's understanding that, when that lead comes off, the very best option is still to remain close. These games are achievable for everyone and can be played every day, everywhere and any time. Even just a couple of minutes a day will pay off.

As with every game we introduce you to throughout this book, play at home first, and build that strong history of rehearsal of what you do want. Remember the importance of training for the situation, not in the situation. Don't be tempted to test it too soon!

ON LEAD/OFF LEAD

This game is very simply about getting your puppy used to being off lead, and teaching them that, regardless of whether they are on lead or off lead, there should be no change in their behaviour. Taking the lead off isn't a big event. Unclipping the lead should not be a cue for your puppy to go. Practise this game in your garden first. If you feel that your puppy is ready, transition to playing somewhere you might be thinking about eventually letting them off the lead, such as a park or a field.

Step 1: With your puppy walking by your side, play a bit of Proximity Zone (see page 160) – rewarding with some of their daily food allowance simply for being close to you.

Step 2: Now unclip the lead, and continue to play Proximity Zone as you walk along. After a brief session of playing off lead, clip the lead back on and – really importantly – continue to play. Your puppy needs to know that the fun doesn't stop when the lead goes back on – and proximity isn't only required until the lead comes off.

Step 3: Repeat!

DROP THE LEAD AND RUN

This game is so much fun, and is really going to help transition from on-lead fun to off-lead fun with your puppy.

It's a game that helps to make the lead a non-event; pick it up, drop it, get your puppy used to lots of different sensations with it. It also guards against those moments that hopefully you will never have, where you accidentally drop the lead. If that happens, this game will make sure that dropping the lead will trigger focus from your puppy rather than them automatically having the urge to run away. What your puppy is going to learn from this game is that if you drop the lead, it's actually a great opportunity to re-engage with you. You become the most fun thing in the environment – not the squirrel in the distance, not the other dog in the park and not the child playing with a football.

Step 1: Start off by playing some Proximity Zone (see page

160) with your puppy on lead. Reward them for being close to you, hanging out with you and not moving too far away.

Step 2: At some point (be unpredictable), you're simply going to drop that lead and dash off! Woohoo! Party on! Your puppy should follow you in pursuit of all that fun to be had with you. When they come and join you, pick the lead up and feed them.

Step 3: Repeat!

TIP: Depending on where you're playing (how much room you have) and how engaged your puppy is, think about how far you choose to dash. Start with small distances and build up. You might need to balance your puppy's energy too. Remember that too much excitement can lead to over-arousal. If your puppy starts jumping and nipping at your clothes when you dash away, lower the energy of the game a little so you are getting the response you want. This might be a good indication that your puppy's dimmer switch needs a little more work. You can think of this as your puppy having a dial in their brain that allows them to access a level of energy that is appropriate to whatever activity they are doing or to whatever event is happening – see chapter 23 for more on this.

ALL EYES ARE ON ME

There are so many things that can draw your puppy's attention when they're out and about, so you need to know their focus is on you. This isn't about insisting your puppy maintains constant eye contact, but about making sure that, whatever your puppy is doing when you're out and about, they have an eye on you and know where you are at all times. In order to do that, you need to make it worth their while.

The first step to being off lead is gentle focus, eye contact and having your puppy look at you and – let's face it – sometimes just being aware that you exist! Remember that you're playing at home in low-distraction environments to begin with. Play on and off lead, always setting your puppy up for success – and play in different locations as your puppy shows they are ready.

Step 1: Place a small piece of your puppy's food on the floor in front of you for your puppy to eat.

Step 2: Providing you've built up a history of playing games with your puppy's food, they should automatically look back at you for the game to restart or to see what's next. Dogs are incredibly cool like that, and your goal is to spot that moment. Be ready to mark the moment your puppy finishes eating the food and looks at you. Use your verbal marker ('Yes!', 'Good!', or whatever comes naturally) to communicate to your puppy that they made a super choice, and follow up with more food to reinforce that look at you.

Step 3: Repeat!

DOUBLE LEAD

This is a powerful and practical game that you will be able to use a lot in everyday life. It's really important that unclipping your puppy's lead doesn't become a trigger of crazy excitement or a cue for your puppy to bog off into the distance. This game safeguards against that, or allows you to change that picture if it has already been created. With rehearsal and practise, this will completely change the emotion that is associated with that lead being unclipped, and it has super cool results. Your puppy is going to learn that good things happen when the lead comes off and removing it becomes a calm event rather than a high-arousal activity. This game could be a true lifesaver!

For this game you will need your puppy on a collar or harness, and either a double-ended lead or two leads if you don't have a double-clipped one available. We love to be resourceful, so whatever you have, you can make it work. The double-ended lead works a little like a safety net, so you can confidently unclip one end and know your puppy is still secure. Not only does this help them out if they consider making the wrong choice (lead off = run off), it means you can take your game out and about, safe in the knowledge that your puppy is still attached to the other end of the lead until they are ready for both ends to be unclipped at once.

As always, play at home first, not somewhere your puppy might have the option of rehearsing the wrong choices.

Step 1: With your puppy wearing their walking equipment and both clips of your double-ended lead (or both leads)

attached, unclip one of the clips/leads and feed your puppy
with your other hand.

Step 2: Clip the lead back on and feed. That's it! Simple. You
are telling your puppy that unclipping the lead means they
should stay close, and that the lead being clipped back on
is a great deal too. Ultimately, hearing the clip of their lead
becomes a trigger of focus.

Step 3: Once you and your puppy are rocking this, mix it up.
You might unclip one end of the lead and feed, then unclip
the other end and feed – then clip one end of the lead back
and feed again. Regardless of whether your puppy is still
attached by one clip or is totally free to zoom off into the
distance, the choice you want to see them making, again
and again, is to stay close.

LEAD OFF, PARTY ON!

This is a really important and FUN game. So many people let
their dog off their lead and immediately worry about where
their dog is going to go. Will they run away? Will they try to
eat someone's picnic or try and chase a bird that they see in
the distance?

You need to communicate to your puppy the concept that
as soon as the lead comes off, you are the most fun and important thing in the environment and not the stranger's picnic or
that super exciting flappy bird. Cue Lead Off, Party On! The
concept is simple – as soon as the lead comes off, the game
starts and the fun is with you. Don't get stuck thinking the

fun only comes from food or toys. Your puppy is looking for fun experiences – you just need to make sure they find them with you! That is what is ultimately going to trump all those distractions the environment might tempt them with and is going to make you the very best source of fun.

Step 1: Start off by unclipping the lead (you can have a long line or double clip lead if required – whatever you feel happiest and most comfortable using).

Step 2: As soon as the lead has been unclipped, have a party with your puppy! Think of the best and most exciting thing you can play and do that. That might be jumping around, racing, playing tug or chase, or a few rounds of one of the games that you've already learned with us. The only 'rule' is that the game involves fun with you, and gets your puppy immediately engaged and having the best time ever. You want your puppy's world to be about you and the FUN.

Getting the balance right is important here. On lead is fun and rewarding for sure (this is really important so your puppy doesn't learn that going back on lead signals the end of the fun, otherwise you are heading for a battle any time you need to get them back on lead), but off lead, the party really starts! This means your puppy is going to learn they need to keep a pretty close eye on you and be ready for that party. In fact, it's their job and their responsibility to do so.

Make sure you keep the fun and the joy of being on lead too, by topping up your game play on lead. When you eventually get to the stage of letting your puppy off lead, be unpredictable about when the lead comes off and goes back on – we will cover this in more detail in chapter 21. Remember how quick dogs are to pair things and learn predictors. Don't make the mistake of only putting your puppy back on lead at the end of the walk, ending the fun and heading back home.

Don't be rushed

There's often a lot of pressure from friends, family and even other dog walkers to let your puppy off the lead. Don't rush it. Wait until you are confident that your puppy is ready. Spend time building valuable foundations, play the games and know that you *are* going to get there, and it *is* going to happen.

When it comes down to it, off-lead freedom is a privilege and carries a level of responsibility that your puppy needs to show you they are ready for. Once you start letting them off lead, assess what you're seeing. Ideally, you are looking for a balance. Some off-lead time where your puppy gets to be a puppy and have that freedom to explore and sniff is lovely – but that needs to be balanced with value for proximity and working with you, and being secure in the knowledge that, if you call your puppy back, they are going to come, every time.

If you find that your puppy is spending much of their off-lead time having a party for one, way in the distance, that's probably telling you that a little more work is needed instilling value in being close.

Set your puppy up for success to ensure they don't rehearse behaviour that you don't want. Under no circumstances do you want them to learn to ignore you and rehearse playing games of 'keep away'. We're going to talk more about teaching your puppy a recall in the next chapter, but when you're thinking about whether the time is right to let your puppy off lead, consider whether there is any chance they are not going to come back. If so, don't give them the opportunity.

Remember – the value needs to tip in your favour. If the environment becomes more exciting and fun than you, recall will quickly become an issue, loose-lead walking will be more of a challenge, and your puppy's off-lead time may quickly become compromised and limited as you have to restrict them from making all those less appropriate choices – which will lead to frustration for both of you. Get the foundations right and your puppy's off-lead adventures will start off on the right paw.

CHAPTER 21
Total Recall

Having a really reliable recall is being able to call your dog back and knowing with absolute certainty that they are going to come, every time, without question. You want to see their eyes literally sparkle, their energy change and an immediate response when they hear their recall cue.

The ideal scenario is that, as soon as you call, your puppy does a whiplash turn, speeds back to you and comes straight into your proximity. They don't stop 10 metres away or even 5, but actually come right up close. That picture is built, first and foremost, by instilling value in proximity. Proximity is the root and foundation of recall and we explored this in more detail in chapter 11.

A 100 per cent reliable recall is fundamental for stress-free walks and joyful dog ownership and it is another key element to truly being able to let your puppy off their lead with confidence.

Lauren's story: Ping-pong Monty

When I first met Linda and her dog Monty, they were in a place of day-to-day firefighting. Walks were not enjoyable in the slightest, and Linda felt like she was spending a lot of time trying to capture Monty, trying to protect the world from him and trying to contain him, constantly having to call him back. So Monty came to us for a crash course in recall, but despite teaching him a brilliant whistle recall, I couldn't get him to stay close. He was constantly pinging over there, recalling, pinging over there, recalling, and I always had to watch for those moments where I would have to call him back. The light bulb for me was seeing the distance he would go — he was always on the other side of the field or park, right on the perimeter and only just in sight. While his recall was great, he was spending more time away than he ever spent close. I was never getting any of those check-ins I see with my own dogs. There was a perfect recall, yet there wasn't freedom, and it still felt quite stressful. It wasn't recall that was the problem, it was proximity.

The fundamentals of truly reliable recall

There are five key considerations for great recall:

1. Build value in proximity
As we're sure you've realised by now, for a great recall you first need your puppy to feel that there is value in being close.

Ultimately, you're looking for a puppy who wants to hang out with you and stay in that proximity zone. When you're on a walk, you want your puppy to be seeking you out. Recall and proximity go hand in hand, so be sure to invest lots of value into proximity by playing the games that grow this skill.

2. Ditch fetch

If your goal is instilling value in proximity and for coming in close, you don't want to be putting lots of fun and value away from you. We see so many owners whose favourite game is chucking a toy or a ball off into the distance for their puppy to chase, but all that does is teach your puppy that the value is away from you. Rather than hurling that toy off into the distance, reward your puppy by making sure you are part of the picture and that the game is played up close. Don't throw your value away! Let's ditch the idea of fetch and instead create a dog that's actively looking to seek out the fun with you.

3. Keep it varied

As dog owners, we can get a bit limited. It can be easy to fall into the trap of playing the same games with your puppy so that piece of food is delivered to their mouth in exactly the same way each time – and then be surprised when a squirrel gets their interest. There needs to be variety in the experiences you are providing in order to keep your puppy engaged. If you had a friend who told the same story every time you saw them, over and over again, would you want to spend time with them? No, because you already know the story. Nobody wants to be bored. Variety is so important!

Does your reward match up to the excitement and lure of the environment? Whether your puppy has discovered the fun of chasing squirrels or playing with a group of doggy friends, handing them a bit of kibble is just not going to cut it when it comes to a choice between you and those other experiences. When you think of the fun factor involved in chasing a squirrel, it comes from the fact that squirrels are masters of evasion. The appeal for your puppy is in that tail shaking, unpredictable elusiveness that makes the idea of a chase so enticing! Put another way, it's the experience that your puppy is choosing. You need to be more fun than the environment if you want your puppy to see value in coming back when you call them.

You need to be really intentional about how you're delivering that daily food allowance to your puppy, or rewarding them for choosing you. When delivering food rewards, make sure you are providing a fun experience that lights your puppy up. That might be a game of Magic Hand (page 180) or a round of Catch Me If You Can (see page 332). There are multiple ways to deliver one piece of food to keep your dog's interest. If your puppy finds toy play more rewarding, build toys into your reward experiences when your puppy comes in close. There's a whole chapter about building toy play (chapter 5).

4. Coming close doesn't mean going home

Dogs are quick to learn that coming in close means they will be put back on the lead. If you only ever call your puppy back at the end of a walk, you may quickly find they start to ignore their recall or actively avoid coming in close, because this means the end of the fun. This is another really important aspect of your puppy's life in which you're going to want to make sure you are ditching the routine. Play games where your puppy comes in close and the fun continues. Mighty Middle (page 182), FUNder (page 163), Typhoon and Tornado (both page 164) are all great options. Make a point of playing games both on and off lead so your puppy doesn't see the lead as a bad deal. When your puppy does come back to you, don't automatically clip their lead on or end the walk straight away. Mix it up. Pop the lead on, play a game and then unclip it again and carry on. Get your puppy used to being handled without your hands reaching towards them always leading to them being restrained or restricted, so that close proximity doesn't end up being a bad deal. A puppy who learns to play keep away and stays just out of reach can be hugely frustrating! You want to make sure your puppy learns that being near you is not a bad option.

5. Don't overuse it

We see a lot of owners who overuse recall and find that, when their puppy does see a bird or a squirrel in the distance, recall has no effect. Because it's used so much, its power has gone.

If your puppy loves being close and values proximity, you shouldn't need to be constantly recalling them to get them away from something. The ultimate aim is to have taught them the skills and concepts, which you've built through games, to be able to hang out with you and make great choices. The responsibility is on them to ignore distractions in the environment and stick with you, rather than being on you to constantly call them back.

Lauren's story: Unintentional signalling

I once taught a lady whose dog would run away at the end of every walk. This dog stayed close throughout the entire walk except when he somehow knew that the walk was coming to an end. This lady made a point of varying the route, the time of day that she took her dog out and how long they were out for, so she couldn't understand how he always knew that they were approaching the end of the walk. I got her to talk me through what she did leading up to this point, and she described how her husband dropped her off at the beginning of the walk and then when she was ready to come home, she would give him a call to let him know where to pick them up. Dogs are so observant. It was the phone call that her dog had come to learn signalled the end of his walk.

We do so many of these little things without really being aware, but our dogs notice and are very quick to pair our subconscious actions and understand when they predict particular events or outcomes. This can be something as simple as walking with the lead around your neck until you're thinking of ending your walk, at which point you change the position of that lead in readiness for clipping it back on to your dog's harness. Don't make it so predictable. Put your lead over your shoulder and then put it back round your neck again. Call your partner and then carry on the walk, or plan the pick-up point in advance. Ditch the routine on a major scale so your puppy doesn't start to notice minor events that they know mean their walk is coming to an end.

Recall Games

So you are building a foundation of awesome proximity and your puppy is learning that you are the very best source of fun, but how do you go about teaching your puppy to come when you call? Recall games are something you can begin right from the very first day, with your puppy's daily food allowance.

Choose a recall word

Before you begin teaching a recall, it's important to think about what word you are going to use. As owners, we often overuse our puppy's name – so much so that it can eventually become like white noise that they learn to ignore. It can also be a little too easy to use a puppy's name in less positive ways, often without realising ('Argh, Poppy, don't chew that!', 'Poppppppyyyyy, what have you pinched now?'). You can't really change your puppy's name if they learn to start ignoring it when you call because of all those other contexts in which it has been used, and overused. To safeguard against this, instead of using your puppy's name for recall, it's a great idea to pick a word that you only use for recall and pair it with really fun stuff. For example, Tom uses variations of his dogs' names, which he only uses when he's calling them. So Thistle's recall is 'Wiss Wiss' and Lava's is 'La La'. Another option we both love is 'Pup! Pup! Pup!'.

I LOVE MY RECALL NAME

Whatever word or phrase you decide on, your first step is to pair it with awesome rewards so your puppy learns how valuable that word or phrase is. Start with some high-value food (whatever your puppy truly loves) so they quickly learn to associate this recall word with really good things.

Step 1: Set up a simple pattern where you throw a piece of food for your puppy to follow, then make your 'Pup!

Pup! Pup!' noise to get their attention so they come back towards you.

Step 2: Feed them really close to you when they come back.

Step 3: Repeat!

Once your puppy has started to recognise their recall word, you need to add a ton of value by reinforcing every time they hear that special word and respond.

Step 4: Throw another piece of food out for your puppy to chase.

Step 5: Just before they turn back towards you, say their recall cue. You will become an expert at spotting that moment they are about to orient back to you.

Step 6: When they come racing back towards you (hopefully FAST!), reward! It sounds simple, right? Too simple almost. But it really is that easy.

Of course, you don't have to use 'Pup! Pup! Pup!'. Pick whatever comes naturally that can be said in a positive, exciting way (and remember you are going to need to yell this in public!). The value of using something other than your puppy's name is that if your puppy's recall happens to hit a blip further down the line and there is a history of that word being ignored, you can use a brand-new one.

TIP: Only throw out one piece of food at a time. This makes it cleaner and more straightforward for both you and your puppy. Make sure you are using food that is easy for your puppy to find so you keep some momentum to your game and can increase the rate of repetitions. This will help to avoid too much sniffing. Above all, don't nag your puppy to come back to you. Learning is most powerful when your puppy makes the right choice and is rewarded for it.

RESTRAINED RECALLS

Adding a gentle restraint into your recall games with your puppy can really power up that drive and desire to come back, because it introduces an element of frustration as your puppy is momentarily unable to get to you. It's worth being aware that not every puppy enjoys being restrained, so make sure your puppy is comfortable with what you're asking before playing this game – and avoid too much frustration, which will turn the game from a fun one to a punishing one for your puppy. Your puppy's recall needs to be joyful.

This is a game you need two people for – and it's really important that your puppy is comfortable with whoever you ask to restrain them.

Step 1: Have your helper gently restrain your puppy, either by holding on to their harness or with a light hand on their chest, while you move a little way ahead.

Step 2: Call your puppy towards you, just as your helper lets go of the restrain. You should see your puppy power joyfully towards you.

Step 3: Depending on what lights your puppy up, reward that super choice to recall to you with an awesome experience – a food game, some toy play or even just a fun game with you.

CHECK ME OUT CIRCLES

This is a super game that teaches your puppy to keep their focus on you and check in with you regularly, rather than all the responsibility being on you to keep your eyes on your puppy. For great off-lead walks and reliable recall, you want to be sure your puppy is seeking you out, hunting you down and keeping their eyes on you.

You can play both on and off lead (and it's great to practise both). Your choice is likely to depend on where you're playing and how confident you are that your puppy is going to remain focused and engaged with you.

The game is played by walking in a circle. The size of circle determines how hard the game is – smaller circles make it easier for your puppy, while larger circles give them more options to check out other things in the environment rather than you.

Step 1: With your puppy walking beside you (on or off lead), throw a piece of food into the centre of the circle you are walking for your puppy to find.

331

Step 2: Your puppy should bounce right back to you after eating the food. Mark that super choice to check back in, then throw another piece of food into the centre of the circle.

Step 3: Repeat, as you keep walking your circle.

Step 4: Add variety by changing the direction you're walking, widening your circle, mixing up your pace and varying how long you ask for your puppy's focus and attention before sending them into the centre. The aim is for your puppy to be actively seeking you out, even if you continue to send them away into the centre of your circle. Using movement and the opportunity to chase food injects fun into the game, especially for puppies that enjoy movement.

CATCH ME IF YOU CAN

This is a fast and fun one – in fact, it may even be our favourite proximity game. It incorporates unpredictability and variety and really does move you towards having a puppy that wants to be with you and not away from you. It teaches your puppy that proximity is FUN, and seeking you out is the very best deal – which is so important when it comes to off-lead reliability and joyful recall.

For this game, you need some kind of obstacle that you can play around. If you're playing at home, that might be a bin or a table. If you're playing out and about, on a walk or in your garden, you could use a tree, a park bench, a bush – whatever is there. Remember to start off somewhere you know your puppy is going to succeed. You want to be sure they are going to be chasing you, not something else that grabs their attention! Depending on how much value you already have for proximity, playing in a secure area with minimal distractions is going to ensure you get those early wins.

Step 1: Start by throwing one piece of food away from you for your puppy to chase. While your puppy is busy locating that food, move around the other side of the obstacle and wait for them to look up and try and find you. You're looking to see that your puppy really wants to locate you and find that area of reinforcement around you.

Step 2: When they catch you, really, really reward them with food and verbal praise. Go crazy! This is your permission to be a little weird – go on, be NUTS!

Step 3: Build up so that you can send your puppy further away and see that they still want to hunt you down. If you're playing with an older puppy, they can get fast pretty quickly, so you may need to get a bit of a sprint on in order to get away from them and give them a chance to catch you.

TIP: If you prefer, and your puppy is comfortable with this, you can have someone restrain them while you dash away rather than throwing a piece of food out for them to find. You can also play this game with a tug or similar type of toy to give your puppy something to chase and catch. This gives you a great reward opportunity to get your puppy playing with the toy when they catch you.

Make sure you give your puppy lots of easy wins. This will boost their optimism as well as reinforcing the value in hunting you down and seeking you out.

Remember that movement and chase can be highly simulating for some dogs, so you may find that this game kicks the arousal up a little too high. If your puppy is showing signs of over-arousal – maybe nipping, or jumping – adapt the speed and energy to suit. Slow yourself and your puppy down – walk rather than sprint.

This is a super game to incorporate into your recall to make it top-level fun.

Impulse control

Playing games to build impulse control (or self-control) is so often the missing piece of the puzzle for real-life recall success. Life can be super exciting, fast moving and enticing for any dog. Without playing games to teach your puppy to be able to listen, think and respond when they are excited, real-life recalls will always be a challenge.

If your puppy struggles with impulse control, you will more than likely see this in lots of areas of life. Maybe they jump at guests, or have been known to indulge in a spot of counter-surfing, or find it hard to contain their excitement when food is present. Chase struggles (a puppy who chases cars, cyclists, joggers, other dogs, squirrels) are often motivated in part by a lack of impulse control and you could already be seeing indications that your puppy's chase drive is strong. A puppy who lacks impulse control is a dog who will chase the squirrel or the jogger in the park, neither of which is conducive to having a reliable, bombproof recall.

Impulse control is taught and inspired (of course) through games. Boundary games (chapter 9) as well as games like Mouse Game (page 118) and Plant Pot Prison (page 344) are not only awesome for teaching some impulse control around food, you will see the benefits of that learning in other areas too – including your puppy's ability to ignore distractions and come when called.

OK . . . GO!

This game teaches your puppy that if they do a little bit of what you're asking them to do (in this case, show a little impulse control around food), you will reward them. But – and here's the key – the permission to engage with the reward (in this case, eat the food) also comes from you. Once they understand this concept, it can apply to anything and everything.

All you need is your puppy, some tasty food and a bowl (yes – you may have ditched the bowl, but sometimes they still come in useful within the context of a game!).

Step 1: Start off by instilling lots of value in your bowl by dropping pieces of food in for your puppy to eat.

Step 2: Once your puppy values the bowl, apply a gentle restraint (hold your puppy by the collar, harness or puppy line or pop a hand on their chest), place a piece of food in the bowl, say 'OK go', pause, then release your puppy to get the food. Repeat!

Step 3: After a few rounds of building that desire and powering up that drive to the food bowl, you are now going to cover it. Can your puppy show some impulse control and back away? You may need to reward even the tiniest movement away from the bowl in the first instance.. The magic comes from your puppy doing this spontaneously – not from you commanding them to 'leave it!' The second you see that, uncover it, then pause before releasing them to the food with your 'OK go' cue. Can they wait for your cue? If not, go back a level.

Step 5: Now you can start to ask for a little more responsibility from your puppy. When the food in the bowl is uncovered, can they show a little impulse control? If you pause for a second before inviting your puppy to engage with the food, do they wait and listen for the 'OK . . . Go!' cue, even if the temptation to dive right in is really strong? Once your puppy is actively waiting for your verbal cue, you are starting to develop that awesome understanding that permission to interact with fun things comes from you, which is the foundation of real-life impulse control.

Step 6: Now you can start to implement 'OK go' in other parts of life, for example to give permission to go through the door, explore a scent on a walk, chase after their friend. This is a huge concept and we teach it very simply with a bowl and some daily food allowance!

TIP: It's really important to keep building the desire. Go back to easier levels to keep your puppy engaged and make sure you don't always make it harder.

What if your puppy ignores you when you call?

If you take the time to instil value in proximity and inject awesome amounts of fun into your recall so your puppy knows without a doubt that coming back is the very best deal, you should find that their recall is robust even in the face of distractions.

Yet there will inevitably be an occasion when your puppy doesn't come when you call, so knowing how to respond if you find yourself in that situation will mean you handle it in the best way possible.

Firstly, don't panic. If your puppy is momentarily distracted by a good sniff or an irresistible distraction, wait them out and see if they can turn their attention back to you without you nagging. The moment you spot that disengagement, call them back and have a party when they come. Never punish your puppy for not coming back.

Top tips for safeguarding your recall

- Make sure your recall isn't being overused or watered down. Don't call your puppy unless you need them – and when you do, make it a really good deal – every time!
- Observe what your puppy is doing when they aren't employed (when you're not asking them to engage in a game, or do a

particular behaviour). Where is their attention? If they are rehearsing lots of what you don't want, change things up. Rehearsal is powerful, and that applies to things you don't want your puppy practising as well as things you do.

- Ditch the bowl and make sure all that value is going into proximity, fun experiences with you and into games that are going to skill your puppy up for those more testing, distracting environments.

- Remember how much influence other dogs can have on your puppy and make sure those lessons are good ones, not bad ones. If your puppy finds other dogs hugely exciting, don't allow them to spend their off-lead time running with dogs who do notvalue for proximity and recall.

- Scatter feeding in proximity can help keep that zone around you a valuable space, not one to avoid.

- Be careful to make sure your puppy doesn't learn to pair being handled and coming close with always being clipped on lead or having their freedom restricted, otherwise it will quickly end up being a bad deal.

- Don't test it too hard or too often. Add value to your recall and leave the testing for when you need it.

- If you find your puppy is showing any level of disregard for your recall, the very best thing you can do is pop them back on lead while you top up their skills. Remember that off-lead freedom is a privilege that your puppy should only be given when they can show they have the skills to make the right choices consistently when given that extra level of responsibility.

The one question you shouldn't be asking yourself

If you are worrying about recall and you have to ask yourself the question, 'I wonder what would happen if I let my puppy off the lead right now?' then *don't do it*! If you are asking that question, then you already know the answer. Don't rush to put your puppy in the big wide world and risk them making poor choices. Once your puppy has practised running off into the distance and interacting with everyone and everything, it is going to be a lot harder rebuilding your recall and persuading them that you are the best deal than if that option was never there.

Some people say that great abs are made in the kitchen. Well, we say great recall is made at home by growing proximity and calmness first.

CHAPTER 22
'That's None of Your Business'

As a dog owner, you want your puppy to learn to focus on you, no matter what the world might be distracting them with – not because they have to, but because they want to. Part of this is about inspiring value in proximity. As you discovered in chapter 11, a puppy who learns to value hanging out close will find it easier to tune out distractions and find the fun with you.

Yet distractions are a part of life, and so teaching your puppy to ignore and work around them is going to be such an important thing for them to learn.

The skill your puppy needs in order to understand that distractions and novelty are none of their business is called disengagement. It helps your dog notice a distraction, or something new and novel in the environment, and continue to move past it without feeling the need to get involved. True disengagement is your puppy's ability to put something out of their mind completely and move on.

The advantages of disengagement are:

- Off-lead freedom.
- Awesome recall.
- Great choices in all situations.

- Ability to work around distractions.
- Appropriate greetings with other dogs.
- Great focus on you.
- An understanding that certain things are 'none of their business'.

Working on your puppy's ability to disengage from things that are both exciting and worrying will set them up for the very best success, and mean they can have much more freedom to make appropriate choices, in spite of temptations and distractions, as they grow up.

Start as you mean to go on

Teaching your puppy the skill of disengagement right from the start can avoid so many struggles.

Puppies are adorable and the temptation is to let them meet every person who thinks they're cute (spoiler: that will be a lot!). We talked in chapter 2 about being your puppy's best advocate. However, if you let your puppy interact with everybody and everything, ultimately you are teaching them that everything in life is their business, which can lead to issues further down the line. You might let your puppy off the lead and discover they want to go and visit every single person in the park. That might seem OK while they're tiny, but it will become less appropriate as they get older and bigger and suddenly have the potential to knock people over or scare them.

They might want to visit every dog, but as you already know from chapter 17, allowing your puppy to meet and greet every other dog you come across runs the risk of putting them in challenging situations. If you've got a puppy that can't disengage, you're unlikely to be able to recall them when they see a squirrel they want to chase, or a bird, or another dog. Suddenly, you find they are running off into the distance.

Why it's important as your puppy gets older

Disengagement tends to become much more of an issue when your puppy reaches 12–16 weeks of age, because they become much more neurologically developed. Their eyesight is fully developed now, so they notice and understand a lot more. They are aware of the world around them and, depending on their natural outlook, may already think the world is full of fun opportunities they want to get involved in. If your puppy is a little more cautious by nature, they will already be aware of things they find scary.

Whether your puppy is beginning to feel confident enough to go and get involved with everything, or is finding novelty something to worry about, this is when you need them to see the value in leaving things alone.

Disengagement is almost a safety net. If your puppy gets really excited about something because you've not grown enough calmness or they become really scared of something because you've not grown enough optimism, disengagement will allow them to move away.

For example, Tom is scared of clowns, but if he sees a clown he doesn't run up to it and punch it in the face. Instead, he minds his own business and gives that clown a wide berth! You want to teach your puppy to do the same.

The root of many behavioural struggles

The most common weakness that we see in behaviour consults is a lack of disengagement. Dogs who struggle with appropriate interactions often have a disengagement struggle. You'll remember that disengagement is the skill required to move from one step of that greeting chain to the next. We delve more into interacting with other dogs in chapter 17.

A dog who doesn't have the skills to disengage from things they find worrying or scary can end up putting themselves in situations they really don't want to be in and find themselves unable to leave again. This can have pretty disastrous consequences. A dog who is fearful of people but who lacks the skill of disengagement might approach a person they are worried about, find themselves 'stuck' and then bite when that person reasonably assumes they wanted to be stroked.

A lack of disengagement is often the culprit for chase struggles because the dog can't disengage from the thing that they're chasing. It can also be the root of separation struggles because a dog is unable to disengage from their owner as they leave the house, and so begins to panic and becomes very distressed at the prospect of their owner going out of sight. Dogs who are unable to ignore other people's picnics they come across on walks lack disengagement too!

Because disengagement is the root of so many struggles, it's such a key thing to work on with your puppy.

How do you teach your puppy disengagement?

By playing games, of course! The aim is to play games that teach your puppy that there's a lot of value in leaving things – and that by leaving things, they get something better.

A good starting point is Mouse Game, which we've already practised in chapter 8 (see page 118). Many of the games we introduced you to in chapter 20 also power up your puppy's disengagement skills and can be applied to any and every distraction, not just other dogs. The following games are going to further inspire and teach this concept.

PLANT POT PRISON

Plant Pot Prison helps your puppy understand that sometimes the best deal comes from moving away from something they really want.

The important thing about this game is to make sure your puppy really wants whatever is under the plant pot, so use something super yummy. If your puppy doesn't really want the food underneath, impulse control will be easy. Having a plant pot (or other object) with a hole in the bottom can help because the smell will waft through the hole and tantalise your puppy's sensitive nose. You can hide a toy underneath instead to add variety, or if your puppy gets more excited about toys than food.

Don't always make it hard either. The idea is to teach your puppy skills that they are going to use in real life – not tricks that look fancy. The key is to keep going back to the early levels and make sure you keep building your puppy's desire to get that reward.

Consider your choice of plant pot for this game. Some puppies will find their own game in running off with a plastic pot, so you may need to set yourself and your puppy up for success with something that can't be picked up.

Step 1: Using a plant pot (mug, cone, jug – be flexible and use whatever you have), pop a piece of food under it, (hold the pot up and don't cover the food at this stage) and encourage your puppy to 'get it'.

Step 2: Repeat this stage until your puppy has a real desire to get the food.

Step 3: Now start fully covering the food with your plant pot, wait until your puppy shows a little bit of disengagement and impulse control (they might back off, sit, lie down, look away), then uncover the food and invite them to 'get it'.

Step 4: There are many layers you can add to this game to work on that skill of disengagement and also teach your puppy to be able to control their impulses, which will come hand in hand with disengagement when it comes to ignoring exciting distractions. Can your puppy move away from the plant pot with you, before you race them back to it and uncover their food reward? Can they do something while the food is uncovered before being invited to 'get it'? If your puppy has learned to sit, or to do a down, can they do that when you ask without catching you out and stealing the food?

DISENGAGEMENT PATTERN

This is a great game to play to build your puppy's ability to disengage from distractions. In real life, that could be a family having a picnic, another dog or a leaf! The predictable pattern of this game helps your puppy understand there is more value in moving away from things they find exciting or worrying than in checking them out, because each time your puppy moves away from the distraction you have set up, you add movement away from it and spell out very clearly where the value is (with you!). Think about where you're playing too – don't start out in an environment with too many other distractions or things that could grab your puppy's attention.

Choose a suitable distraction. This will depend on your puppy. You want to use something they are interested in but not something that is so exciting they are going to struggle to leave it alone. This might be a toy, or some low-value food, or even a person. When you're first playing this game, keep your puppy on a lead or long line.

Step 1: Place one piece of food towards the distraction. Your puppy should go towards the distraction to find that piece of food, and then look back to you to see if you've got any more on offer.

Step 2: The moment they check back in with you, start moving away so they have to follow you. When they catch up, feed, feed, feed (give them several pieces of food). This tells your puppy very clearly that the choice to disengage is the best deal. By marking the moment they turn to look at you and giving them a jackpot reward (lots of pieces of food), your puppy learns that there is more value in moving away from the distraction than in checking it out.

Step 3: Repeat. The more repetitions you do, the faster your puppy should disengage from the distraction. If you find they're struggling, help them out to begin with. Make the distraction less distracting, or play a little further away from it. You can also have your puppy on a trailing puppy line to help guide their choices.

Step 4: To progress from this level, you can make the distraction gradually more exciting, until you can take it out and about and play with real-life distractions that you come across on a walk or in the park. Once your puppy has a clear understanding of the game and is playing like a pro, you will find there are situations where you can use it to give them a little extra responsibility for making that great choice to disengage from something they might previously have wanted to investigate.

If you have a particularly 'sniffy' puppy, think about how you deliver those pieces of food. Instead of feeding your puppy on the floor when they disengage from the distraction, you could throw the food to keep their nose off the ground, or have a fun game of Magic Hand if your puppy has mastered the art of catching (see page 180).

WALKING ON SUNSHINE

As well as being a super game to add to your repertoire for encouraging loose-lead walking, Walking on Sunshine is a great one to play to help your puppy learn to disengage from exciting distractions up ahead, and focus on you instead.

To play, you need your puppy on a lead and two food bowls, placed a short distance from each other on the floor.

Step 1: Start with nothing in the bowls. Walk slowly around the bowls, looking for any moment of upward focus. As soon as your puppy offers that focus and control, race with them to the nearest bowl and drop a piece of food in for them to eat.

Step 2: Carry on walking around the two bowls and marking moments of focus on you by rewarding your puppy with food dropped into the nearest bowl. Once your puppy associates the bowls with food, they might find it harder not to pull towards them, so you're really starting to test their disengagement skills.

Step 3: Next try dropping food into one or both bowls before you start walking. Can your puppy walk calmly towards or past the bowl even when they know something yummy is inside? If they do, race them to the bowl for their reward.

How DMT helps teach disengagement

In chapter 10 we looked at DMT (Distraction, Mark, Treat). DMT is a really valuable game for teaching your puppy to be optimistic about novelty, because you are pairing new and unexpected events with a positive outcome.

It's also a game that you can use to build your puppy's skill of disengagement. By pairing novelty with a calm marker and a calm, positive reward, DMT helps your puppy learn to ignore distractions rather than engage with them.

We previously introduced you to the basic format of DMT, but there are many levels that we'll now explore. The most important thing to understand about these different levels is that your puppy will make it clear when they are ready to go to the next level. Be aware that your puppy may move up and down between the levels, depending on how tricky the distraction is, on their level of arousal (see chapter 23 for more on this) and on how full their bucket is.

Level one
At this level, you notice the distraction and you mark ('Niiiiice' or the marker word of your choice) and reward, no matter what your puppy is doing. Your puppy might be barking or whining or pulling towards it. They might be rooted to the spot, unable to take their attention away from it. Mark and treat anyway. If they're unable to take food, that's just information. Your puppy is finding it too hard to disengage from the distraction.

It might feel like you're rewarding your puppy for barking at something they find scary or exciting, but in that moment your puppy's brain doesn't have the skills to do anything else. Your job is to change your puppy's emotional response to distractions and teach them that ignoring them is the very best option.

If you do end up in a situation where your puppy is finding a distraction too challenging (either because it's way too exciting to ignore or way too scary), don't let them continue rehearsing that reaction. Get your puppy out of that situation by picking them up or leading them off to somewhere they feel better. The T in your DMT doesn't have to be a food reward. For your puppy, the most positive outcome in some situations might be distance from the thing they were reacting to. Remember that disengagement is a skill that needs to be practised – and sometimes dogs can't remove themselves from situations they aren't comfortable with.

Level two

At level two, your puppy will notice the distraction, but rather than pulling towards it or yapping excitedly and spinning at the end of the lead, they don't react. They may still be struggling to remove their attention from it, but the emotion it has triggered is not so high that it is driving your puppy's behaviour. As with level one, mark and treat.

Level three

At level three, your puppy hears your marker word and looks back to you. At this level, your puppy is able to hear and respond to you. They will probably be more receptive to taking food. They acknowledge the distraction, but when they hear your marker, they know now that distractions mean a yummy treat. This level is where you start to feel like you and your puppy have some teamwork going on.

Level four

This is where it gets exciting. Your puppy looks at the distraction and then looks at you before you have even said your marker word. Woohoo! Mark and treat. At this point, you see that your puppy is really starting to disengage from distractions. They are still aware of them, but they are no longer quite so important.

Level five

When your puppy reaches level five, they don't acknowledge the distraction at all. They are aware of it, but all those layers mean they immediately think, 'That's none of my business. I'm not worried about it!' Your puppy has perfected the art of disengaging from distractions and moving on. Even at level five, you should still mark that win and follow up with food.

It is worth remembering that the level your puppy is at on one day may not be the level they are at on another. There may be a day where your puppy's bucket is fuller than normal and it takes a little less to trigger a reaction. That's OK. Keep topping up the optimism and building their skills of disengagement, and you will have more and more days where your puppy is able to disengage from distractions that previously worried them or got them fizzy with excitement.

Don't just pick the 'villains'

One really important thing to remember about DMT is that you need to use it for all distractions, not just things you know your puppy will react to, or struggle to ignore. If you can teach your puppy to tune out all those small events and easier distractions that are happening every day, they will have much less paying into their bucket on a day-to-day basis. This will help them have the capacity to deal much better with the 'villains' (the really exciting or really scary things) when they do happen.

Making sure you DMT distractions (noises, people, other dogs) your puppy isn't all that interested in also ensures that your marker doesn't accidentally become a trigger for your puppy – a signal that something has appeared that they need to worry about.

Work on all these games and make sure your puppy isn't put into situations they find too challenging before they understand the value of disengagement, and you'll be creating a super cool pup who can tune out distractions and focus on you. Your puppy seeing value in leaving things alone is the secret to having a dog that you can go through life with, that can stay safe and is enjoyable to be around.

CHAPTER 23
Your Puppy's Dimmer Switch

In the same way that not every puppy naturally understands or is able to choose calmness, not all puppies come knowing how to access a level of energy that is appropriate to different events that might happen over the course of a day. We refer to this as arousal.

Whenever something happens that your puppy considers to be important or interesting, their arousal increases. Ideally, when that event is pretty small and insignificant, it should result in a small increase in arousal – and a small response. When that event is bigger and more significant, you should expect to see a bigger increase in arousal – and a bigger response.

If you walk into a room, it would be entirely reasonable for your puppy to give you a sleepy glance or a gentle thump of their tail while remaining calmly on their bed. If you dropped a pen on the floor, you would expect your puppy to notice, but otherwise that really shouldn't be a big deal. It really wouldn't be appropriate for your puppy to leap off their bed and do zoomies around your living room. That reaction would be a little over the top. Even a knock on the door shouldn't trigger all that much of a reaction. By contrast, if a firework went off close to your puppy, you would expect a big response. You'd want your puppy to react, and to get themselves out of danger.

The dimmer switch

As well as those boxes inside your puppy's brain that contain all the behaviours they might select when experiencing excitement, fear or frustration, there is also a part of your puppy's brain that has the job of setting their level of arousal correctly for different situations. However, in some puppies their dial is either on or off and they don't have the little gradations in between those two extremes. They are either on (full of energy, game on, go go go – or sometimes full of reactivity) or they are off (crashed out, snoozing).

These are the puppies who typically flip between chaos and calmness and seem to have nothing in between. If you've ever known a dog who can be snoozing soundly until a tiny sound or movement causes them to leap from their comfy spot, barking and zooming around the house in a way that seems entirely disproportionate to the event that has triggered that reaction, that dog is is lacking a dimmer switch!

It can be common for puppies to arrive without a dimmer switch. This is often established in those early weeks while they are part of a litter. Depending on the environment those puppies were raised in, they may have had lots of opportunities to learn to respond to events (feeding time, play time) and had littermates doing the same. They quickly learn from each other, and may have spent much of those first weeks of life either asleep or reacting to those events that they have learned are significant. It's really important to help your puppy discover all the middle levels in between those two extremes.

Why does my puppy need a dimmer switch?

Not every activity your puppy is going to be doing needs them to be operating at full throttle – and in fact, the more your puppy gets to practise flip-flopping between full on and zonked out, the more polarised those extremes will become. If your puppy only ever goes from calm crate time to full-on high-energy play, those extremes are going to be rehearsed and reinforced.

If you have a puppy who finds the whole of life exciting (a leaf moved – party on!), it's going to be particularly important for them to learn that there are levels of energy (arousal) that exist between full-on disco and asleep.

The more they get to rehearse that on-off response to events, the less chance they will have of accessing the more appropriate energy levels they might need for walking calmly on lead, or playing a game without tipping into over-arousal and bucket over-flow. It can affect their relationships with people and other dogs. Imagine having a conversation with someone who's either asleep or swinging from the chandeliers. The conversation isn't going to go well in either case.

Life without a dimmer switch is stressful and exhausting for a puppy.

Why is arousal so significant?

Every behaviour struggle you could encounter as your puppy grows up – whether that's barking, lunging, pulling on lead, noise reactivity or chasing – is going to be impacted by their state of arousal. Whenever your puppy's arousal level is not correctly matched to the situation they find themselves in, their behaviour choices are less appropriate.

If your puppy tends towards higher levels of arousal, they can become increasingly reactive to the environment. Helping them learn to manage and control their arousal in different environments will keep their stress bucket as empty as possible and allow them to live a happy, healthy life in which their interactions with the world are entirely appropriate.

Your puppy's arousal level will influence:

- Their ability to recall when other dogs or distractions are present.
- Their ability to have appropriate interactions with other dogs.
- Their vigilance to sounds and events in the environment.
- Their ability to greet you calmly and politely when you come home from work.
- Their response when something worrying or ambiguous happens.

The skill that influences how easy it is for a dog to go from high arousal to low arousal, back to high arousal, and then to low arousal again – and for their bucket to empty – is called arousal up, arousal down.

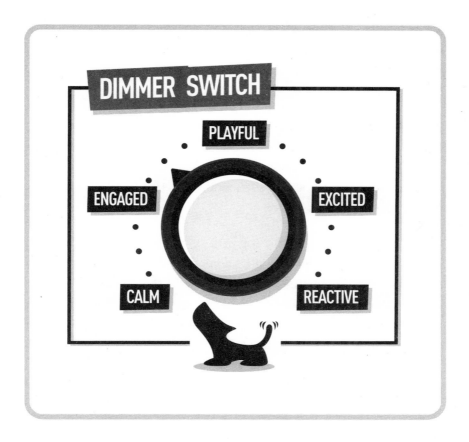

When thinking about those increments of arousal that sit between calmness and craziness, it can help to split the dial on that dimmer switch into four ranges.

0–25 range – At the bottom of the dial is low arousal – what you might think of as calmness. Every dog should have a foundation of calmness. If your puppy is calm, the behaviour choices they make – as well as their emotional state – are all appropriate.

357

25–50 range – At this level, your puppy is more alert and engaged. This might be a nice, calm, loose-lead walk or a gentle mooch around the garden.

50–75 range – In this range, arousal is much higher. For many puppies, this might be the range of playing games. For older dogs, this is the level of arousal they might exist in while running an agility course or doing other high-energy activities. Every dog is different when it comes to their ability to think and perform in higher levels of arousal.

75–99 range – This is the top end of the arousal scale. If your puppy currently acts like a light switch and flips from snoozing to barking at people passing the window or to the sound of a knock on the door, you may already be very familiar with this range on their arousal dial. At this level, the choices a dog makes are likely to be less appropriate and their ability to listen and respond to cues may be compromised.

100 – When they reach this level, they have tipped into reactivity and over-arousal. This is the point of bucket overflow and unde-sirable behaviour.

Questions to ask yourself
Think about a typical day and consider what percentage of the day your puppy spends in each of the ranges. What do the different arousal levels look like for your puppy? What behaviour do you see when they're in each range? This will be different for every dog. Are there certain events – either things you do or things that happen – that trigger particular levels of arousal in your puppy?

> ## Signs that your puppy might not have a dimmer switch
>
> - Energy levels that switch from zero to one hundred.
> - A very small window to work with your puppy before they get overexcited. You might start playing a game and they quickly get overstimulated and move to barking, mouthing or biting you and generally not listening.
> - Reactions that aren't really proportionate or appropriate to the thing that has triggered them.

Four strategies to find your puppy's dimmer switch

Repetition is the mother of skill when it comes to growing a dimmer switch. The more your puppy rehearses those levels in between on and off, the more efficient their dimmer switch will become. The main way to grow your puppy's dimmer switch is by giving their brain the opportunity to learn at different levels.

Strategy one: lead walking and pace changes

You can teach your puppy to transition more seamlessly between lower and higher levels of energy and arousal by something as simple as the way they move. Energy and movement creates and perpetuates arousal.

Think about your own energy. If you're feeling sluggish and sleepy, getting yourself moving will wake you up and help you feel more energised. If you've ever done a sprint, you will be familiar

359

with how a brief session of quick movement can get your energy up. Exercise does the same.

Use this knowledge to help your puppy grow a dimmer switch. Once you and your puppy are heading out for walks (even if it's just into the garden), try to incorporate changes of pace into your sessions. So you might walk quickly for a few seconds and then slow down a little. You are looking for your puppy to match your pace. As well as testing whether your puppy values proximity (do they mirror and match your pace in order to stay close?), this will gradually flex that skill of moving up and down through different levels of arousal.

Your puppy will have to learn to adjust their dimmer switch in line with how fast or slow you are walking. This variety in pace and speed should become part of your day-to-day walks.

Strategy two: food

Think about the way you deliver your puppy's food and the experience that you create with it. Remember that your energy affects your puppy's energy, so if you want to decrease arousal, keep your voice and your movements low, slow and calm. If you want your puppy to be working at the lower levels of arousal, try kneeling down and putting your puppy's food calmly in front of them, or bring it slowly towards their mouth, only letting them take it when they are able to be calm and controlled.

If you want to inject a little more energy and bring your puppy's arousal up a notch, delivering the food with more animation will achieve that. Rolling it, flicking it or throwing it for your puppy to chase will all add energy because you are adding animation and creating movement. Vary up and down the different levels of animation and arousal each time you play, so your puppy is practising going up and down and flexing that dimmer switch.

PAINT THE TOWN RED

This is a fantastic food-follow game that will help boost your puppy's focus and fun. Play it at different speeds to help grow that dimmer switch.

Step 1: With the food in the palm of one hand, move your hand from side to side. Imagine you are holding a paint brush and do smooth, horizontal strokes. Make sure your puppy's nose is right on the food so you keep them connected to your hand as you move it backwards and forwards.

Step 2: When they have followed your hand for a couple of strokes, release the piece of food from your hand.

Step 3: Reload with another piece of food and play again. Vary the speed of your painting motion so your puppy is changing their pace to keep their nose on the food reward in your hand.

Keep your hand at your puppy's head height so they can comfortably follow your painting motion. You don't want your puppy to have to reach their head up for the food.

TIP: If you're playing games with food, the choice of food is likely to have an impact on your puppy's level of arousal too. High-value food that your puppy LOVES will probably make them more excited than something a little lower in value.

Strategy three: vary your games

You can help your puppy cultivate a dimmer switch within your game sessions too. Whenever you and your puppy play games, alternate between games that are exciting (arousal up) and ones that are a little calmer (arousal down) so your puppy learns to regulate themselves and transition between the different energy levels required for those different games.

Play a few repetitions of a game that involves faster movement (games that involve chasing food like FUNder are great for this), followed by some slower movement games. Even varying how far and how fast you throw food while playing the same game can achieve this. You might do a little bit of Catch Me If You Can (page 332), then you might move to do Mouse Game (page 118) and see if your puppy can bring their energy levels down to be able to win at that game. Think about how much energy you inject into the games you choose, too, in order to get the picture you want – and when deciding what games to play, always work with what you're seeing. The aim is to gently increase and decrease arousal and help your puppy access those middle levels they might currently be missing – not to go from crazy chaos to complete calmness. Do that, and you will actually make their dimmer switch more efficient!

Think about the pace and energy you inject into a game – most games can be tweaked and adjusted to create different levels of arousal in your puppy.

TIP: Use the boundary

Boundary games are really useful for teaching your puppy the dimmer switch skill of arousal up, arousal down. When your puppy is on the boundary, the focus is on being calm. Use that between short sessions of higher energy play, where you call them off the boundary for a short game (chasing food, a gentle game of tug) before hopping them back on the boundary and bringing that energy back down with some calm feeding. Again, your aim is not to go from calm to crazy – gentle increases and decreases in energy are the way to hone that skill and develop that really efficient dimmer switch. To begin with, it might be enough to get your puppy moving gently and then see if they are able to transition to calmness on a boundary, with some Aeroplane Game or Mouse Game to help lower the arousal.

Strategy four: massage

Believe it or not, you can actually teach a dog a dimmer switch through massage. This is a great way to get puppies used to coping with different levels of arousal – the middle ground between zero and a hundred.

At first, massage your puppy with long, calm, slow strokes in the direction of their fur. Do this for a few minutes – they should find this very relaxing. Then switch to stroking them against the direction of their fur or change from slow strokes to more energetic rubs or pats. Just by changing the direction and energy, you are going to cause an increase in arousal. Put a hand softly on your puppy's harness if they're struggling to regulate themselves or they are getting too jumpy and excitable. Alternate massaging your puppy in both directions – with and against their fur.

Depending on how stimulating your puppy finds touch, you may find even gentle stroking sends them into a wriggly excitable bundle of energy. The more you get to know your puppy, the better you will be at recognising what kicks their arousal up – and the more you'll be able to adapt your games and strategies to get the picture you're looking for.

Variety is the key

As well as being intentional about growing a dimmer switch within your training sessions and when you play games, try and incorporate differences in energy levels throughout your puppy's day too. Make sure each day is a mix of doing calm activities and medium-arousal activities as well as more exciting ones. If you were to imagine your puppy's day like an ECG, you want to see gentle peaks and troughs of arousal over the course of the day.

Calmer parts of your puppy's day that aren't spent sleeping are likely to include things such as long-lasting chews, boundary games and non-event car journeys. Intersperse those with short sessions of games, walks or trips out and about, depending on what your puppy is able to cope with (always thinking about their bucket). Aim for the activities you do over the course of a day to create different levels of arousal in your puppy.

NOSE TARGET

This is a great 'arousal down' behaviour that is also brilliant for teaching your puppy to value proximity and focus.

Step 1: With your puppy's attention on you, hold your hand out to the side at your puppy's eye level, perhaps 2–3 inches away from their nose, palm facing your puppy. You are looking for your puppy to move towards your hand and touch your palm with their nose (don't nose bop your puppy – you need them to offer the behaviour). Initially, your puppy might just look at your hand or take a step towards it. Whatever interaction they offer, give your verbal marker ('Yes', 'Nice', 'Wow', 'Good') and use your free hand to feed your puppy by popping a piece of food in the open palm of the hand you were asking them to target.

Step 2: Now put your hand behind your back before presenting it again for your puppy to have another go.

Step 3: Repeat this until your puppy gets the idea and is touching their nose to your palm each time. Reward when they do, so they begin to understand the rules of the game. Moving your hand away and popping it behind your back between repetitions makes sure your puppy doesn't learn to ignore it. Your hand becomes a cue to your puppy to practise the behaviour.

Step 4: Once your puppy understands what you are looking for and is touching their nose to your hand, you can make it a little tougher by moving your hand further back. Can they still push their nose into your hand?

Step 5: Take it up a level by holding your hand at different heights and different angles. Be careful not to bring your hand towards your puppy. You want to see them seeking out your hand with their nose. Try really hard to deliver the food into that hand while your puppy's nose is still touching your palm. You want your puppy to understand that the value comes to them. This will help your puppy figure out that the reward is for touching your palm with their nose, and will mean you can add duration (teach your puppy to keep their nose there for longer) by gradually adding more of a pause before marking and rewarding.

Games medley: Developing a dimmer switch

Think about the top ten games you play with your puppy. We've introduced you to lots of games already. Your puppy might also enjoy some toy play or a gentle game of tug. Each one of those games is going to create a certain level of arousal and excitement in your puppy.

Write your games in a list, and next to each one write a number from 10 to 100 that corresponds with the level of arousal that game creates. This will very much depend on your puppy's personality and the current shape of their brain, and is an exercise you will find easier the more you play and the better you get at identifying how excited (and potentially how close to being overexcited) your puppy is. For example, Magic Hand might create an arousal level of 50, whereas tug kicks your puppy right up to arousal level 100.

Aim for a game that hits each level between 10 and 100 (one game for level 10, one game for level 20 and so on). You're then going to incorporate a mix of these games each time you play with your puppy, so they are learning to transition between different levels.

Mixing up the length of your sessions will be important here too. You might play a really short game of whatever your puppy finds super exciting (often games involving toys, or lots of movement) and a slightly longer game of something slightly calmer. At no point do you want your puppy to tip into over-arousal – that headspace where they can't think, can't hear you and resort to the behaviours you tend to see in moments of bucket overflow.

The witching hour

There is a certain time of day, typically around 6–7 p.m., when your puppy enters what we like to call 'the witching hour'. This is the time of day they might start to steal things, pester you, do zoomies, hump things and generally get a little bit naughty.

Why does this evening witching hour happen?

Perhaps the day has been quite relaxed for your puppy and not much has happened. Then all of a sudden, the family comes home. Maybe you finish work or children come home from school and suddenly there's a lot of activity and energy. There is noise and movement and people. Early evenings, when you finish work, might also be the time when you usually play with your puppy, or do a training session.

As we already know, dogs are creatures of efficiency. Not only do

367

they predict events, they increase their energy levels in anticipation of those events. If you predictably take your puppy for a walk at the same time every day, or do a fun play session at the same time every evening, guess what? Leading up to that time, your puppy's arousal and energy levels will increase.

Your puppy is gearing up for the energy they need to play with you, interact with you and be trained by you.

This becomes a challenge if you get home from work or come home after a particularly busy day and just want to sit down and relax. Because of that predictable routine, your puppy has got their energy ramped up and their arousal has increased, ready for this interaction they are anticipating. If not channelled into a focused activity, that excess energy might turn into your puppy doing zoomies or barking or pawing at you or stealing things. This becomes self-fulfilling. You didn't bring the disco so your puppy has created it instead. This pattern carries on and becomes more established as the days go on.

What can you do about it?

The first thing you need to do is ditch the routine. Get rid of the predictable events that you have with your puppy throughout the day. Mix up what you do and the time that you do it.

New puppy owners are often told that it is important to be consistent and have a routine in order to have a well-behaved dog, but we believe the opposite. Inconsistency creates a well-behaved dog, because it avoids this prediction, this anticipation and this constant level of arousal up. Some days you might not have the time or the energy to follow the usual rhythm, but your puppy does. It's actually pretty stressful for them to have a routine.

The second step to combating this witching hour is to swap times of the day where these exciting activities have happened in the past for calmness. This might be a great time to give them a long-lasting chew or a lick mat, or to do a calm session of boundary games. Can they settle on their bed and be rewarded for chilling out and relaxing?

The first time you try this, your puppy is going to object. They may be pretty insistent that it is party time. Persevere, and over time you will be able to move them more and more towards calmness. Your aim is to replace these spikes in arousal (the witching hour) with something calmer.

Think of zoomies or the witching hour as your puppy's energy level and rhythm being totally incompatible with where your energy level is at the time. The worst thing you can do is become frustrated and angry. That's only going to reinforce this rhythm and create conflict. Ditch the routine, swap in calmness and the witching hour will disappear.

CHAPTER 24

Troubleshooting Common Puppy Problems

You are coming to the end of this book and you have absolutely rocked this! You have ditched the bowl, ditched the routine and have been learning and having fun through games. Your puppy is cool, calm, optimistic and wants to be close to you. You feel as though you're winning at life. And then . . . BAM! Perhaps your once well-behaved puppy has suddenly started to question the deal? Maybe they have started pulling on lead and reacting to other dogs on walks, causing havoc in your garden, terrorising other pets in the house or they've stopped being motivated by their daily food allowance. You might be left wondering what the heck has happened!

When your puppy first came home with you, they didn't know what a good deal or a bad deal was. Their eyesight wasn't fully developed and everything in the world was new to them. You could feed them a piece of kibble and they would more than likely think it was AMAZING. Now they're a little older, their eyesight has developed and they have become more aware of the world around them. They've started to realise that actually it *is* fun to chase that squirrel or run off to the other side of the park and snaffle that half-eaten hamburger. Suddenly, offering them a boring old piece of kibble is no longer a good deal.

Many owners find that at around 3 to 6 months, their puppy starts to have a few 'blips'. You might describe them as being 'into everything'. This is also a time when you might start to take your eye off the ball a little. Your puppy is older, they're toilet trained and they fit into your life a little more seamlessly, and so there is a tendency to think that your training is 'done'. Your puppy is bigger and more adaptable, so perhaps you start taking them to more places without a second thought – but going to more places can equally be more testing and bucket filling for your puppy.

If you're experiencing behaviour struggles, don't panic!

It's common that as your puppy gets older, different challenges will pop up along the way. Remember, everything is changeable. When things go wrong, it's also a reminder to you as an owner that your training is never 'done' and your puppy is still learning. It's a good time to revisit the earlier chapters of this book and refresh some of the key concepts. Your puppy is discovering the fun of the world, so you have to remind them of your fun. YOU are the good deal.

Here are some common puppy problems that might start to emerge as your puppy grows and some simple strategies to solve them.

Common Puppy Struggles

1. Help! My puppy's ignoring their recall!

Has your puppy's recall become a little less instant? Perhaps they have started looking at you to assess if you've got something good on offer, before sauntering back slowly, coming most of the way back before zooming off again, or even deciding not to come back at all. Your puppy has discovered the value of things in the environment. They know it's fun to chase that squirrel or go and say hello to another dog, so as an owner you have to top up your value. You have to remind your puppy how much fun you can be.

Strategies for success

- For a 3-week period, make sure that you only call your puppy back if you can give them a really good deal. Perhaps you play their favourite game when you recall them, get them chasing you or chasing their food. Be inventive and have fun with your puppy. Reward them for coming back, either with food or a toy or another game. Think about what you do on their return to make it the best deal. Don't just call them back and clip their lead on. Start to top up their bank of good deals so they actively want to come back to YOU.
- Limit rehearsal of what you don't want. This might mean that for a few weeks your puppy goes back on a lead so they don't have the opportunity to practise ignoring you or choosing distractions over coming back when called. If they're showing they are responsive to you on a lead then

move to a long line, where they have a little more responsibility but you still have that safety net of being able to direct their choices if necessary. If your puppy is missing some of the skills for that level of freedom, the very best thing you can do is manage the situation while you top up those skills.

- Focus on proximity. Revisit chapter 11 and put the majority of your puppy's daily food allowance into playing games that encourage your puppy to see value in being close to you, such as Proximity Zone and Proximity Vortex (pages 160 and 162).

- As your puppy becomes more responsive with their recall, reinforce the idea that if they come back then they will get a good deal. Call them into Mighty Middle (page 182) and let them go again. Or play some FUNder (page 163) so they're reminded that if they come back, they get to go again.

- Change your recall word. In chapter 21 we talked about using 'Pup! Pup! Pup!' or another word to recall your puppy, rather than using their own name. If they have learned to ignore their recall word, then choose a different one and build the value for that word using exactly the same steps you used before. Starting afresh and reinforcing the value in coming back is way better than trying to rebuild value in a word your puppy has learned to ignore. When teaching your new recall cue, make it really clear to your puppy that if they come back, they get an amazing reward.

2. Help! My puppy is becoming reactive!

Maybe you've noticed that your puppy is suddenly becoming reactive to the world. Perhaps walks have become a nightmare as your puppy is barking and lunging at things they previously ignored, or maybe your puppy has started to become unpredictable around other dogs or people.

Strategies for success

- If you've got a reactivity struggle then 80 per cent of your puppy's daily food allowance needs to be focused on DMT, optimism and calmness games.
- Calmness conquers all! A calm puppy is not going to be barking, lunging or reacting. Make sure you are not doing things with your puppy on walks that are getting them overexcited. Too many high-energy chase games or overly stimulating environments can quickly fill your puppy's bucket and create the anticipation that means walks lead to over-arousal.
- If you find you're on a walk and your puppy is reacting, the best thing you can do is give them a few days' break. Give them a bucket holiday (see page 35). Let their bucket empty and then reintroduce walks in a structured way. Think about the environments you visit and the level of challenge these give your puppy. Lots of rehearsal of short outings where your puppy only practises feeling optimistic is much better than longer walks where bad experiences stack up.
- If your puppy is reacting and you have tried DMT and your puppy is still struggling, A to B (page 261) is a super option for getting your puppy out of a situation they are finding too tricky. Practise at home with your puppy first so you're ready if you need to utilise it when you are out and about with them.

- Take a breath and don't worry. If your puppy starts to behave in this way, don't panic. Humans can be quick to label this kind of behaviour, and you would be forgiven for thinking you now have a reactive dog for life. Reactivity *is* changeable with the right strategies and the right games. It isn't always going to be this way – you will transform this struggle. We have done so many consults with dogs who have extreme reactivity struggles, from biting other dogs to lunging at people, but their behaviour has always changed. Your current situation is not a predictor of the future.

- It can help to remind yourself of this: your puppy is not giving you a hard time; they are having a hard time. Their behaviour may be challenging, but your puppy does not want to feel the way they may currently be feeling. At the end of the day, poor behaviour is just information. Your puppy is simply telling you, in the only way they know how, that they don't currently have the skills to deal with a particular situation. That's OK, because it means you can work on those skills outside of those more challenging situations, and you and your puppy will end up feeling much better about things.

TURN AND FEED

This is a super cool game to add to your toolkit if your puppy has started reacting to things in the environment. It's a brilliant one to have on hand for those occasions where you can't get out of the situation you're in and you have to make the best of it in that moment.

375

As with every game, it's one to play and build at home first, outside of the situations your puppy may have started struggling with. Just like you wouldn't try and teach a recall for the first time when your puppy was already running full pelt after a rabbit, you don't want to try and teach this game in an environment your puppy is finding tricky.

Step 1: With your puppy on lead, slide your hand down the lead towards their harness (exactly the same way as you do when you're playing A to B), slip a finger underneath your puppy's harness or collar and gently turn them towards you so you can feed them in the space between your feet. You might choose to crouch down to give them even more of a visual barrier from whatever they might find worrying in the environment.

Step 2: While your puppy is in that really protected place between your legs, keep feeding. Drop multiple pieces of food down on that patch of floor between your feet so your puppy's focus stays down, ready for the next piece to drop. In this way, you are effectively telling your puppy to forget about the environment and just focus on that small area between your feet.

Step 3: Once they're eating food and their arousal levels are reducing, throw a piece of food out towards the environment so your puppy has to turn around to locate that piece of food. This means your puppy can take the environment in for a second before coming back in towards you and feeding between your feet again. By doing this, you are effectively making the environment more bite-sized for your puppy.

3. Help! My puppy's household manners have started to deteriorate!

Perhaps your puppy has started barking at things out of the window or counter-surfing.

Strategies for success

- A calm dog in the house is going to be a well-behaved dog, so you need to divert 80 per cent of your puppy's daily food allowance to calmness and the Calmness Triad (see chapter 8).
- As well as growing calmness, think about where your puppy is rehearsing a lack of calmness. What events in the day are triggering them? It might be that you, as their owner, have inadvertently reduced calmness. Perhaps you've started playing exciting games in the living room with your puppy and now they think the living room is an exciting place. Remember to rehearse the room. If you want calmness in the living room, remember only to do calm things there and go to a different room or the garden to play the exciting, high-arousal games.
- Make sure that your puppy is getting enough true rest. Do they need to spend more time apart from you in the house? Revisit the idea of presence ≠ access (page 191).
- A really useful exercise is to get a piece of paper and write on the left-hand side anything your puppy is currently doing that you don't want. For example, you might not want your puppy to jump up at the kitchen counter and steal food. On the right-hand side of your paper, write what you do want instead. So, instead of stealing food, you might want your

puppy to lie calmly on their boundary whenever they are in the kitchen. Perhaps your puppy has started to bark at the living room window. Reframe that into what you do want, which might be for them to hang out calmly in the living room away from the window. How can you achieve that? You might put a baby gate over the living room door for a few weeks to restrict access when you're not able to supervise, or reward your puppy for being on a boundary instead of being at the window, or DMT those barking triggers, or have your puppy on a lead in the living room to limit their access to the window. Sometimes working out what you DO want helps to give you a logical solution to the problem.

Tom's story: Remote thief

My mum's dog would always steal her glasses and the TV remote. It was his way of getting my mum's attention, because he knew it would always get a reaction from her. It was charming at first, but it got to the point where it was so extreme, her dog wasn't allowing her any access to her remote at all. It is in situations like this where the 'what do I want?' exercise comes in really useful. What you want is for your dog to learn to ignore the glasses, so perhaps you have the glasses on the table or on the floor while you play some boundary games, or you reward your dog for walking past the glasses without taking them. It's all about about focusing on what you DO want. In this case, though, my mum enjoyed her dog's behaviour so much that she refused to take my advice! So he carried on doing this right up until he passed away, at age 13.

- Draw a rough floor plan of your house and really think about where you want your puppy to spend their time. Pinpoint any problem areas. You might want your puppy to be away from the work surfaces in the kitchen, the front door or the living room window, so you need to make sure your boundaries are all well away from those areas. Rethink where your puppy is spending their time. Boundaries are anchor points for your puppy and it's really crucial to think about where they are placed. Revisit Suction Boundaries (page 303).

BOUNDARY BASEBALL

The aim of this game is for your puppy to move from boundary to boundary. You're teaching them that there is value in hunting out a boundary and for being on it. If they're on a boundary, they're not doing less appropriate things like counter-surfing, stealing your slippers or barking at the window. It's a great game to help you re-establish household manners. You can create a boundary from anything by playing the steps of boundary games.

Step 1: Create a boundary in each room of your house. This could be anything from a dog bed to a chair to a box or a towel.

Step 2: Pick a room, reward your puppy for being on the boundary in that room, release them and walk to another room.

Step 3: Your puppy's job is to find the next boundary and get onto it so you can reward them again.

4. Help! My puppy's getting up to mischief in the garden!

Gardens are common places for puppies to run riot. They might bark, dig, run up and down the fence if there's another dog next door or chase things such as birds, squirrels, foxes and cats. We once had a behaviour consult with an owner who was in tears because his puppy had dug up his lawn, which was his pride and joy.

Strategies for success

- If you're having trouble with your puppy's behaviour in the garden, decrease the amount of time they are spending outside and supervise them. That way, they can't rehearse things that you don't want.
- It's important to establish calmness in the garden, so follow the same process that you do in the house. Work through the Calmness Triad outside in the garden. You might give your puppy a passive calming activity out there or reward them for spontaneous moments of calmness. You want to be very clear about what they should be doing in the garden, so make sure you employ them in something appropriate rather than allowing them to create their own mischief. Occupy them with a chew, employ them on a boundary, take them to the toilet on lead and use their verbal cue. Make it really clear to your puppy what they should be doing and then bring them inside.
- If you've got a dog who is really interested in what the neighbours are doing or is reacting to things on the other side of the fence, play Disengagement Pattern near the fence (page 346). Throw one piece of food towards the fence, walk away from it and then feed, feed, feed your puppy. Your puppy is

going to be actively suctioned away from the fence and is learning that the value is away from it and not near it.

- If you've got a puppy who likes to dig, limit rehearsal. Put a boundary in the garden away from where they dig and put loads of value there, so they want to go on the boundary more than they want to dig up your lawn.
- If your puppy is doing something in the garden that you don't want them to do, use your Attention Noise (page 216) to interrupt them in a positive way so you can direct them to something more appropriate.

5. Help! My puppy is reacting to my other pets in the house!

It's common to find that as your puppy gets older, they start to pester another pet (that isn't a dog) in the household. At first, everything was new so your puppy might have ignored your other pets, but as they've got older (and braver) they might start to take more of an interest in your other pets. If your puppy has approached your cat and your cat has run off, your puppy might have suddenly discovered the fun in chasing them.

Strategies for success

- Create a gated community so you can separate your other pets from your puppy. If you've got a cat in the house and you want some shared space, think vertically as well as horizontally. You might want to have some shelves on the wall that the cat can jump up onto so they are safely away from your puppy at ground level.

- Think about where you place the resources for each animal so they can co-exist without conflict. For example, if your puppy spends a lot of time in the kitchen but this is also where your cat's litter tray and food are, this may create unnecessary conflict, or make it harder for your puppy to learn to ignore your cat. Think about putting your pets' food and rest places in different locations.

- Work on calmness with your puppy whenever they are in the presence of your other pet. Employing your puppy in a passive calming activity and working through your calmness protocol will teach your puppy the value of calmness around other pets and make it easier for your puppy to disengage.

- If your puppy has learned how much fun it can be to chase your cat, then stop rehearsal by having 3 weeks where your puppy is on a lead in the house whenever your cat is around. Reward your puppy for proximity to you or for being on a boundary whenever the cat is present.

Lauren's story: Six dogs and a parrot

I once worked with an owner who had six dogs and a parrot. The parrot knew that the dogs barked at the doorbell so it learned to mimic the sound and would do it regularly throughout the day so the dogs would go crazy. I did a lot of work DMTing the doorbell with the dogs and getting them to go to their boundaries whenever they heard it. We also worked on the parrot's enrichment so it had other things to do rather than wind the dogs up! There is always a solution to your struggle, and your puppy can learn to live harmoniously with other pets in your home.

6. Help! My puppy is pulling on the lead!

Walks with your puppy might suddenly become challenging if they start pulling on the lead.

Strategies for success

- Is your puppy pulling on the lead because they don't value proximity enough? If so, 80 per cent of their daily food allowance needs to be going into proximity games.
- Rehearsal is king when it comes to pulling on the lead. If your puppy has had the opportunity to rehearse pulling, they will keep doing it, so rather than long walks where your puppy practises what you don't want, aim for quality over quantity. A 30-second session of your puppy walking nicely on a lead outside your front door is preferable to half an hour of determined pulling. You'll be able to build up to longer sessions as your puppy only rehearses what you want.
- Where is your puppy's brain when you head out for a walk? If your puppy has learned that the on-lead part of your walk is the build-up to an exciting destination ahead where they're allowed off lead to play and run, their brain might already be way up ahead, anticipating that fun. If your puppy is anticipating the joy of a particularly delicious-smelling lamp post several streets ahead, that's going to create pulling on the lead, because your puppy's brain isn't with you, calmly in the moment, but is somewhere way up ahead. Check where your puppy's brain is before you head out to make sure they are able to focus calmly on you. It can help to play a game before you even leave the house or garden, or start with

a scatter feed – something to really bring that brain back to where it should be. If in doubt, ditch the walk and play games at home instead.

- Keep your puppy focused by keeping their brain engaged. As you leave the house, can your puppy do Mighty Middle (page 182)? Great! Then carry on walking. Sense your puppy starting to lose focus or beginning to pull? Can they put two feet up on an object (page 224)? Great! Carry on walking. This is all about keeping your puppy focused and engaged with you, rather than pulling ahead.

- Change the equipment that you walk them on. If your puppy has lots of rehearsal of pulling while wearing a particular harness, change the picture by introducing a new harness or lead – something your puppy will notice is different and that has no history of pulling. Start from fresh with this new set-up and go back to putting value in proximity and calmness.

7. Help! My puppy is resource guarding

Resource guarding happens when your puppy has something that they might value – it could be food, a toy or an object that they've stolen – and they are unable to disengage from it. You might try and take it off them but they refuse to let it go. They might growl, snap or bark at you, or run away with their stolen treasure.

Strategies for success

- If you notice that your puppy is showing signs of guarding resources, be mindful not to give them anything that they are likely to guard while you're growing their skills. Don't leave washing hanging somewhere your puppy can reach so they have the opportunity to pinch a sock! Be careful not to leave items lying around that your puppy could be tempted to pick up – anything from TV remotes and spectacles to tea towels and children's toys can be valuable treasure to a puppy. If your puppy is starting to guard food items, consider whether high-value chews are appropriate for the time being – and if your puppy does have them, make sure you allow plenty of space for your puppy to enjoy them in peace. The last thing you want to do is create a situation where your puppy starts to guard because they think you are trying to take a food item away from them.

- If they are already guarding, don't try and take the object away. This will create a bigger problem and your puppy will find it even more difficult to disengage. Walking away is not going to cause your puppy to do it more in the future, but it will avoid an escalation in the moment. If you really need to get an item away from your puppy, move away and do something to draw their attention away from what they have. Use your Attention Noise, walk out of the back door into the garden or into a different room, open the cupboard where their snacks are, or pick up their lead. Do anything you can to interrupt them, and then give them something more appropriate to occupy them while you calmly retrieve the stolen item without your puppy noticing. Keep everything as calm as possible. Adding more energy to the situation is likely to make it worse.

- Resource guarding struggles don't normally happen because your puppy loves whatever object they have stolen. Socks aren't really that valuable! Some puppies will even guard stolen toilet roll tubes or bits of paper. The root of the problem is that your puppy is unable to disengage from whatever item they have, so go back to chapter 22 and refresh your learning. Build up your puppy's disengagement skills. Play lots of games with your puppy where they disengage from one thing then engage with something else.

TOY SWITCH

Toy Switch is a great game for teaching your puppy that what you have is always the best deal. It also builds the skill of disengagement. When you and your puppy are first learning this game, it's best to play with two identical toys. It's important to play with toys you know your puppy isn't going to resource guard. If your puppy has previously struggled to let go of a particular toy, use something completely different.

Step 1: Sit on the floor so you are at your puppy's level and have two identical toys, one in each hand.

Step 2: Start with one toy behind your back and move the other in a fun way to entice your puppy to play. Make the toy exciting. Move it around the floor like it's a squirrel.

Step 3: When your puppy grabs hold of the toy, let them tug on it for just a couple of seconds, and then stop tugging with that toy, make it go very still, and bring the other toy out from behind your back.

Step 4: Animate the second toy and make that one super

exciting instead. The aim of the game is that your puppy disengages from one toy and engages with the other. As soon as your puppy lets go of the first toy, put it behind your back so that you avoid any confusion and encourage them to tug for a few seconds on the second toy.

Step 5: Then stop tugging with the second toy (just like you did before) and present the first toy again. Can your puppy switch back to the first one?

This is a great game for teaching your puppy that there is fun and value in switching from one activity to the next.

You can play with different toys or even with food – we love to play with two hard tripe sticks early on with our puppies. You can even add a word in. When one toy goes still before you animate the next one, say 'switch'. Your puppy will learn when they hear the word 'switch' they stop what they're interacting with and switch to something else.

This is a high-energy game, so play in really short sessions, especially if toy play is something your puppy finds very exciting. A full bucket and higher levels of arousal can feed into a resource guarding struggle, so don't play for more than a few minutes at a time. One successful switch is better than a long session where your puppy goes beyond their ability to think and struggles to disengage from the game.

For some dogs, immobilising the 'dead' toy actually increases their inability to disengage and switch to the new toy, which can very quickly cause arousal levels to escalate. You might find you have greater success letting go of the 'dead' toy, so your puppy no longer has that reflex response of tugging against it, and then animating your second toy so that it becomes the exciting one.

> **TIP:** If, despite all the above strategies, your puppy is still frequently resource guarding, look at the possibility that your puppy has a full bucket. What's paying into their bucket? What can you do to reduce that? You might find resource guarding gets better that way.

8. Help! My puppy isn't motivated by food!

If you're using your puppy's daily food allowance to put the value into games and learning, what do you do if your puppy isn't motivated by food?

Strategies for success

- If this is a sudden change and your previously 'foodie' puppy becomes indifferent to food, a vet check is always recommended to make sure there is nothing medical going on.
- As an owner, you can get into a trap of constantly switching food to see if that makes a difference to your puppy's food motivation, but generally we find it doesn't. If your puppy becomes disinterested in kibble, you might switch to chicken, until they start refusing chicken, and all of a sudden they are fine-dining on fillet steak! But at some point, fillet steak won't work any more either and you're going to be stuck. Not only that, your puppy needs a balanced and varied diet. If

your puppy has no motivation to work for their food, it's the experience of feeding your puppy that you need to look at rather than the food itself. What can you do with that food to create a more rewarding experience?

- Observe your puppy. What do they like to do? Are they really into chase or do they love jumping up in the air? Think about all the ways you deliver that food to them and turn every piece into an experience. Roll or throw the food or get them to chase it. Throw it into the air so they have to catch it. Hide the food so your puppy has to sniff it out. If you need to reignite your puppy's interest in their food, consider spending 2 weeks where there are no rules and instead it's just about having fun. It's the experience around the food that matters to your puppy. This is what will keep them interested, rather than the food itself. If you have to work for something, then you value it much more than if you are handed it for free. It's the same for a dog and their food. Think about what your puppy enjoys and try to deliver their food in a way that appeals to them. If you think your puppy isn't naturally 'foodie', you may just need to work a little harder and adapt the way you deliver their food to them.

The end!

Wow, wow, wow! What an epic journey you have been on, and you have been AMAZING! Think how far you've come from first getting your puppy to where you are now. You really are a true Gamechanger – you've played games, had fun and turned your puppy's struggles into strengths. But this is not the end, this is only the beginning of a truly beautiful journey with your special dog. You're now becoming a Gamechanger and a Concept trainer, and you're changing the face of the dog-training world step by step, day by day, game by game! You are on the right path, you are armed with the learning and the knowledge to make sure you have a long, happy and stress-free life with your puppy. So keep having fun, enjoy being together and remember that whatever you face in life, there's a game for that! Together we can do this, we've got this – let's do it!

For more fun, games and information on how to train your puppy as they get older, go to www.absolute-dogs.com

Index

Note: All entries for games appear in bold throughout the index.

Access your free Perfect Pet Dog Programme here!

Watch us work with real dogs and level up your learning with video demonstrations that support what you've learnt in this book. You've got access for life!